A...
Theory and practice

AUDITING
Theory and practice

SECOND EDITION

JOHN DUNN

Department of Accounting and Finance
University of Strathclyde, Glasgow

PRENTICE HALL

LONDON   NEW YORK   TORONTO   SYDNEY   TOKYO   SINGAPORE
MADRID   MEXICO CITY   MUNICH

First published 1996 by
Prentice Hall Europe
Campus 400, Maylands Avenue
Hemel Hempstead
Hertfordshire, HP2 7EZ
A division of
Simon & Schuster International Group

Typeset in Stone Serif and Stone Sans 10/12pt
by Photoprint Typesetters, Torquay
Printed and bound in Great Britain by
Redwood Books, Trowbridge, Wiltshire

Library of Congress Cataloging-in-Publication Data

Dunn, John, 1959–
    Auditing : theory and practice / John Dunn. — 2nd ed.
        p. cm.
    Includes bibliographical references and index.
    ISBN 0–13–240896–1
        1. Auditing. I. Title.
    HF5667.D76 1996
    657'.45—dc20   95–46383
                                                     CIP

British Library Cataloguing in Publication Data

A catalogue record for this book is available from
the British Library

ISBN 0–13–240896–1

1 2 3 4 5   00 99 98 97 96

For Richard, Iain, Andrew and Jonathan

Contents

Preface

Most of the large accounting firms derive more income from auditing than from the provision of any other single service. Despite this, auditing is sometimes regarded as one of the less exciting branches of accountancy. The image of Michael Palin trying to exchange a career in chartered accountancy for one in lion-taming has persisted through the years. However, this attitude ignores the rapid changes and controversies which have affected the auditor during the five years since the first edition of this book was published. Company law has changed because of the influence of the European Union. The well-publicised failure of several major companies, such as the Maxwell Corporation and BCCI, and heightened competition within the profession have led to the development of increasingly stringent regulatory standards and auditing techniques which are both more efficient and effective.

Auditing is a practical discipline. It has, however, been the focus of much research and debate, both in the United Kingdom and overseas; this text aims to make this material more accessible to students. It is, to some extent, a compromise between the books which are devoted exclusively to the theory of auditing and those which are rooted in its practical aspects. By embracing both the theoretical and practical strands of auditing, and by explaining and illustrating their linkages in a succinct and clear style, the text seeks to provide a balanced and pertinent framework for the study of auditing.

The text is written for undergraduate students on courses in auditing; however, it will also be of use to students preparing for the examinations of the professional accounting bodies.

Structure

As with the previous edition, the text is organised into four parts, as follows:

    I   The Regulatory Framework of Auditing
    II   Audit Reporting

III   The Collection of Evidence
IV   Other Roles for Audit

The purpose and structure of each part, and its component chapters, are outlined at the start of each section.

Teaching and learning features

Each chapter begins with a set of **learning objectives** to highlight what students should be able to accomplish after reading the chapter. In recognition of a trend towards the more flexible provision of courses and a greater emphasis on students for self-learning, each chapter is interspersed with short self-assessment **activities**, the suggested answers to which follow on immediately. This feature is designed to encourage students to interact with the text to check their progress and understanding of key concepts and techniques. **Worked examples** and **illustrations** are integrated throughout the text. Chapters end with a **summary** which highlights and reinforces the main topics covered by the chapter, and an extensive annotated list of **references** to books and articles that might be consulted to enable particular topics to be studied in more depth. Assessment material comprises a range of **review questions** and **exercises**.

Changes to the second edition

In addition to the provision of the learning objectives and self-assessment activities within each chapter, the content of the text and the illustrations have been comprehensively revised and updated to take account of the latest regulatory changes and new Statements of Auditing Standards issued by the APB. In particular, the chapters in Part II on the Audit Report and Qualified Audit Reports have been completely rewritten; the chapters on Auditor Independence and the Auditor's Duties in Part I have been substantially revised. Much of the material in Parts III and IV still holds and remains largely unchanged from the previous edition; however, a new and final chapter on environmental auditing has been included, given the growing awareness that businesses have a much broader responsibility than the creation of wealth for their shareholders.

John Dunn

Abbreviations

ACCA	Chartered Association of Certified Accountants
AICPA	American Institute of Certified Public Accountants
APB	Auditing Practices Board
APC	Auditing Practices Committee
ASB	Accounting Standards Board
ASC	Accounting Standards Committee
CAR	Commission on Auditors' Responsibilities
CICA	Canadian Institute of Chartered Accountants
CPA	Certified Public Accountant
FRC	Financial Reporting Council
FRS	Financial Reporting Standards
ICAEW	Institute of Chartered Accountants in England and Wales
ICAI	Institute of Chartered Accountants in Ireland
ICAS	Institute of Chartered Accountants of Scotland
IIA	Institute of Internal Auditors
SAS	Statement of Auditing Standards
SEC	Securities and Exchange Commission
SI	Statutory Instrument
SSAP	Statement of Standard Accounting Practice

PART I

THE REGULATORY FRAMEWORK OF AUDITING

This section contains the material which forms the basis for the rest of the text. It places auditing in its theoretical perspective. This is partly because this is an important issue in itself and partly because it will be difficult to discuss the issues of reporting and testing discussed in later sections without knowing why these activities are undertaken.

This part of the book is split into four chapters. Chapter 1 deals with the definition of audit and lays down some of the principles and postulates which underlie the discipline. Chapter 2 discusses the topic of auditor independence. This is important because auditors cannot give credibility to the reports if they themselves lack credibility. This chapter highlights some of the problems associated with ensuring that auditors are independent and also that they are seen to be independent.

Chapter 3 discusses the auditor's duties to the users of audited financial statements. This is an aspect of auditing which has received a great deal of attention in recent years, partly as a result of a number of alleged audit failures. This chapter is interesting precisely because of the passions and arguments which the topic raises. Chapter 4 concludes this part of the book by discussing some of the different approaches to auditing around the world.

CHAPTER 1

Why have an audit?

The audit of a large company can require the efforts of a large team of accountants for an entire year. This could result in an audit fee of many hundreds of thousands or even millions of pounds.

In the United Kingdom, company law requires virtually every company to have an audit, regardless of the cost and regardless of whether the directors and shareholders wish one. It is, therefore, important to introduce a text on auditing with a discussion of the reasons for having an audit.

By the time you have completed this chapter you should be able to:

- Describe the agency problem.
- Explain the role of the auditor and the legal framework within which audit operates.
- Describe the role of the professional accounting bodies in the regulation of audit.
- Decribe some of the main auditing postulates.

1.1 The agency problem

In most of the Western world, wealth is created by businesses which harness the savings of investors and the energy of employees. Industrial concentration has led to the creation of companies which are larger, and arguably more complex, than many of the sovereign states which act as their hosts. It is necessary for the control of large businesses to be delegated to a small number of directors. It would be impossible, for example, for every shareholder in a large company such as British Gas to become involved in its management. These directors may, therefore, find themselves taking decisions which have enormous implications for the investors and employees of the organisations which they manage.

This separation of ownership from control can create conflict in that the directors will often be forced to choose between the shareholders' welfare and their own. In order to protect themselves, the shareholders must implement mechanisms to protect their interests. The cost of these safeguards, along with the effects of those abuses which could not be prevented, have been described by Jensen and Meckling as 'agency costs'.[1] Their work has been followed by a whole series of papers on the agency problem and the ways in which it can be controlled.[2]

1.1.1 *Agency costs*

The limited company would almost appear to have been specifically designed to enable corrupt managers to profit at the expense of the shareholders and other investors. It was created with the intention of attracting widespread share-holdings. Control of the company is delegated to the board of directors, who usually have total discretion over business strategy, investment and financing decisions. The directors may also be tempted to award themselves excessive remuneration packages, either in the form of substantial salaries or in fringe benefits such as expensive cars, lavish offices and so on.

Another feature of the limited company is the lack of any direct responsibility by the shareholders or the directors for the amounts owed to the creditors. If a company's future was threatened it could, at least in theory, be quite sensible for the directors to invest its remaining assets in a high risk venture. If the gamble is successful, the directors' jobs will be saved and the shareholders will enjoy the resultant profit. If the venture fails, then the owners and managers will be no worse off than they would have been if the company had simply collapsed. The creditors will, however, suffer because the assets from which their debts would have been settled have been squandered.

1.1.2 *Solutions to the agency problem*

There are two main ways in which a principal can prevent an agent from abusing his position of trust. First, it is possible to remunerate agents in such a way that their interests coincide with those of the principal. Second, the principal can monitor the agents' actions and penalise for any exploitation.

ACTIVITY

Suggest some of the ways in which agents might be motivated to work in the best interests of their principals. Will these work?

It is extremely difficult to reward managers in such a way that their interests coincide with those of the shareholders. If bonuses are linked to performance, managers may be unfairly penalised because of events which were outside their control. If a manager's bonus or salary is linked to profit, then he could suffer because of an increase in interest rates or movements in foreign currencies. Even if the profit figure is adjusted for the direct effects of these events, the company's competitive position may have been undermined by them, thus reducing sales. A further problem is that the manager's attention may become focused on the performance measures which are built into the bonus calculation. This could discourage investment in research, advertising and even in fixed assets because of the short-term effects of this type of expenditure on profit. In the longer term, the shareholders would, of course, suffer as a result.

Another type of incentive is to give shares to the managers. Bonuses could take the form of either shares in the company or options to purchase shares at fixed prices. While this would encourage managers to maximise the share price, conflicts of interest would remain. If a director built up, say, a 5 per cent holding in his company, he would be entitled to only 5 per cent of the profits. He would, therefore, bear only 5 per cent of the cost of the perquisites which he awarded himself.

While incentive systems go some way towards reducing the agency problem, they must be supplemented by close monitoring of management's behaviour. Major shareholders can sometimes insist on having a representative on the board of directors. This tends to happen when a company is taken over by another or when a venture finance organisation provides a relatively small company with finance. Major shareholders may also be able to request informal meetings with management, so that the company's progress can be discussed. Such arrangements are, however, only available to large shareholders.

1.1.3 *Published accounts*

Company law attempts to provide the shareholders with the means to monitor the behaviour of their directors:

- Sections 221–222 of the Companies Act 1985 require companies to keep proper accounting records.
- Sections 223–225 of the Act define a company's accounting reference period and make the directors responsible for the preparation of a profit and loss account for this period and a balance sheet as at its end.
- Sections 226–234 deal with the form and content of these statements.
- Sections 238–239 give the members and debenture holders the right to receive copies of the statements.
- Section 241 requires the directors to hold a general meeting at which these accounts are laid before the shareholders.
- Section 242 requires that a copy of the accounts should be delivered to the registrar of companies.

If the shareholders are unhappy with the directors' stewardship of their company then they will have the opportunity to question them at the annual general meeting. They may ask for their resignations. Indeed, many companies require each director to retire from office and offer himself for re-election at least once every three years.[3]

Thus, the Companies Act ensures that the shareholders have the right to regular reports about the performance and financial position of their company. This should enable them to make intelligent use of their power to remove the directors from office. The problem is, of course, that the directors are themselves responsible for the preparation of the financial statements which are used to assess their stewardship. Furthermore, any performance-related bonuses and the value of any share options are also likely to be related to the profit figures which are published in the statements. Thus, the directors may be tempted to manipulate the figures in the annual report. This can only undermine the credibility of the financial statements.

1.2 The role of the auditor

> In the most general sense, an audit is the means by which one person is assured by another of the quality, condition or status of some subject matter which the latter has examined. The need for such an audit arises because the first-mentioned person is doubtful about the quality, condition or status of the subject matter, and is unable personally to remove the doubt or uncertainty.[4]

This quotation would appear to describe the shareholder's circumstances. He is in obvious need of assurance regarding the quality of the information in the financial statements. Furthermore, there is no way in which any individual shareholder would have the opportunity to verify the content of a set of financial statements. An audit would appear to be the obvious solution to this dilemma.

1.2.1 *What is an audit?*

Several definitions of an audit have been proposed:

> An audit is the independent examination of, and expression of opinion on, the financial statements of an enterprise by an appointed auditor in pursuance of that appointment and in compliance with any relevant statutory obligation.
>
> (APC[5])

> An audit is a methodical review and objective examination of an item, including the verification of specific information as determined by the auditor or as established by general practice. Generally, the purpose of an audit is to express an opinion on or reach a conclusion about what was audited.
>
> (Miller[6])

> Auditing is a systematic process of objectively obtaining and evaluating evidence regarding assertions about economic actions and events to ascertain the degree of correspondence between those assertions and established criteria and communicating the results to interested users.
>
> (ASOBAC[7])

ACTIVITY

Review the definitions shown above. Try to identify some common themes or elements.

Auditors must be independent. The APC definition actually uses this word, while the others say that the auditors' examination must be 'objective'.

Auditors must collect evidence to support their opinion. This is implied by the description of an audit as an 'examination' by the APC. The other definitions are even more explicit.

Auditors must report to the users of the financial statements.

Strangely, none of the definitions mention the need for the auditor to be qualified to express an opinion on the matter under consideration. This could, however, have been taken for granted in the sense that each definition has been taken from a document which is addressed primarily to professional accountants.

The purpose of an audit is not to provide additional information. It is intended to enable users to rely more heavily upon the information which has already been prepared by others.

> The objective of an audit of financial statements, prepared within a framework of recognized accounting policies, is to enable an auditor to express an opinion on such financial statements.
>
> The auditor's opinion helps establish the credibility of the financial statements. The user, however, should not assume that the auditor's opinion is an assurance as to the future viability of the entity nor an opinion as to the efficiency or effectiveness with which management has conducted the affairs of the entity.
>
> (IFAC[8])

Thus, the user of the audit report must examine the financial statements to which it relates if he wishes to discover whether the company has been properly managed.

The word audit must be used with care because it can have several different connotations. Senior managers, for example, may employ internal auditors to monitor the operation of the accounting system and to check on the honesty of junior staff. In the public sector, auditors may be employed to ensure that an organisation is obtaining 'value for money'. Throughout this book, it should be assumed that an audit is an independent investigation into the quality of published accounting information, unless it is otherwise stated.

1.2.2 *Support for the need for an audit*

An independent audit is not the only means by which the actions of a company's management can be monitored. Furthermore, audits are often expensive. It is, therefore, surprising that relatively little evidence exists to support the need for this mechanism.

A number of models have been developed to explain the role of the auditor. Ng developed a mathematical model of the financial reporting process, assuming that the manager's remuneration is related to the reported earnings figure.[9] He established that managers can maximise the value of their remuneration and minimise the variability of their income by selecting a reporting function which is biased towards overstated profits and which tends to be as uninformative as possible. The manager's gain would be at the expense of the owner of the company who would, under these circumstances, prefer an earnings function which tended to understate income and provided as much information as possible. While the existence of GAAP[10] should reduce the extent of possible distortion, there is always the possibility that managers will not comply with GAAP. An audit should ensure that the information produced by managers is not misleading. Thus, the owner will benefit from an audit because it will reduce the cost of management remuneration.

A paper by Ng and Stoeckenius[11] extended the agency model to look at the effects on the truthfulness of reporting of different methods of rewarding managers. The model suggested that the only method of remuneration which did not provide a motive for biased reporting was a fixed salary. Fixed salaries are regarded as unsatisfactory because they provide very little incentive to maximise the owner's profit. The authors conclude that there has to be a link between reported profits and management compensation and that some means of ensuring that managers report truthfully must be found. They proceed to demonstrate that a costless audit, which was guaranteed to detect every error in the information produced by management, would optimise the manager's decisions with respect to the wealth of the owner. It could, therefore, be in the owner's best interests to commission an audit, provided that it was not too expensive.

Antle points out that the auditor is an economic agent in his own right.[12] He used game theory to model the auditor's behaviour, assuming that the auditor would wish to minimise the cost of the audit. One of the insights gained from this model was the way in which the owner could benefit from the auditor's ability to compensate him for any costs which resulted from an error in the audit report. The auditor could be viewed as an insurer who would be willing to bear part of the owner's risk in return for a fee.

Relatively few studies have been able to support the need for an audit with empirical evidence. This is hardly surprising, given the complexity of the relationships between the various parties involved. Chow's study[13] examined the effects of four hypothetical factors which could have an effect on the decision for a company to have an audit. The study was based on 1926 data collected for 165 publicly traded American companies. The year was chosen because there were no statutory audit requirements at that time. Chow's four hypotheses were as follows:

H1   The smaller is the manager's ownership share in the firm, the higher is the probability that the firm voluntarily engages external auditing.

H2   The higher the proportion of debt in a firm's capital structure, the higher is the probability that the firm voluntarily engages external auditing.

H3   The greater the number of different accounting measures in a firm's debt covenants, the higher is the possibility that the firm voluntarily engages external auditing.[14]

H4   The larger a firm's total size, the higher is the probability that it voluntarily engages external auditing.

The first three hypotheses are based on the assumption that the need for an audit will increase with the potential for conflict of interest. This may be because the owners or lenders will insist on an audit. An audit could also be in the manager's best interests. One of the implications of agency theory is that the owner will estimate the cost of the manager's selfish actions and will take this into account when deciding on the manager's remuneration. The manager might wish to have an audit in order to prove that he is not acting in this manner and so to justify a higher salary.

The fourth hypothesis is based on the assumption that the cost of an audit is not directly related to the size of the company. There are certain fixed costs which do not vary from audit to audit. Even the variable costs do not increase in direct proportion to company size. H4 implies that a large company will find an audit relatively inexpensive, while the absolute cost of the benefits to be obtained are more likely to be substantial. Chow's results supported H2, H3 and H4. Measurement problems prevented any meaningful tests on H1.

An empirical study by Francis and Wilson[15] attempted to identify the link between certain variables which would have an effect on agency problems and the selection of an accounting firm to act as external auditor. It was hypothesised that a company which had a greater incentive to signal that certain types of abuses had not been committed would be more likely to employ one of the large, highly prestigious accounting firms.

Francis and Wilson selected 196 companies who had changed their auditor during the seven-year period from June 1978 to June 1985 and collected data on the following:

1   The amount of stock owned by management.
2   The existence of a bonus system for senior managers which was linked to accounting variables.
3   The diffusion of ownership, proxied by the size of the single largest shareholding.
4   The ratio of long-term debt to equity.
5   The size of the company, measured in terms of total assets.
6   The amount of finance raised from the issue of shares or borrowing during the three years before the change of auditor.

In all but the final case, the authors measured changes in the variables during the three years before the change of auditor.

The study concentrated on companies which had changed auditors in order to control for the effects of variables such as the type of industry the company was in and so on. The results of the study suggested that there was a link between the agency variables and the choice of auditor. In other words, a company which is likely to be seen to have a motive to publish misleading accounting information is more likely to engage one of the 'Big Eight' accounting firms to act as auditor.[16]

Neither the Chow nor the Francis and Wilson articles prove that an audit is the most effective solution to the agency problem. The fact that companies volunteer to have audits or deliberately choose auditors whose opinions are more likely to be persuasive does not rule out the possibility that other, possibly more efficient, mechanisms exist.

Briston and Perks attempted to estimate the total amount spent on audits during 1976 and arrived at a total of £109.7m.[17] This, they argued, was an unacceptable burden for society to bear.[18] They felt that there was little merit in such an investigation and that most of the benefit of an audit could be obtained from an internal investigation. There has been virtually no public support for their proposal to abolish the requirement for an external audit.

1.3 The legal requirements relating to audit in the United Kingdom

UK company law is virtually unique in that it requires all limited companies to have their accounts audited. Only dormant and certain very small companies are exempt. The Companies Act 1985 deals with the auditors' appointment and their duties.

The auditors' duties revolve around the audit report. Auditors are required to make a report to the members stating whether, in their opinion, the financial statements show a true and fair view of the company's performance and position. The content and meaning of the audit report are major issues which fall outside the scope of this chapter. They will be covered in Chapter 5. It is, however, important to note that the auditor has very few duties which are not directly associated with this report.[19]

The extent to which the shareholders and the other users of the financial statements can rely on the auditor's report will be examined in Chapter 3.

1.3.1 *Small companies*

Companies are exempt from compulsory audit if they have a turnover of less than £90,000. Companies with a turnover between £90,000 and £350,000 require only an independent accountant's report on whether the financial statements correctly reflect the company's books. This is a recent exemption. Formerly all active companies were required to have an audit regardless of their size or their owners' wishes.

ACTIVITY

Suggest why it might be argued that the audit of a small company is unnecessary. Is it possible that small companies will choose to continue with audits on a voluntary basis?

It is common for the owners of small companies to be actively involved in their management. This means that the agency problems referred to above do not arise.

Banks and other third parties who deal with small companies can usually protect their interests in other ways than requiring an annual external audit. This could, for example, involve the shareholders and directors providing personal guarantees for any advances.

It is unlikely that many small companies will continue to have an audit on a voluntary basis. They might, however, feel that doing so would reduce the risk of internal frictions between individual shareholders or provide a useful source of credible information about the company's financial history if they ever decided to sell it as a going concern.

1.4 The professional accounting bodies

The vast majority of practising auditors are members of one of the following bodies:

The Institute of Chartered Accountants in England and Wales (ICAEW)
The Institute of Chartered Accountants of Scotland (ICAS)
The Chartered Association of Certified Accountants (ACCA)[20]
The Institute of Chartered Accountants in Ireland (ICAI).

These bodies have a statutory duty to ensure that those of their members who are involved in audit work do not act in a dishonest or negligent manner.

1.4.1 *Educational requirements*

It takes several years to become a qualified accountant. While each body has slightly different rules, in general, one has to obtain the minimum entry requirements (typically a degree in the case of ICAEW and ICAS) and then complete a period of practical training of roughly three years' duration. Students must pass a series of demanding examinations during the training period. Thus, a school leaver who sought a career in accountancy would have to commit himself to a course of study and training which could take six years or more to complete.[21]

Having become a qualified accountant, one is still unable to act as an auditor. Each of the professional bodies insists that its members do not provide professional accounting services unless they are in possession of a practising certificate. Again, the rules differ from body to body. In general, one has to obtain at least two years of appropriate experience before being granted a practising certificate. This period has to be spent in the employment of a suitably qualified member of the profession. In fact, very few professional accountants ever obtain a practising certificate and are content to spend their careers working as employees in professional offices or in industry.

1.4.2 *Professional pronouncements*

The professional bodies would be reluctant to relinquish their regulatory role to a state organisation. To this end, they have established programmes for setting ethical and auditing standards. These have been in response to a number of audit failures caused by a lack of objectivity or technical competence. These had led to a great deal of adverse publicity and had created a lack of confidence in the value of the audit opinion.[22]

Auditor objectivity is regulated by the Guide to Professional Ethics. This covers a number of ethical issues including the auditor's independence. The detailed content of these rules will be considered in Chapter 2.

The professional bodies have also set up the Consultative Committee of Accountancy Bodies (CCAB). This body has a number of sub-committees which have specific roles in the setting of standards on accounting and its related subjects. The Auditing Practices Board (APB) is one of these. The APB's publications include series of Statements of Auditing Standards (SAS).[23] SASs contain basic principles and essential procedures with which auditors are required to comply. The intended structure of the SASs is shown in the appendix at the end of this book. Many of these standards are already in place and others are being developed. The standards themselves are contained in longer documents. The standards are highlighted and the other material is meant to provide guidance.

The APB has also taken over the Auditing Guidelines published by the Auditing Practices Committee, the APB's predecessor. These guidelines are being phased out as and when they are replaced by SASs.

This book will contain a critical appraisal of the standards and of many of the guidelines. The professional standards of other countries, notably those of the United States and Canada, will also be referred to throughout.

Each of the professional bodies has its own disciplinary procedures which would be invoked if a member does not comply with the requirements of the professional standards. In addition to these, the ICAEW, ICAS and the ACCA have created a Joint Disciplinary Scheme. If any one of the three bodies is of the opinion that a matter has arisen which gives rise to public concern and which should be investigated, it can report the matter to the Executive Committee which will in turn appoint a Committee of Inquiry. If the Committee finds a complaint against a member or firm proven then it will release the details of its findings to the press.

1.5 Auditing postulates

It could be argued that auditing does not require a theoretical background. The need for an audit could be demonstrated without the mathematical models described in 1.2.2 above. Indeed, given that company law requires an audit to be conducted, one could be forgiven for believing that pragmatism would be sufficient to explain the manner in which the auditor conducts his investigation and expresses his opinion. Such a view would, however, be misguided.

There have been a number of attempts to develop a cohesive theoretical framework for the audit process. The most influential of these has been that of Mautz and Sharaf.[24] They argued '. . . one sees something incongruous in the existence of a professional group drawing its status primarily from auditing, but having no perceptible body of theory to support that practice'.[25] These words are as relevant now as when they were first written in 1961.

The accountancy profession faces a variety of pressures. At the time of writing, these include the pursuit of international harmonisation of standards, increasing competition between accounting firms driving the development of more efficient auditing techniques and the constant manufacture of manipulative accounting policies. These challenges must be dealt with in the light of a cohesive theoretical framework, otherwise auditing will lose all credibility.

Mautz and Sharaf went on to state the following 'tentative' postulates of auditing:[26]

1 Financial statements and financial data are verifiable.
2 There is no necessary conflict of interest between the auditor and the management of the enterprise under audit.
3 The financial statements and other information submitted for verification are free from collusive and other unusual irregularities.
4 The existence of a satisfactory system of internal control eliminates the probability of irregularities.
5 Consistent application of generally accepted principles of accounting results in the fair presentation of financial position and the results of operations.
6 In the absence of clear evidence to the contrary, what has held true in the past for the enterprise under examination will hold true in the future.
7 When examining financial data for the purpose of expressing an independent opinion thereon, the auditor acts exclusively in the capacity of an auditor.
8 The professional status of the independent auditor imposes commensurate obligations.

A set of postulates is a set of fundamental assumptions from which propositions can be drawn. Postulates do not lend themselves to direct verification, although the validity of the propositions drawn from them can be challenged. These postulates are based partly on the experience of their authors and are also, to some extent, normative statements on the nature of auditing.

Mautz and Sharaf used their postulates to develop five primary concepts in auditing:

1   Evidence.
2   Due audit care.
3   Fair presentation.
4   Independence.
5   Ethical conduct.

These could be said to form a theoretical foundation for auditing, although care has to be taken in making such a statement about any model. The role of the auditor has evolved over time and this process of change is likely to continue, perhaps requiring the framework to be updated.[27]

A more recent framework, entitled the 'Enduring principles of auditing', appeared as an appendix to the APB's McFarlane report:[28]

> *Integrity*
> Auditors should observe high standards of integrity.
> *Independence*
> Auditors should at all times be objective, expressing opinions which are free from influence, independent of the company and its directors, and unaffected by commercial conflict of interest.
> *Competence*
> Auditors should act with a high degree of professional skill.
> *Rigour*
> Auditors should apply a high degree of rigour to the audit process, maintaining a stance of professional scepticism in their assessment of evidence.
> *Accountability*
> Auditors should act in the best interests of shareholders whilst having regard to the wider public interest.
> *Judgement*
> Auditors should apply sound professional judgement.
> *Communication*
> Auditors should openly disclose all matters necessary for a full under-standing of the opinion they express. Auditors may make disclosure in the public interest to the appropriate authorities when they become aware of matters indicative of fraud or a breach of law or regulation with which the business is required to comply and consider it necessary to do so.
> *Providing value*
> In providing their service, auditors should ensure that they provide value to shareholders.

The above frameworks have the advantage of being rooted in pragmatism. This might, however, undermine their claim to be 'theoretical'. A number of attempts have been made to model the role of audit. For example, Power produced a monograph on the 'audit explosion' which analysed the growing emphasis on audit (not just financial audit) throughout society. He identified four difficulties:

1 Audits are increasingly concerned with abstract systems of control rather than first order operations and risks.
2 The growth in different types of audit has tended to bring about greater expectations about audit and control.
3 It is difficult to observe audit success or failure.
4 Audits are not neutral. They act on organisations to make them auditable. Audits can either become ineffective rituals which examine procedures implemented for the sake of the auditors (and which are divorced from actual operations) or they can harm the operations of the organisation by placing undue emphasis on control.[29]

1.6 Summary

The audit of published financial statements is a response to the agency problem. Shareholders require some means of ensuring that the information upon which they base their investment decisions is credible.

The need for an audit has been demonstrated by means of mathematical modelling. It has also been established that companies which are more likely to experience agency problems are more likely to employ an auditor.

In the United Kingdom, most active companies are required by law to publish audited accounts. The auditor's duties are laid down in the Companies Act 1985. The accountancy profession has also published a series of standards and guidelines to ensure that the auditor's work is of acceptable quality.

A number of theoretical models of the audit process have been published, the most influential being that of Mautz and Sharaf.

———— REVIEW QUESTIONS ————

1. Examine the list of factors investigated by Francis and Wilson (section 1.2.2). Why would each of these factors be likely to affect management's desire to report the company's performance honestly?

2. The auditor is employed to add credibility to the published accounting information. What attributes would the auditor have to possess in order to achieve this objective?

3. Very few countries require all companies to have an audit. Why are the agency problems likely to be different in smaller companies? Are small companies less likely to require an audit?

4. What are the implications of requiring the auditor to seek reappointment on an annual basis?

═══════ EXERCISES ═══════

1. ABC Ltd is a wholly owned subsidiary of Alphabet plc. ABC manufactures and sells a range of double glazed windows and doors for domestic and industrial premises within fifty miles of its factory and offices. Other subsidiaries supply the remainder of the country. Alphabet has a minimum performance target for each of its subsidiaries. If a company cannot meet this, then it is closed down and its market area is served by neighbouring companies. All of ABC's managers, from the sales and factory supervisors up to the directors, receive an annual bonus which is based on reported profit. All of the bookkeeping is done on a micro-computer at ABC and the company employs full-time accountants to prepare all accounting statements.

Assume that there is no audit function. Identify five individuals within ABC who could have a motive to manipulate the bookkeeping records within the company or the statements which are prepared from them. In each case, suggest how the the desired distortion could be achieved.

2. Universities usually involve external examiners in the process of setting and marking examination papers.

(a)   Suggest why this should be.
(b)   Draft a job description for an external examiner.
(c)   List a set of criteria which could be used to select an external examiner for a degree course in accountancy.

3. The historical development of any subject is often a useful starting point for any student who is embarking on a course devoted to it. As an exercise, a great deal could be gained from reading brief descriptions of the history of both financial accounting and auditing.[30] Have the disciplines of financial reporting and auditing developed in parallel?

References and further reading

1. Jensen, M.C. and Meckling, W.H., 'Theory of the firm: managerial behaviour, agency costs and ownership structure', *Journal of Financial Economics*, October 1976, pp. 305–60.

2. A useful summary of this branch of the literature can be found in Chapters 8 and 9 of Watts, R.L. and Zimmerman, J.L., *Positive Accounting Theory*, Prentice Hall, 1986.

3. The internal relationships within a company are governed by a constitution entitled the articles of association. A specimen set of articles is contained in Table A, contained in a statutory instrument 'Companies (Tables A to F) Regulations 1985' (SI 1985/805). Each regulation in Table A is deemed to be part of the company's articles unless an alternative rule regarding the same matter has been adopted by

the company's shareholders (Companies Act 1985, s8). Paragraph 73 of Table A requires that one-third of the directors retire at each annual general meeting.

4. Lee, T.A., 'The nature, scope and qualities of auditing', in Carsberg, B. and Hope, A., *Current Issues in Accounting*, 2nd edition, Philip Allan, 1984, p. 84. This essay provides a very readable description of the many examples of auditing which are to be found in all aspects of everyday life.

5. Auditing Practices Committee, *Auditing Standards and Guidelines: Explanatory foreword*, 1980, paragraph 2. The Auditing Practices Committee has been superseded by the Auditing Practices Board. Surprisingly, this new body has not published its own formal definition of audit.

6. Bailley L.P., *Miller GAAS Guide 1994*, Harcourt Brace Jovanovich, 1994, p. 1.03.

7. Committee on Basic Auditing Concepts, American Accounting Association, *A Statement of Basic Auditing Concepts (ASOBAC)*, 1973, p. 2.

8. International Federation of Accountants, Guideline 1, *Objective and Scope of the Audit of Financial Statements*, 1980.

9. Ng, D.S., 'An information economics analysis of financial reporting and external auditing', *The Accounting Review*, October 1978, pp. 910–20.

10. Generally Accepted Accounting Principles. GAAP is an American term which refers to the various accounting standards and other rules which must be adhered to by the preparers of accounting statements. In the United Kingdom, this phrase does not have quite the same meaning because the system of standards is not as comprehensive as in the United States, although its use has become more commonplace since the publication of a book entitled *UK GAAP* (Davies, M., Paterson, R. and Wilson, A. *UK GAAP*, Macmillan, 1994).

11. Ng, D.S. and Stoeckenius, J., 'Auditing: incentives and truthful reporting', *Journal of Accounting Research*, Supplement 1979, pp. 1–24.

12. Antle, R., 'The auditor as an economic agent', *Journal of Accounting Research*, Autumn 1982, pp. 503–27.

13. Chow, C.W., 'The demand for external auditing: size, debt and ownership influences', *The Accounting Review*, April 1982, pp. 272–91.

14. This is because lenders may attempt to protect their interests by writing restrictive covenants into the loan agreement. Some of these may be based on accounting numbers (the directors could, for example, agree to maintain a certain relationship between debt and equity). If the accounting figures upon which the covenants are based are audited, then the lenders may be prepared to accept a lower rate of interest. The reduced cost of interest could exceed the cost of an audit.

15. Francis, J.R. and Wilson, E.R., 'Auditor changes: a joint test of theories relating to agency costs and auditor differentiation', *The Accounting Review*, October 1988, pp. 666–82.

16. The accountancy profession has, for many years, consisted of a relatively small number of large and medium-sized firms and a very large number of small firms. Historically, the eight largest firms have each been particularly dominant. These have been described as 'The Big Eight' despite their identity (and number) changing over recent years because of mergers. It would be unfair to suggest that the work done by the smaller firms is of a lower quality. The large firms are, however, considered more credible by a number of potential users of the accounts, particularly financial institutions.

This dominance of the audit market was underlined by a report which was published in 1989. This estimated that the Big Eight firms received approximately

35 per cent by value of the annual aggregate audit fees paid to UK accountancy firms. The top twenty firms received about 50 per cent. (Likierman, A., *Professional Liability: Report of the study teams*, HMSO, 1989, p. 18.)

17. Briston, R. and Perks, R., 'The external auditor – his role and cost to society', *Accountancy*, November 1977, pp. 48–52.

18. The estimated cost of audit was regarded as rather conservative in a subsequent article which put the total for 1976/77 at £416.02m. (Fanning, D., 'How slow are the auditors in Britain?', *Accountancy*, August 1978, pp. 44–8.)

19. The other reports which auditors are obliged to make from time to time are dealt with in the APB Practice Note 8, *Reports by Auditors Under Company Legislation in the United Kingdom*, 1994.

20. The preferred abbreviation for this body is ACCA, even though the letters would appear to be in the wrong order.

21. The requirement for a degree is not universal. The ACCA is particularly flexible about the range of entry qualifications which it will accept. The bodies which restrict themselves to graduates do not insist on degrees in accountancy. In fact, the accountancy profession annually takes 10 per cent of the United Kingdom's output of graduates, drawing from all disciplines.

   Minimum entry requirements and the training and examination systems of the professional bodies are constantly changing. The careers advisory service of any university should be able to provide the latest details.

22. A useful discussion of the various problems faced by the accountancy profession in the late 1970s, when the standard setting process really began, can be found in Hay Davison, I., 'The future of auditing is in our hands', *Accountancy*, July 1977, pp. 84–91.

23. APB, *The Scope and Authority of APB Pronouncements*, 1993.

24. Mautz, R.K. and Sharaf, H. A., *The Philosophy of Auditing*, American Accounting Association, 1961.

25. *ibid.* p. 1.

26. *ibid.* p. 42.

27. Robertson, J.C., 'A defence of extant auditing theory', *Auditing: A Journal of Practice and Theory*, Spring 1984, pp. 57–67. This article contains a detailed justification for the retention of the Mautz and Sharaf concepts as a theoretical framework for auditing.

28. APB, *The Future Development of Auditing*, 1992.

29. Power, M., *The Audit Explosion*, Demos, 1994.

30. Two particularly readable accounts can be found in Lee, T.A., *Company Financial Reporting*, Van Nostrand Reinhold, 1982, Chapter 4 and Lee, T.A., *Company Auditing*, Van Nostrand Reinhold, 1986, pp. 21–30.

CHAPTER 2

Auditor independence

It is vitally important that the auditor enjoys the shareholders' confidence. They will be unable to place any confidence in the audit report if they feel that its content has been influenced by the directors.

By the time you have completed this chapter you should be able to:

- Define independence and explain why it is important.
- Distinguish between real and apparent independence.
- Describe some of the ways in which auditors might be influenced by the directors.
- Explain the independence regulations in force in the United Kingdom.
- Explain some of the suggestions for the enhancement of auditor independence.

2.1 What is independence?

The objective of an audit has been described as enhancing 'the credibility of the financial statements by providing reasonable assurance from an independent source that they present a true and fair view'.[1] An audit is necessary in order to add credibility to the financial statements. This objective will not be met if the readers of the audit report believe that the auditor could have been influenced by the directors of the company.

ACTIVITY

List some of the ways in which the directors might be seen to be able to influence the auditors.

There are a number of ways in which the auditor could come into conflict with the directors. Broadly, they can affect the auditors' fee income by removing them from the audit or from some other activity. Replacement and public criticism can also affect the auditor's reputation.

The auditors can be considered independent if they resolve this conflict honestly, without shirking their responsibility to the shareholders. This could involve demanding that the directors change their stance over some accounting matter or insisting on the publication of an audit report which expresses reservations about the figures which the directors have published. In either case, the directors could retaliate. If the auditors are not supported against the directors then they could be penalised for their honesty.

There are three main ways in which the auditors' independence can manifest itself:

1   Programming independence.
2   Investigative independence.
3   Reporting independence.[2]

Each of these is vital to the auditors' credibility.

2.1.1 *Programming independence*

Obviously, the audit report will be of little value unless it is supported by a thorough investigation. A thorough investigation may not, however, be in the directors' best interests. If they wish to conceal something then they will wish to minimise the possibility of its discovery. Even if they have nothing to hide, the directors may wish to reduce the audit fee or publish the financial statements as quickly after the year end as possible. If the auditors can be persuaded to curtail their enquiries then this could have a beneficial effect on the cost or on the completion date of the audit.

The auditors must be free to approach the engagement in any manner which they see fit. This freedom is particularly important in the context of an ongoing relationship between an accounting firm and the company. The auditors' approach must adapt as the client company grows and develops new activities. Furthermore, new auditing techniques are constantly being developed. It would not be acceptable for the directors to hinder the auditors in their choice of the basic strategy which they intend to take to the engagement.

2.1.2 *Investigative independence*

Programming independence protects the auditors' ability to select the most appropriate strategy for their audit work. Investigative independence protects the manner in which they implement this strategy. The auditors must have free access to the documents and records of the company. Any questions about the company's business or the accounting treatment of its transactions must be answered.

Underlying the argument that the auditors should not be restricted in the collection of audit evidence is the idea that the audit should be conducted with the full cooperation of the company's management and staff. This is obviously in the shareholders' best interests. If the auditors have difficulty in obtaining the information which they require, the audit will become more expensive. Impeding the auditors could also act against the directors' interests in that it could create the impression that they have something to hide when their actions are disclosed in the audit report.

2.1.3 *Reporting independence*

If the directors have been trying to mislead the shareholders by publishing accounting information which is incorrect or incomplete, they will certainly wish to prevent the auditors from making this public. This is when auditor independence becomes absolutely crucial. Most disagreements are likely to arise over subjective decisions such as the interpretation of an accounting standard or an estimate such as a provision for bad debts. If the auditors insist on disagreeing with the directors, there is no guarantee that their treatment will be popular with the shareholders. In the case of an estimate, they may also find that subsequent events prove them wrong. If, on the other hand, the auditors suppress their doubts, it is possible that their willingness to concede to the directors will never be discovered.

The auditors will often be tempted to follow the line of least resistance by simply complying with the directors on all but the most fundamental differences. By doing so, they will avoid the sanctions which could be imposed by the directors. They are, of course, risking the possibility of even more severe penalties if they are discovered, but this will not necessarily happen. This would, of course, be disastrous for the users of the financial statements. Audit reports would be incomplete or would be expressed in ambiguous language. There would be no point in having an audit under such circumstances.

2.2 Real versus apparent independence

Independence has been described as being 'essentially an attitude of mind characterised by integrity and an objective approach to professional work'.[3] It has also been suggested that 'The two most essential personal qualities for an auditor are probity and strength of character'.[4] This means that independence, despite its importance, will always be difficult to measure. After all, it would be virtually impossible to observe a person's mental attitude or his personal integrity. The auditors' guidance does, however, go further. We are told that an auditor's 'objectivity must be beyond question . : . . That objectivity can only be assured if [the auditor] is, as is seen to be, independent'.[5] It is not enough for auditors to be independent; they must also ensure that there is nothing which would cast doubt on their impartiality. It is, of course, necessary to ensure that auditors are seen to be independent. It would be difficult for the users of the audit report to trust the honesty of someone whom they did not know personally, especially if that person had an obvious vested interest in misleading them. Even if auditors could approach an assignment in which they had a clear conflict of interest with complete detachment, the shareholders could be forgiven for questioning their objectivity. This doubt would completely undermine the credibility which the audit was supposed to add to the financial statements.

The importance of the auditors' attitude towards the client was underlined in a paper which discussed the effects of culture on auditor independence in Japan.[6] This paper pointed out that the auditors' natural inclination was to cooperate with the directors of the company, despite the independence regulations which were based on those in force in the United States. This stemmed from the fact that the Japanese tend to view themselves in the context of the groups to which they belong. It is simply alien for someone to view himself as being independent of an organisation with which he is involved. Unfortunately, this has led to documented cases where the auditors' independence had been constrained to such an extent that a number of unacceptable accounting practices have been condoned.

It will be shown in the sections which follow that the rules which are designed to protect the appearance of independence are not particularly effective in eliminating the auditors' dependence on the company's directors. It would be unfair, however, to suggest that the shareholders' faith in the auditors' objectivity is misplaced. In practice, most auditors approach their work in an independent manner, regardless of the very real pressures which the directors may try to exert. It is, however, ironic that the shareholders can rely on the auditors' integrity despite the rules which are intended to support it rather than because of them.

2.3 Restrictions on independence

It has already been suggested that there will be occasions when the auditors will be in conflict with the directors of the company. It is difficult to ensure that the auditors are able to resist any attempt to influence their judgement in such circumstances because the balance of power tends to lie with management.

It must always be remembered that the auditor earns a living by providing a service. In order to survive, a firm of accountants must be able to attract and retain clients. If the directors of a company are able to threaten the auditors' income then they have the ability to undermine their independence. The problems regarding independence stem from two main sources, the auditors' relationship with the company and the nature of the accountancy profession itself.

2.3.1 *Relationship with the client*

It is impossible to overcome the fact that the auditors receive a fee for the audit. This creates an immediate and pressing need for them to make sure that they do not endanger this source of income. In practice, the amount of the fee tends to be negotiated with the directors. This means that the directors can attempt to pressurise the auditors into restricting the extent of their investigations or punish them for expressing an honest opinion in the audit report by refusing to pay a realistic fee. The directors can also influence the likelihood of the auditors continuing to receive this fee in future years by attempting to have them replaced by another firm. This means that the auditors are faced with a clear conflict of interest. If they upset the directors, they run the risk of losing their livelihood.

It is, of course, difficult to measure the extent to which the auditors and the directors disagree and the effects of this conflict. One study did manage to do so by looking at qualified audit reports and their effect on auditor retention. The evidence suggests that an auditor who expresses doubts about the figures which the directors have published is more likely to be replaced.[7] Auditors will only be truly independent if they can be protected from unfair removal from office. It would, however, be unrealistic to give auditors a permanent position with the company as this would reduce the incentive for them to provide an efficient service at a reasonable cost. The shareholders must always be free to select the most appropriate firm of accountants to conduct the audit. This means that there will always be an opportunity for the directors to influence the shareholders' choice of auditor.

The audit fee is not the only incentive to cooperate with the directors. Accounting firms earn an increasing proportion of their total income from the provision of consultancy services.[8] In the United Kingdom it is common for a company's auditors to provide tax advice as well as acting as management consultants on various other aspects of business. These other contracts may vary from executive recruitment to the implementation of information technology. The directors are also free to award the contracts for these services without seeking the permission of the shareholders. This means that the auditor of the company may be totally dependent on the goodwill of the directors for the continuation of a lucrative consultancy contract. This can hardly reassure the shareholder who has doubts about the auditor's independence.

Following the Companies Act 1989 a statutory instrument was published which requires the publication of remuneration received by auditors for non-audit work.

A related problem is the fact that the other services which the auditor provides could be incompatible with the auditor's main role. If, for example, the auditors are being paid to minimise the company's tax charge, this task could be made more difficult if they express any doubt about the accuracy of the figures in the published financial statements. It is not, perhaps, surprising that many countries refuse to allow the auditors of a company to serve it in any other capacity.

2.3.2 *The structure of the accountancy profession*

It has been suggested that competition within the accountancy profession has intensified.[9] This can put pressure on auditors in a number of ways. If the directors are displeased with them then it will not be difficult to find a replacement.

The cost of the audit is another factor. Accountancy firms are constantly trying to improve the efficiency of their techniques so that they can reduce the time taken to complete the audit and their fees. This could lead to the temptation to cut corners in the conduct of the audit in order to avoid the loss of the audit to a more efficient firm.

The competition between the accounting firms is also making them more publicity conscious. The loss of an audit tends to be publicised in the accountancy and business press, particularly if a large company is involved. This can create further pressure to avoid the displeasure of the directors.

The subjective nature of accountancy is a further source of friction between the auditors and the directors and is also another means by which pressure can be exerted. In deciding whether the accounts show a true and fair view, the auditors must decide whether they agree with the policies which have been adopted by the directors. If they disagree over a contentious issue, then they run the risk of being replaced. There is also the possibility that they will face public criticism if the directors make known the reasons for their choice of accounting policies and cast doubts on the auditors' understanding of the issues. This could be done through the chairman's statement in the accounts themselves, by an announcement at the annual general meeting or even through the press.

In the United States a practice has developed which has become known as 'opinion shopping'. This involves the directors of a company who disagree with their auditors over a contentious accounting issue asking another firm of accountants for their opinion on the matter. It will, of course, be more difficult for the auditors to sustain their position if the other accountants support the directors' argument. It could also lead to the fear that the directors will favour the other firm when they are deciding on the appointment of an auditor for the incoming year. An attempt has been made to curb this practice by requiring firms who are approached for a second opinion to contact the auditors to see if there are any relevant facts that they ought to know.

2.4 Independence regulations in the United Kingdom

There is a host of regulations which exist to govern auditor independence in the United Kingdom. The Companies Act 1985, the accountancy profession's Rules of Professional Conduct and Auditing Standards and Guidelines all contain provisions which are intended to strengthen the appearance of independence. The regulations relating to the preparation of financial statements are also relevant.

2.4.1 *Companies Act rules on the appointment of the auditor*

S 384 of the Companies Act places the responsibility for the appointment of the auditors firmly in the hands of the shareholders, rather than the directors. This section states that the auditors shall be appointed at the general meeting of the company at which the accounts are laid before the shareholders and will hold office until the next general meeting at which accounts are to be laid. In theory, therefore, the directors cannot bribe the auditors with an offer of reappointment or intimidate them with the threat of replacement because they do not have the authority to carry out these acts.

The shareholders usually reappoint the retiring auditors. They are not, however, obliged to do so. If they feel that another firm could provide a better service then they would be free to appoint it instead.

The directors can only appoint the auditors in exceptional circumstances. They can appoint the company's first auditors and can also appoint someone to fill a casual vacancy. These appointments would, however, come to an end when the statements were laid before the company in general meeting. The shareholders would then be free to appoint another firm if they wished.

The shareholders of a private limited company are entitled to dispense with the requirement to appoint auditors every year. They can make an election under s 386 of the Companies Act 1985. Effectively, this election deems the auditors to have been reappointed whenever they would normally have retired. This election can continue indefinitely. It is likely that a company which has made this election will also have dispensed with the requirement to hold an annual general meeting. This means that it would be necessary to have a special shareholders' meeting to remove the auditors from office and appoint another firm.

Part II of the Companies Act 1989 further protects the auditors' independence in a number of ways. Independence is specifically mentioned in s 24 of the Act.

Every auditor must belong to a 'recognised supervisory body' (RSB) and be entitled to act as an auditor under that body's rules. ICAEW, ICAS, ACCA and ICAI have been granted this status. Schedules 11 and 12 of the Companies Act 1989 describe the duties of the RSBs and the entry requirements which they must impose. All of these rules serve to protect the auditors' programming and investigative independence by ensuring that they have the necessary knowledge and skills.

Holders of overseas accounting qualifications which have been approved by the Secretary of State can also practise as auditors in the United Kingdom. This is granted by s 33 of the Companies Act 1989. The approval may be subject to the person taking additional education in UK law and accounting. Historically, this provision tended to be exploited by accountants from some of the Commonwealth countries. In the future, it is likely that the number of overseas bodies whose members are approved will increase because of the EC's directive on the mutual recognition of professional qualifications. The safeguards built into this provision should prevent it from affecting the quality of audits.

Officers and employees of a company, and the business partners and employees of these people, are barred by s 27 of the Companies Act 1989 from acting as its auditor. If anyone is barred from acting as the auditor of a company which belongs to a group then that person is also barred from acting as auditor of the other companies in that group. These requirements are necessary to prevent the appointment of someone who has an obvious vested interest in seeking to please the directors.

A person who is barred from acting as auditor should refuse any offer of nomination and should resign immediately if he or she becomes ineligible during the appointment. If the audit was conducted by someone who was ineligible then s 29 empowers the Secretary of State to order the appointment of another auditor to conduct a second audit or to review the first audit and report on the need for a second. The cost of this will be borne by the company, but can be recovered from the ineligible auditor.

2.4.2 *The auditor's rights*

The Companies Acts contain a number of rules which are intended to protect the auditor's investigative independence. The most important of these are contained in s 389A of the Companies Act 1985. This section states that:

- The auditors of a company have a right of access at all times to the books, accounts and vouchers, and are entitled to require from the company such information and explanations as they think necessary for the performance of their duties as auditors. Thus, the directors cannot suppress information on the grounds that they do not consider it relevant to the audit.
- It is a criminal offence for an officer of the company to make a misleading, false or deceptive statement to the auditors in respect of a material matter relating to the audit. This applies whether the statement is written or oral. It also applies whether the statement was knowingly or recklessly misleading.
- The company's UK subsidiaries and their auditors are obliged to provide such information and explanations as the auditor of the parent company may reasonably require. In practice, the same firm of accountants will usually be retained to audit the statements of all of the companies in a group. This provision will, however, be useful if other accounting firms are involved.
- The company is obliged to take all reasonable steps to obtain informa-

tion and explanations required by the auditors from the company's overseas subsidiaries.

This legislation prevents the directors from restricting the collection of evidence in a blatant manner. This does not, however, prevent more subtle attempts to do so by, say, imposing reporting deadlines which would be difficult, but not impossible, to meet. Alternatively, the directors could try to negotiate a fee which would barely allow the auditors to conduct a full investigation. The shareholders are unlikely to be sympathetic towards auditors who have been accused of unduly delaying the publication of the financial statements or of over-charging for their services.

The auditors' reporting independence is protected by the fact that s 236 of the 1985 Act specifically requires that the auditors' report should state whether the accounting statements have been prepared in accordance with the Act and also whether the financial statements give a true and fair view of the company's financial position and performance. This means that the directors cannot attempt to resolve a disagreement over an accounting matter by asking the auditors to word their report in a vague manner which simply avoids the expression of the auditors' opinion about the statements.

While this protection is to be welcomed, the problem is that there is considerable debate about the definition of truth and fairness. At any given time, there are usually a number of contentious areas in accounting which have not been dealt with by an accounting standard or specific legislation. This means that there is considerable scope for the directors to interpret the rules in such a way as to ensure that the statements portray the company in a favourable manner. This has led to the creation of the phrase 'creative accounting'. If the auditors qualify their report over such a difference of opinion, it could be argued that they are being unrealistic and obstructive.

The auditors are also entitled to communicate with the shareholders in person. According to s 390 of the Companies Act 1985, the auditors are entitled to receive notice of any general meetings. The auditors are entitled to attend these meetings and to be heard on any matter concerning them as auditors.

2.4.3 *Companies Act rules on the removal of the auditor*

The auditors can be removed from office or could wish to resign. This might be because the firm cannot provide an adequate service or because its credibility has been impaired by some bad publicity. The Companies Act 1985 contains a number of provisions which are intended to ensure that the directors cannot undermine the auditors' independence by threatening to remove them from office. The dismissal of the auditors and their possible replacement with another firm are left in the hands of the shareholders. The relevant legislation is contained in sections 391 to 394A of the Companies Act 1985.

The auditors can be removed from office at any time. This simply requires an ordinary resolution at a general meeting, regardless of any agreement between the auditors and the company. Special notice has to be given for a resolution for the removal of the auditors from office before the expiration of their term of office or for the appointment as auditor of a person other than the retiring auditor.

The company must send a copy of the notice to the auditors. The auditors are then entitled to make written representations and request that these be distributed to the members. Any notice of the resolution which is sent to the members should state that these representations have been received. The company must also send a copy to every member unless there is insufficient time to do so before the meeting. If they are not sent out then the auditors have the right to have them read out at the meeting itself.

This right to communicate with the members will make it more difficult for the directors to remove the auditor unfairly. This will, however, be less effective if they are not posted to the members but are simply read out at the meeting. This is because it is unlikely that all of the shareholders will be present. The directors, or anyone else who claims to be aggrieved, can also apply to the court to have the right to distribute the representations withheld. This application will be granted if the court is satisfied that the representations are being abused to secure needless publicity for defamatory matter.

The auditors retain the right to attend and be heard at the general meeting at which their removal or replacement is to be decided. If they are removed from office then they can attend the meeting at which the statements which they would have reported on are laid before the members and the meeting at which their replacement is to be appointed. They have the right to be heard at these meetings on any matters affecting them as a former auditor.

ACTIVITY

In theory the auditors should have no fear of upsetting the directors. If the directors do threaten them with replacement then they can write to the shareholders at the company's expense and speak against the resolution at the meeting. The members of the company can then decide on the resolution to remove or replace the auditors with all of the facts at their disposal.
Do you think that these procedures will be effective in practice?

It is debatable whether this legislation is likely to be effective. First, the directors will almost certainly be able to influence the shareholders in their choice of auditor. Very few of the members will have strong feelings about which particular firm should conduct the audit. Second, the auditors' representations might be viewed as an attempt to retain a lucrative appointment. If the directors wish to remove the auditors from office because they refused to assist them to mislead the shareholders then they will almost certainly create some pretext for doing so – saying, for example, that their work was unsatisfactory or that their fees were too high. This could lead to a great deal of adverse publicity for the audit firm and could discourage the auditors from fighting to retain the appointment. Third, the mechanics of the rules tend to leave the initiative with the directors. It is they who are responsible for copying and despatching the auditors' response. This means that they are forewarned of their arguments and can respond accordingly.

There is one final provision which effectively makes it pointless for anyone to remove the auditors in order to suppress some damaging information. Any auditor who ceases to hold office must deposit a statement. This statement must list all of the circumstances connected with ceasing to hold office which should be brought to the attention of the members or creditors of the company. Alternatively, the auditor must deposit a statement to the effect that there were no such circumstances.

If the auditors' statement contains a description of circumstances then the company must distribute copies to the members and debenture holders. This can only be avoided if the company can convince the court that the statement is being used to secure needless publicity for defamatory matter. If the company does not make an application to the courts, or if the court insists on the distribution of the statement, then the auditors are also obliged to send a copy to the Registrar of Companies.

It is an offence for the auditors to fail to comply with this requirement. It does, however, remove any temptation to remove the auditors in order to conceal something from the shareholders or creditors. Such an attempt would, if anything, draw even more attention to the matter.

These provisions apply even if the auditors resign from office. In fact, the resignation is not considered effective until the auditors deposit the statement of matters connected with the resignation at the company's registered office. This prevents the auditors from resigning instead of reporting some embarrassing facts. The auditors might, for example, be tempted to resign quietly if they discovered that the statements had been materially misstated in previous years. It would reflect badly on the firm if the irregularity was reported because the shareholders would want to know why it had not been revealed sooner. It would, however, be a breach of the auditors' statutory and professional duties to allow the misstatement to continue. The auditors would, however, have to disclose the inaccuracies in the statement of matters connected with the resignation and could not, therefore, escape the dilemma by resigning.

This safeguard suffers from many of the deficiencies which exist in the regulations regarding the replacement of the auditor. The directors would be forewarned of the auditors' statement as they would be responsible for its distribution and could easily produce their own counter-claims.

Thus, the Companies Acts go to great lengths to protect auditors from the influence of the directors. These safeguards would prevent the blatant abuse of the auditors and would ensure that the auditors' views were made available to the shareholders. Unfortunately, these rules are not capable of giving total protection to the auditors.

2.4.4 *The Guide to Professional Ethics*

The Guide to Professional Ethics is published by the bodies whose members are authorised to conduct audits.[10] The rules cover several aspects of professional behaviour, including independence. They attempt to protect auditor independence in two main ways. First, they prohibit auditors from entering into certain proscribed relationships with the client company which would detract from the appearance of independence. Second, they give auditors the right to communicate with anyone who is asked to take the appointment over from them.

An audit firm cannot be considered independent if it is so heavily dependent on the fees paid by a client that its directors can effectively put it out of business by removing it from office. The rules suggest that the fees from any given client should not exceed 15 per cent of the gross recurring fee income of the practice or 10 per cent in the case of a public interest company (e.g. a quoted company).

The logic behind this guidance is sound. The problem is that it ignores the reality of the way in which accounting firms operate. Most of a firm's business expenses will consist of fixed costs, such as salaries and administrative expenses. The loss of 10 per cent, or even less, of annual fee income could have a disproportionate effect on the firm's short-term profits. Even in the longer term, an accounting firm cannot lay off staff without incurring adverse publicity.

Even if the firm as a whole could survive the loss of a relatively small client, the audit partner who was responsible for the loss could suffer enormously. His or her share of the partnership profits could be linked to the number of audits for which he or she is personally responsible. The loss of an audit could also affect his or her standing within the firm. Thus, the loss of an audit could have very little effect on the firm as a whole, but could be a serious matter for the partner concerned.

The auditor must also avoid a situation where a personal relationship with a member or members of the client's staff would impair objectivity. Thus, it is suggested that it would not be appropriate for the partner or a member of the audit team to be a relative of a senior member of the client's staff. While it is easy to avoid this type of involvement, little can be done about the problems of close friendships developing between the partner in charge of the audit and the senior management of the company over a number of years.

Auditors should not be shareholders in client companies. If this arises because of the gain of a new client or through inheritance then the investment should be disposed of as quickly as possible at the open market price. In avoiding a financial stake in the company, auditors should also refrain from making loans to or accepting loans from clients.

Auditors are advised to avoid conflicts of interest. Thus they should take care when providing services in addition to audit. If they agree, for example, to assist in the negotiation of a loan contract, the auditors could be tempted to accept a set of financial statements which was misleading because a more accurate set would present the company in a less favourable light to a potential lender.

Auditors should also be extremely wary of participating in the preparation of the financial statements or the underlying bookkeeping records upon which they are based. The rules accept that a small private company may require the assistance of the auditor in this respect and permits the preparation and audit of the same figures. It is, however, suggested that the auditor should not be involved in the preparation of statements for a public company.

The guidance also lays down some procedures for auditors who are asked to take over an appointment from another firm. Before taking up the appointment, they must request permission to contact the outgoing firm and write asking for all information which ought to be made available to them to decide whether they should be prepared to accept the nomination. If the company does not permit them to contact the other firm, or if the other firm replies that it has not received permission to reply to the request, then the appointment should be refused.

ACTIVITY

How does this requirement assist auditor independence? Is it likely to be effective?

Effectively, this means that auditors have the right to contact anyone who is asked to replace them and to inform them of any professional reasons why they should refuse the appointment. It is to be hoped that the other firm would not condone any unprofessional behaviour by the directors of a company, such as an attempt to coerce their auditors into accepting an unacceptable accounting policy by threatening to replace them.

Unfortunately, the rules do not go beyond ensuring that the other firm is contacted. There is no requirement that an auditor should refuse an assignment just because the present incumbent asks him to.

2.4.5 Auditing and accounting standards

The APB has published a number of Statements of Auditing Standards (SASs). These deal with reporting and the collection of evidence. The standards on audit testing assist the auditors' programming and investigative independence by requiring, amongst other things, that their work is properly planned and their opinions adequately supported. Auditors are constrained by these requirements and cannot bow to pressure from the directors to disregard them. Furthermore, the directors would have little to gain in this respect from replacing the auditors with another firm who would, after all, be bound by the same rules.

The reporting standard protects the auditors' reporting independence by prescribing the form and content of the audit report, stating in very precise terms what wording should be used in each of the circumstances where the normal audit opinion cannot be expressed. The directors cannot ask the auditors to modify the report because they would then be in breach of their professional standards. This makes it difficult for the auditors to mask any uncertainty or disagreement by resorting to the use of vague language.

The explanatory foreword to the Financial Reporting Standards requires auditors to consider whether the accounts have been prepared in accordance with the requirements of the FRSs when deciding on the truth and fairness of the draft financial statements prepared by the client. Again, this supports the auditors' reporting independence. If the directors try to publish a statement which is based on a misleading accounting policy, the auditors can resist their arguments by referring to the FRSs.

The problem with the both the reporting standard and the FRSs is that they are open to interpretation. The reporting regulations permit the auditors to disregard any disagreement or uncertainty provided the problem is not material. Unfortunately, there is very little practical guidance on the definition of materiality in the real world. The FRSs are equally subjective and ambiguous.

2.4.6 *Are auditors independent?*

It would appear from the foregoing arguments that auditors have a vested interest in cooperating with the directors of the company. This begs the question – are auditors independent? If not, then there is very little point in having an audit.

The rules which are intended to protect auditor independence are flawed. This does not mean, however, that they are totally ineffective. At the very least they lay down a mimimum standard against which auditors' work can be measured. If the auditors fail to comply with the provisions of an SAS or accept figures which are in direct contravention of one of the FRSs, then they could face severe penalties. Quite apart from the immediate possibility of having to pay damages to anyone who suffers, the firm will also lose a great deal of credibility in the eyes of other clients and could lose a great deal of business.

Thus, at worst, auditors could only be influenced in subtle ways and only over matters of opinion. The penalties for a direct breach of the rules would almost certainly outweigh the value of retaining any single client.

2.5 Some possible developments

The Canadian Institute of Chartered Accountants commissioned a survey of the public's perception of the audit function.[11] One of the questions in the survey asked whether respondents believed that the auditor would be prepared to 'bend the rules' in order to justify an audit report which would be acceptable to management. The response to this question was not particularly encouraging. Almost half (45 per cent) of the sample disagreed with this suggestion and a further quarter (24 per cent) were neutral about it. This means, however, that a quarter of the investing public are unsure about auditor independence and almost a third of the investing public have doubts about independence.

It would appear that some action is required to remedy the imbalance in the relationship between the auditor and management. A number of suggestions have been put forward, some of which have been rejected outright, others of which are still under consideration.

2.5.1 *Audit committees*

An audit committee is

> A committee of the board normally comprising three to five directors with no operating responsibility in financial management. Its primary tasks are to review the financial statements, the effectiveness of the company's accounting and internal control systems, and the findings of the auditors, and to make recommendations on the appointment and remuneration of the external auditors.[12]

The basic role of the audit committee is to improve the quality of financial reporting. This would be achieved by increasing the level of debate and awareness about accounting matters at board level and also by enabling the auditor to communicate more effectively with the directors.

If a company did not have an audit committee, the finance director would often be expected to take total responsibility for the preparation and audit of the financial statements. This means that it is possible for the other directors to have very little involvement in accounting. This is undesirable for a number of reasons. The finance director could feel that he is under pressure to ensure that the figures appear satisfactory, even if this means that they have to be distorted. Any disagreements which he has with the auditor might not be brought to the attention of the board and so the company could suffer a qualified report or be charged an excessive audit fee because of the finance director's intransigence. The other directors could be accused of shirking their responsibilty for the truth and fairness of the accounts.

Ideally, an audit committee should consist largely, or even entirely, of non-executive directors. This is because non-executives are seen to be less dependent upon the company for their livelihoods. They will not look at areas such as the selection of accounting policies with the same degree of self-interest. The executive directors depend on the company for a much larger proportion of their total income. Inevitably, they will be tempted to publish misleading figures in order to satisfy the shareholders' desire for profits, particularly if the results would be disappointing.

Even if the members of the committee are not accountants, they ought to have sufficient knowledge and experience of business to be able to study the broad concepts underlying the draft accounts which are to be presented to the main board for approval. They would be able to consider the merits of the various accounting policies which could be adopted. They could arbitrate between the finance director and the auditor, particularly over areas requiring subjective judgement. This means that the board will be able to take the advice of the audit committee and will, therefore, be able to arrive at an informed decision about any contentious accounting matter.

It has been suggested that non-executive directors are as dependent on the goodwill of the executive directors for the continuation of their appointments as the auditor. Thus, the audit committee could be ineffective because the members are afraid to support the auditor. A study was conducted to investigate this possibility.[13] The results of this work indicated that the committee would be more likely to support the auditor rather than the finance director, particularly if the disagreement between them was over the application of an objective, technical standard.

A further analysis of the study's findings indicated that committee members who hold full-time management posts in other companies are even more likely to support the auditor than members who are retired managers or those who have no managerial experience. This could be because a full-time executive has more to lose from being associated with a scandal or it could be because he will have a greater awareness of accounting matters.

One of the recommendations arising from the CICA report is that there should be legislation to require every public company to have an audit committee. The principal reason for this would be to strengthen auditor independence.[14]

2.5.2 *Restriction on range of services offered*

One of the proposals which was contained in the EC's Eighth Directive, which was concerned with the regulation of auditors, was that auditors should be prohibited from offering any additional services to their clients. An accounting firm would, therefore, have to decide whether it was going to serve any given client as an auditor or as a consultant. This would solve two of the problems associated with independence. Each client would provide a smaller proportion of total income and the conflicts of interest inherent in providing other services in addition to audit would cease.

Despite the apparent advantages which this would offer, the Department of Trade and Industry faced vigorous lobbying from both auditors and their clients who feared that the suggestion would lead to additional cost and a great deal of disruption. It was pointed out that the knowledge gained from audit could assist in the provision of tax and financial planning advice. The opposite was also true: the auditor could use the insight gained from consulting in order to plan a more effective audit. The reaction would certainly appear to have been persuasive because the DTI have withdrawn the proposal.

2.5.3 *Compulsory rotation of auditors*

Another suggestion contained in the Eighth Directive was that there should be an upper limit on the number of years for which an accounting firm could act as auditors to any given company. After a maximum of five years, the company would have to find another auditor.

This would mean that the auditor would not have to worry about the effects of upsetting the directors because he would know that he was going to be replaced after five years anyway. Furthermore, the auditor would also be aware that another firm was going to be taking over from him in the foreseeable future. The incoming firm could discover any shortcomings in his audit work and might report them. This would provide the auditor with an additional incentive to resist any attempt to influence him.

Again, this proposal was considered unacceptable by the accountancy profession and the companies themselves and was withdrawn as a result. Again, this was on the grounds of the time and cost. Every five years, the directors would have to select a new firm of auditors. The company would then be faced with the disruption of a new audit team having to familiarise itself with the workings of the company for the first time. It could also be argued that an auditor is more likely to miss something during the early years of an appointment when he is relatively unfamiliar with the client.[15]

This proposal was certainly unpopular, although it is not totally unworkable. In Italy, for example, an auditor cannot serve the same client for any more than nine years. After this period has elapsed, he cannot be reappointed by the company for at least five years.[16]

2.5.4 *Peer review*

In the United States, any accounting firm which wishes to act as an auditor of a company which is supervised by the Securities and Exchange Commission must have their quality control procedures reviewed at least once every three years. This review can be conducted by either another firm of CPAs or by a team from the AICPA. Such a review will ensure that the overall quality of audits is maintained throughout the profession. It will also encourage the auditor to ensure that he does not permit his standards to slip in the face of pressure from clients as he could, effectively, lose his licence to practise as a result.

There is no direct equivalent to the peer review system in the United Kingdom. It has, however, been suggested that larger accounting firms could conduct their own internal reviews by using staff from other offices to review the quality of audit work.[17]

2.5.5 *Conceptual framework*

The problems created for the auditor by the enormous subjectivity inherent in accounting were discussed in 2.4.5 above. Accounting as a discipline has evolved over time. This means that there is no widespread agreement on such apparently fundamental issues as the precise definition of basic terms such as assets and liabilities, nor is there any general agreement on the information needs of the users of accounting statements. This means that the auditor is required to form an opinion on the truth and fairness of a set of accounting statements when, in fact, the term 'true and fair' does not have an agreed working definition.

One response to this problem, which has serious implications for the preparers and users of accounting information as well as the auditors, has been to attempt to design a cohesive set of theories to underpin the development of accounting standards and to guide the preparers and auditors of statements when dealing with matters which are not the subject of formal standards. This set of theories has been described as the 'Holy Grail' of accountants.[18]

It has been suggested that the auditor would be the greatest beneficiary of the conceptual framework project. This is because it is extremely difficult to argue against a proposed accounting policy which is not specifically prohibited by law or one of the FRSs. Even where a policy would appear to be in breach of these regulations, it is often possible to circumvent the rules. In 1986, for example, a company took counsel's opinion about the way in which the definition of extraordinary items was being abused. It was argued that this standard had been ignored to such an extent that the company had to ignore it too in order that the accounts should comply with 'general accounting practice'. The company's audit report was unqualified, even although it would appear that the statements contained a clear breach of SSAP 6.[19]

2.5.6 *The Cadbury Report*

The Committee on the Financial Aspects of Corporate Governance ('The Cadbury Committee') was established in 1990 by the Financial Reporting Council, the London Stock Exchange and the accountancy profession. This was in response to concerns about the criticisms of financial reporting and other aspects of corporate governance. This led to the publication of a wide-ranging report in 1992.[20] Auditor independence was one of the issues covered in this report.

The committee made the following recommendations in respect of auditor independence:

- Both auditors and directors should acknowledge a responsibility to maintain an objective working relationship.
- More effective accounting standards should be developed.
- Every listed company should form an audit committee.
- Companies should disclose the fees paid to auditors in respect of non-audit services.
- Audit firms should rotate the partner in charge of individual audits on a periodic basis.

While the sentiments contained in the report are admirable, it did little more than express further support for the status quo.

2.6 Summary

Independence is of vital importance to auditors. Audit reports will have no value unless auditors can programme their work in the most appropriate manner, conduct investigations without restriction and report their findings clearly and objectively.

The appearance of independence is at least as important as the auditors' attitude, although it may be that the readers of the report are forced to rely on the auditors' integrity to a greater extent than they would wish.

A number of proposals have been put forward to improve the quality of auditor independence. The most practical of these would be the creation of audit committees and the improvement of the standard setting process.

REVIEW QUESTIONS

1. Describe the procedures which would have to be undertaken by the directors of a company who wished to appoint an auditor to replace the present holder of the post. Assume that the auditor does not want to be replaced.

2. 'The auditor is only as independent as the directors allow him to be'. Discuss.

3. If independence is essentially an attitude of mind, why is it necessary to have the auditor's behaviour regulated by so many detailed rules?

4. The Automobile Association (AA) will, in return for a fee, have an engineer inspect a used car on behalf of one of its members. Compare and contrast the independence of the AA from the garage selling the car with that of an auditor from the company whose accounts he is auditing.

5. Discuss the extent to which the provision of non-audit services could impair or enhance the independence of the auditor.

6. Considerable amounts of time and effort have been devoted to the development of a conceptual framework for accounting, so far without success. To what extent would the auditor's independence be enhanced by the adoption of an agreed conceptual framework?

EXERCISES

1. Whinge and Grovel is a small firm of Chartered Accountants, which employs approximately fifty professional staff and provides a range of management consultancy services as well as traditional audit and accounting work. The firm has recently been appointed as the auditors of Bigg Bisness PLC, a major quoted company. This has been hailed as something of a coup for such a small firm and the partner in charge of the firm has issued a press release claiming that this prestigious new appointment is likely to be followed by others.

The audit was obtained by a tendering process. The firm has committed itself to conducting the audit for a fee which is 20 per cent lower than that paid to the outgoing firm for the previous year's audit. The engagement letter restricts fee increases to a maximum of 5 per cent for each of the next two years.

Bigg Bisness has appointed the firm to provide tax advice and to negotiate the final amount of corporation tax payable. The tax partner has given the board of Bigg Bisness an informal undertaking that the tax liability will be at least 30 per cent lower than that of the previous year.

Whinge and Grovel also gave a great deal of assistance during the replacement of the company's computer system, which took place during the first two months of the financial year. The firm provided a systems analyst who designed the detailed systems specifications for the software house which wrote the programs for the accounting function. One of the firm's managers has also been seconded to supervise the operation of the new system until a permanent manager with the appropriate qualifications and experience can be found. Discuss the ways in which Whinge and Grovel has compromised its independence.

2. You are the technical partner in the executive office of a major firm of Chartered Accountants. You are concerned that the audit staff in some of your provincial offices could be acting in a manner which could impair the appearance of the firm's independence.

Draft, in note form, a series of rules regarding professional independence for circulation to professional staff working on audits.

3. You are the partner in charge of a firm of accountants. You have returned from holiday and found a number of memos, each of which relates to a different audit:

(a) The audit senior in charge of the audit of A plc has become engaged to the chief accountant of the company. The happy couple met during the interim audit. The final audit is scheduled to commence in two weeks time.

(b) The audit partner in charge of B plc has been taken ill. Another partner has been asked to take charge of the work on an interim basis, but has refused on the grounds that she owns shares worth £1,000 in the company. The company's market capitalisation is approximately £500,000.

(c) The audit manager in charge of the audit of C Ltd, a garage, has recently purchased a new car from the company, taking advantage of their low interest finance package.

(d) A friend of one of the firm's partners is also the finance director of D plc. He is dissatisfied with the service provided by his present auditor and he would like your firm to accept nomination for appointment at the next annual general meeting.

(e) The directors of E plc have invited you to offer yourself for election as auditor at their next annual general meeting. They have indicated that the audit fee will be approximately £150,000. The gross recurring fee income of your firm is just over £1.5m per annum.

(f) The directors of F Ltd, a small manufacturing company, are thinking of retiring and have asked you to assist them in the preparation of a package of information which will be presented to support the sale of their controlling interest in the company.

They have offered to pay you a percentage of the amount raised by the sale in return for your help.

What action should you take with regard to each of these memos?

4. During the annual general meeting of a large, quoted company, the directors have been asked the following questions regarding the reappointment of the auditor:

(a) The auditor is supposed to be appointed by the shareholders and to act on our behalf. Why is it that we are simply asked to rubber stamp your recommendation every year? To make matters worse, the reappointment would always seem to have been agreed with the auditor in advance because he always seems to have indicated that he is willing to accept the post.

(b) How can the auditor be independent anyway? You negotiate his fees. You give him all sorts of lucrative consultancies which we never hear about. He would sign anything which was put in front of him!

Frame a (polite) response to the shareholder's complaints. Suggest why the shareholders tend to delegate so many of their powers regarding the appointment and remuneration of the auditor to the directors.

5. Mr Tick is the auditor of G plc, a medium-sized manufacturing company. He is rather perplexed. The chief accountant of the company has prepared a draft set of accounts which clearly fails to comply with several of the FRSs. The chief accountant is apologetic, but refuses to change the figures because he has been ordered to ensure that the profit figure comfortably exceeds the amount stated in the press release which the managing director issued several weeks before the year end.

Mr Tick spoke to the managing director, who holds an accounting qualification, and was told that the interpretation of the FRSs was a matter of personal opinion. His view was that the accounts were as true and fair 'as they had to be'. He refused the auditor's request for a meeting with the entire board of directors on the grounds that none of the other directors knew anything about accounting matters and always followed the managing director's advice anyway.

The managing director countered Mr Tick's threat to qualify the audit report by stating that it would not be difficult to convince the board and, indeed, the shareholders that another firm of accountants would provide a better service. Mr Tick does not feel that he should have to resign over this issue. Effectively, this would mean that he was being penalised for someone else's dishonesty.

State the ways in which the creation of an audit committee would improve the quality of the financial statements and the independence of the auditor of G plc. How should such a committee be constituted in this case? What barriers could exist to its effectiveness?

References and further reading

1. APB, SAS 100, *Objective and General Principles Governing an Audit of Financial Statements*, 1995.
2. Mautz, R.K. and Sharaf, H.A. *The Philosophy of Auditing*, American Accounting Association, 1961, pp. 206–207.

3. ACCA, *Professional Independence*, 1984, paragraph 1 (a).
4. Flint, D. *Philosophy and Principles of Auditing*, Macmillan, 1988, p. 64.
5. ICAEW, *Integrity, Objectivity and Independence*, 1993.
6. McKinnon, J. 'Cultural constraints on audit independence in Japan', *The International Journal of Accounting*, Fall 1984.
7. Chow, C.W. and Rice, S.J., 'Qualified audit reports and auditor switching', *The Accounting Review*, April 1982.
8. See *Accountancy*, July 1995, pp. 18–20.
9. Zeff, S.A. 'Does the CPA belong to a profession?', *The Accountant's Magazine*, October 1987.
10. The Rules of Professional Conduct are contained in the *Accountants' Guide*, published annually by the Certified Accountants Educational Trust.
11. CICA, *Report of the Commission to Study the Public's Expectations of Audits*, 1988, Appendix B. Telephone interviews were conducted with 540 individuals, who had been selected on the grounds that they were 'knowledgeable' users because they had read audited financial statements or had invested in publicly traded shares.
12. Marrian, I.F.Y., *Audit Committees*, ICAS, 1988.
13. Knapp, M.C., 'An empirical study of audit committee support for auditors involved in technical disputes with client management', *The Accounting Review*, July 1987.
14. CICA, *Report of the Commission to Study the Public's Expectations of Audits*, 1988, p. 38.
15. A study in the United States of lawsuits against accountants revealed that 23 per cent of the cases analysed involved accountants with three years experience or less with the client. (St. Pierre, K. and Anderson J.A., 'An analysis of the factors associated with lawsuits against public accountants', *The Accounting Review*, April 1984, pp. 242–63.)
16. Oldham, K.M., *Accounting Systems and Practice in Europe*, Gower, 1987, p. 167. Article 56 of the EC's Fifth Directive states that the auditor should be appointed for a period of not less than three or more than six financial years. Reappointment should be restricted so that the same auditor cannot hold office for more than twelve consecutive years. At the time of writing, it would appear that the UK government is opposed to this suggestion.
17. APC Auditing Guideline, *Quality Control*, 1985.
18. Nobes, C., 'Through mists in search of the Holy Grail', *Accountancy*, November 1985, pp. 75–6.
19. Cunningham, E., 'The prickly problem of accounting practice', *Accountancy Age*, 21 August 1986.
20. *Report of the Committee on the Financial Aspects of Corporate Governance*, Gee and Co., 1992.

CHAPTER 3

The auditor's duties

The auditor's duties are laid down by the Companies Act 1985. Essentially, these revolve around the auditor's report on the truth and fairness of the financial statements. The interpretation of these requirements has been the subject of a great deal of controversy. Specifically, there has been a great deal of debate about the extent to which auditors should be held responsible to the users of the financial statements if it is subsequently discovered that they failed to discover an error. This is a very topical area. It is also one in which the attitude of the courts has changed significantly in recent years.

By the time you have completed this chapter, you should be able to:

- Describe the auditors' duties.
- Explain what is meant by reasonable care and skill in the context of audit.
- Explain the auditors' duties with respect to the detection and reporting of fraud.
- Explain the effects of the audit expectations gap.
- Explain how auditors maintain the quality of their work.
- Explain the extent of the auditors' liability to readers.

3.1 The nature of the auditor's duties

The audit report is addressed exclusively to the shareholders. It has, however, been suggested that the auditors' responsibilities extend to other groups of users. Lee, for example, argues that the auditor has three different levels of responsibility:

1   A SPECIFIC responsibility . . . to the shareholders and their company.
2   An ETHICAL responsibility . . . to his profession and to the public.
3   A TENTATIVE and INFORMAL responsibility . . . to other persons making use of company financial statements.[1]

This notion of a broad responsibility to society as a whole was the central theme of an essay by Flint which argued that '[t]he practice of auditing cannot evolve satisfactorily in a changing world if it is not conceived and exercised in the context of a social philosophy of audit and accountability'.[2]

It could be argued that the enlightened attitude displayed in the foregoing quotations forms a stark contrast to the current attitude which prevails within the accountancy profession, which is one of denying responsibility to all but the narrowest group possible. There has, however, been a growing tendency for lenders and investors to blame the auditors for decisions which have had an unsatisfactory outcome.

ACTIVITY

Suggest why auditors are likely to be blamed for bad investment decisions.

There are two main reasons for this. One is that readers often misunderstand the auditors' role and may genuinely believe that they were entitled to a duty of care. The other, more cynical suggestion is that accounting firms are backed by professional indemnity insurance and may, therefore, be the only parties involved who are able to afford compensation. This is sometimes called the 'deep pockets' theory.

3.2 The auditors' statutory duties

The auditors' principal duty is to make a report to the company's members on the company's annual accounts. They must state whether, in their opinion, the statements have been prepared an accordance with the Companies Act 1985 and whether they give a true and fair view of the profit or loss for the year and state of affairs at the year end.[3]

The auditors must also consider whether the information in the directors' report is consistent with the information in the profit and loss account and balance sheet. Any inconsistency should be disclosed in the audit report.[4] The auditors are also required to form an opinion on several other matters. They do not have to make a positive statement about them in the report, but must bring any reservations to the shareholders' attention. They must consider whether:

- proper accounting records have been kept by the company;
- the company's balance sheet and profit and loss account are in agreement with the accounting records and returns;
- all the information and explanations which considered necessary for the purposes of the audit have been obtained and whether adequate returns for their audit have been received from branches not visited during the audit; and
- the requirements of Schedule 6 to the Companies Act 1985, which is

concerned with the disclosure of the directors' emoluments and other benefits, have been complied with.

The auditors are not required to make a positive statement if they are satisfied with these matters. They must, however, state any reservations in the audit report. If the company has not made full disclosure of the directors' emoluments then the audit report should, if possible, contain a statement of the required particulars.[5]

The auditors' principal duties centre round the report on the truth and fairness of the financial statements. This chapter will examine the nature of the auditors' responsibilities with regard to this report, concentrating on two key issues:

1 To what extent does the auditor have to be certain that every error or irregularity in the financial statements has been discovered?
2 To whom is the auditor responsible?

There are no clear answers to either of these questions. It would, however, be difficult to overstate the importance of either of them. Increasing the level of assurance which the auditors are expected to provide will have a corresponding effect on the amount of evidence which must be collected, especially if auditors are to uncover fraudulent misstatement. This, in turn, will increase the cost of the audit to the shareholders. An extension of the auditors' responsibilities to third parties will also increase the cost of the audit. This is because the auditors must protect themselves by means of professional indemnity insurance. Broader responsibilities will increase the likelihood of a claim and so the insurance premium will rise. This cost will be passed on to the company in the form of higher fees.

3.3 'Reasonable skill and care'

The sections of the Companies Act 1985 which deal with the auditors' duties make constant use of the word 'opinion'. Auditors must form an opinion on the truth and fairness of the financial statements, on the adequacy of the company's accounting records and so on. Auditors are not, therefore, obliged to provide a guarantee. This reflects the subjectivity inherent in accounting. There is always the possibility that someone will disagree with some of the assumptions upon which the figures have been based. It is also a response to the limitations of time, cost and availability of evidence which prevent the auditor from checking every transaction and balance recorded in the company's records. This leaves the auditor with a certain amount of discretion about the amount of testing which must be done in order to support the opinion.

While the audit report is not a guarantee that the figures are free from error, the auditor must conduct the audit in such a way that it stands a reasonable chance of discovering a material error in the figures. The ICAEW published guidance for its members in which it was stated that there was a general presumption that the supplier of a service would carry it out with 'reasonable skill and care'.[6]

ACTIVITY

What does 'reasonable skill and care' mean to you? How might you go about measuring this in relation to audit work?

> It is difficult to determine what is meant by reasonable skill and care. Claims of negligence have often been settled out of court. This is partly because accountants tend to be afraid of adverse publicity and partly because their insurers have been reluctant to risk setting legal precedents which would increase the level of their exposure.[7] This means that there is very little recent case law in this area. A further difficulty is that many of the principles which have been applied in the past were established so long ago that they would no longer be considered applicable. Many apparent precedents could, in fact, be misleading.

The requirement that the auditor should apply reasonable skill and care has not changed over the years. The development of new auditing techniques and changes in the business environment have, however, led the courts to expect higher standards. In the famous case of Re Kingston Cotton Mill Co. (No. 2) (1896) 2 Ch. 279, it was held that the auditor had not been negligent, despite the fact that he had failed to attend the company's stock-count and had failed to detect a substantial error because of this. Nowadays, auditors who failed to attend a stocktaking would find little comfort in the Kingston Cotton case. Such an omission would be considered unacceptable. The accountancy profession has, for example, issued an Auditing Guideline which suggests that the auditor should always attend stocktakes when the value of stock is likely to be material.[8] Mautz and Sharaf have argued that the publication of professional pronouncements on ethical and auditing standards constitutes a public acceptance of responsibility.[9]

This attitude was echoed in the judgement in the case of Re Thomas Gerrard and Son Ltd (1968) Ch. 455 in which it was stated:

> I am not clear that the quality of the auditor's duty has changed in any relevant respect since 1896. Basically that duty has always been to audit the company's accounts with reasonable care and skill. The real ground on which Re Kingston Cotton Mill Co (No. 2) is, I think, capable of being distinguished is that standards of reasonable care and skill are, upon expert evidence, more exacting today than those which prevailed in 1896.

It is unlikely that a court would be satisfied with the work of an auditor who had failed to comply with professional auditing standards and guidelines. This does not, however, mean that the application of the rules contained in these documents will provide absolute protection against accusations of negligence. A court could find, for example, that the professional pronouncements were themselves too lax.[10] The application of the standards also requires a great deal of subjective judgement.

The techniques available to the auditor are developing at a considerable pace. The introduction of computerised accounting has, for example, created opportunities to conduct very comprehensive tests at relatively little cost. Statistical sampling techniques which enable the auditor to quantify the risk of arriving at an incorrect conclusion have been developed. Many accounting firms have adopted the so-called 'risk-based approach' to auditing. This has the advantage of forcing the auditor to examine the company's circumstances and to identify possible pressures or opportunities for error or deliberate manipulation. These techniques are becoming more widely used. It is possible that, in years to come, failure to apply them will be considered indicative of negligence.[11]

3.4 Fraud

The shareholders expect the directors to take care to protect their company's assets. They will, therefore, expect to be informed of any significant losses because of fraud. One of the main criticisms directed at auditors is that they frequently fail to detect fraud or to notify the shareholders that fraud has occurred.

ACTIVITY

Try to suggest why auditors would be unwilling to accept a duty to detect and report fraud.

The distinction between fraud and error is one of intent. Errors occur in a random manner. This may mean that their effects will tend to cancel each other out. Errors may be obvious, in which case they will probably be detected and corrected by the company's staff. Fraud, on the other hand, is deliberate. It involves the falsification of records in order to conceal either a theft or some other form of misconduct. This means that the inaccuracies in the financial statements will occur in a systematic manner, with a greater likelihood of significant misstatement. Fraud will usually be much more difficult to detect than error because the culprit may have taken care to conceal it.

3.4.1 *Professional guidance on the auditor's responsibilities for the detection of fraud*

Paradoxically, professional auditing standards would appear to be placing less emphasis on the detection of fraud as time passes while the courts are becoming stricter with auditors who fail to discover it.[12] The SAS on the auditors' duties with respect to fraud states that the prevention and detection of fraud and other irregularities rest with management and that the auditors' duties do not require a specific search for fraud. The auditor's only duty is to plan the audit so that there is a reasonable expectation of detecting any material misstatements which have resulted from fraud.[13]

The SAS suggests that the directors are responsible for the prevention and detection of fraud. The auditor should, however, take care to ensure that the truth and fairness of the financial statements has not been distorted by fraudulent misstatement. The procedures which auditors should adopt with regard to fraud will depend on the risk that fraud could occur and remain undetected and also the risk of that fraud impairing the truth and fairness of the statements. The SAS contains an appendix which lists some of the factors which the auditor should take into account in evaluating this risk. The auditor should also bear in mind the effectiveness of the different audit tests which can be carried out. Fraudulent employees could have used forged documents or acted in collusion so that the misstatement will not be discovered by normal audit techniques. Auditors cannot, after all, apply any more than reasonable skill and care. It would be unusual for an auditor to test, say, the authenticity of a document which had apparently been created by a third party.

Thus, the professional standards would appear to suggest that the auditors should not be too concerned about the possibility of fraud unless something is discovered to indicate that an irregularity has occurred. If, however, the auditor becomes suspicious then further work should be done to clarify the situation. It may be that the suspicions were groundless. If a fraud is discovered then all of its implications should be considered. The financial statements might have to be altered in order to give a true and fair view. Any evidence obtained from the person or persons responsible for the fraud will have to be re-examined.

The auditors will normally report any fraud to the management of the company. If it appears that the fraud has been committed by management itself then the auditors ought to seek legal advice as to the most appropriate action to take. In general, auditors will not have to report direct to the shareholders provided the matter is properly accounted for. If the directors refuse to adjust the financial statements then the auditors might not be able to state that the accounts give a true and fair view and would, therefore, be forced to modify the report to the shareholders accordingly.

Auditors might have to report the fraud or other irregularity to a third party, possibly the police. This will, however, happen only in the most extreme circumstances. The auditor has a professional duty of confidence towards the company.[14] The auditors must weigh the damage to the public interest which would be caused by a breach of this duty against the effects of suppressing the information about the fraud or irregularity. This is unlikely to be an easy decision. It might help to consider the number of people who are likely to be affected by the matter and the amount which they are likely to lose. It is also worth considering the extent of the certainty that the fraud or irregularity has been committed.

The auditors should ensure that they are not exposed to the risk of legal action by reporting the matter to a third party. It may be necessary to demonstrate that the report was made in the public interest and was not motivated by malice. The auditors must also have reasonable grounds for suspicion. If possible, the directors should be persuaded to report the matter themselves.

The Cadbury Committee points out that many of the difficulties associated with reporting fraud would be resolved if companies established audit committees. The audit committee would provide the perfect means for the auditors to communicate any suspicions regarding senior executive management.[15]

3.4.2 *The attitude of the courts*

The courts would appear to view the detection of fraud in the same light as the detection of any other inaccuracy in the financial statements. Auditors are expected to apply reasonable care and skill to the search for fraud. There is, however, a double problem associated with this. The shareholders are likely to view the existence of fraud as indicative of poor stewardship on the part of the directors. Thus, the theft of, say, £500,000 could have virtually no impact on the profitability of a large company but could still be viewed with alarm by the shareholders simply because it is a reasonably substantial sum. The auditors may, therefore, be expected to discover relatively small misstatements. This is compounded by the fact that the fraud could have been very carefully concealed by employees, who may hold a position of trust.

The courts do not, however, expect the auditor to conduct an exhaustive search for fraud. All that is required is a degree of healthy scepticism. In the Thomas Gerrard case, for example, the auditors argued that they had no grounds to suspect the assurances of the company's managing director when, in fact, he had fraudulently overstated the value of stocks. This argument was rejected, mainly because the auditors had failed to conduct a rudimentary examination of the stocks themselves and had, therefore, been negligent. Such basic errors of judgement would appear to be common to most of the cases in which the auditor has failed to detect fraud. Another example arose in a Canadian case, where the auditors of an airline ticket agency had failed to detect a scheme to mislead the owner of the business and the airline. The court held that the auditors would have discovered the problem if they had conducted a simple reconciliation of the tickets issued during the year.[16]

It has been pointed out that senior management may be able to benefit from a distortion of the figures even if they do not enjoy any direct gain as a result. An improvement in the profit figures could, for example, lead to an increased bonus or prevent a takeover bid. The fact that such a manipulation could be very difficult to detect means that the auditor should always consider the factors which could indicate a relatively high risk. This could mean that additional testing will be required in certain areas or even that the accounting firm should not accept the appointment.[17]

3.5 Expectation gaps

There have been a number of suggestions that the users of audit reports do not fully understand the nature and purpose of an audit and the extent of the auditor's duties. In 1970, for example, Lee published the results of a survey of the beliefs of auditors, auditees and the beneficiaries of audits.[18] This revealed, *inter alia*, that many investors thought that the auditor guaranteed the accuracy of the financial statements. Substantial numbers also thought that the auditor was supposed to provide advice and assistance on accounting and, to a lesser extent, non-accounting matters.

Beck conducted a study into the beliefs of Australian investors.[19] This was done by means of sending a list of assertions regarding possible roles of the auditor. This revealed the following:

- 93 per cent of the respondents thought that the auditor provided assurance that there have been no frauds perpetrated by company officials.
- 92 per cent thought that the auditor ensured that management had discharged all of their statutory duties.
- 71 per cent expected the auditor to warn of any inefficiency in management.
- 81 per cent thought that the auditor gave assurance that the company was financially sound.
- 71 per cent expected the auditor to ensure that all of the directors' actions were in the shareholders' best interests.

ACTIVITY

Who could suffer as a result of the expectations gap?

This widespread ignorance of the precise role of the auditor was seen as the source of much of the adverse press comment about the quality of audit work. Such ill-informed criticism could undermine the credibility of the accountancy profession.

These misconceptions are damaging to the users of the audit report, who may be placing an excessive amount of reliance on the figures in the accounts.[20] They are also damaging to the auditor, whose credibility will be damaged when it becomes apparent that he is unable to satisfy many of the users' expectations. It is important, therefore, that differences in expectations are identified and eliminated, either by the introduction of

more stringent auditing standards or by educating the readers of the
audit report.

The accountancy professions in both the United Kingdom and Canada have
made some attempt to inform users by the publication of booklets aimed at the
non-accountant.[21]

3.5.1 *The psychology of the expectation gap*

A theoretical model of this expectations gap was devised and tested using the
psychological theory of causal attribution.[22] Any failure by a professional person
may be caused either by an error of judgement or by external circumstances
which could not have been controlled. When attributing responsibility for this
failure, an observer will take three sets of information into account when
deciding on the extent to which the professional should be blamed:

Consensus
This concerns the extent to which the behaviour of the person under
observation (the 'actor') conformed to that of other actors in similar
circumstances. If an auditor had displayed a high level of consistency
with professional standards, then this would tend to imply that the
failure was because of some external circumstance. Suppose, for example, that auditors do not investigate the extent to which major weaknesses in the company's system of accounting controls have been
exploited. If observers use only consensus information, then an auditor
will not be held responsible if he fails to discover a fraud which has been
caused by such a weakness.

Consistency
This concerns an actor's past record of successes and failures. He is more
likely to be held responsible if he has already been blamed for errors in
similar circumstances. Thus, the auditor in the previous example is more
likely to be criticised if he has already been blamed for failing to discover
fraud in other companies.

Distinctiveness
If it is recognised that a certain task is difficult, then the actor is less
likely to be held responsible for any failure. If, for example, it was
recognised that it was particularly difficult to discover a carefully concealed fraud, then an auditor who had not been able to do so would be
less likely to be blamed.

The distinction between these different types of information is an important
one. If users rely heavily on consensus information, then the problem of the
expectation gap can be resolved by modification of auditing standards. If the
other factors are more important, then much more work will have to be done to
establish the manner in which users measure previous success rates or the degree
of difficulty associated with each aspect of an audit.

The authors created seven cases in which the auditor had failed to detect an error or irregularity in the financial statements. For each case, a variety of combinations of consensus, consistency and distinctiveness information was developed. Two samples, one of qualified accountants and the other of small business owners, were asked to examine the cases. The businessmen were used as a surrogate group for the users of audited statements. Each participant was given 100 points for each case. He was asked to allocate these between: auditor ability, auditor effort, task difficulty, and 'luck'. This enabled the authors to measure the extent to which the auditor was being held responsible for the failure.

The initial examination of the responses to these cases revealed that the accountants tended to attach much more importance to the auditor's compliance with auditing standards. This meant that the accountants were also much less likely to find the auditor responsible for the failure. The users tended to place a great deal of emphasis on the consistency and the distinctiveness information.

A further study based on this same information considered the interaction between the various sources of information. This suggested that the users tended to pay relatively little attention to the consensus information, unless the two other sources implied that the auditor was not responsible. It would appear that both auditors and users must be informed about the importance attached by the other to compliance with auditing standards. It would also tend to confirm the fear that compliance with professional standards is not necessarily an adequate defence against charges of negligence.

3.5.2 *The accountancy profession's response*

The American Institute of Certified Public Accountants established the Commission on Auditors' Responsibilities in 1974. This Commission was asked to investigate whether there was a gap between what the public expected of the auditor and what the auditor provided. The Commission reported in 1978, concluding that there was a gap in expectations and that the auditors should be made responsible for reducing it.[23] The Commission made a number of suggestions which suggested ways in which the audit could be changed so as to accommodate users' needs and also suggested that there was a need for auditors to extend the audit report so that the extent of their responsibilities was more clearly defined.

With regard to fraud, the Commission stated that the auditor should be expected to detect those frauds that the exercise of professional skill and care would normally uncover. The auditor should also pay careful attention to the controls within the company's system and ensure that steps are taken to eliminate any weaknesses which could be exploited. Traditional audit techniques may not always provide the assurance which is required of them. The auditor should always pay attention to the effectiveness of their tests and to the availability of new methods.

More recently, the chairman and senior partner of one of the major international accounting firms, speaking in the United States, stated that there was still a major gap in expectations.[24] While he did not accept that the profession had failed to meet its responsibilities, he still felt that too much was expected both in terms of the detection of fraud and error and also in terms of the forecasting of impending business failure. This, he felt, was the reason for much of the criticism directed at the auditing profession. He suggested that the auditing standards should be extended so that the auditor was required to evaluate the company's system of management controls and to identify aspects which were especially defective. At that time there were no specific requirements for the auditor to examine the control systems. It was also suggested that the auditor should be required to consider the company's business environment and to identify any symptoms which suggested that there was a higher than normal risk of misstatement.

The Canadian Institute of Chartered Accountants (CICA) has also conducted a survey of users' needs.[25] This confirmed the results of the previous studies in that there was a gap between the service provided by the auditor and the expectations of users. Concern was expressed about the following:

> auditor independence;
> proficiency;
> the quality of accounting information and the standards upon which they are based;
> the lack of warning given about risks, particularly about business failure;
> the discovery of fraud, and
> the auditor's desire to limit responsibility to a narrow group of users.[26]

Again, the report went on to make a number of suggestions about improvements which could be made by the auditor in order to reduce this gap.

The Auditing Standards Board (ASB) of the AICPA has produced several new auditing standards in response to these studies. These are Statements of Auditing Standards (SASs) numbers 53 to 61. These cover four main areas:

1 SAS 53–54
   Clarify the auditor's responsibilities with regard to fraud and illegal acts by the client. In particular, the auditor is required to look for indicators that these problems exist and to inquire into any suspicious circumstances.

2 SAS 55–57
   Attempt to improve the effectiveness of the audit by requiring a more effective response to weaknesses in the company's system of internal controls, by providing guidance on analytical review techniques which ought to be applied, and by discussing the problem of auditing accounting estimates.

3 SAS 58–59
   Strengthen communication between the auditor and the users of the report by augmenting the information given in the audit report so that

the reader is better informed about the relative responsibilities of the auditor and management. The limited nature of the audit testing is also made more apparent. Guidance is also given on the auditor's responsibilities with respect to the going concern concept.

4   SAS 60–61

Strengthen communication between the auditor and the company by suggesting ways in which management can be informed about problems with the company's accounting system. The development of links with the company's audit committee is also covered.[27]

The ASB still perceives an expectations gap, despite the introduction of this substantial number of new SASs. In particular, it is believed that the auditor should produce additional reports on internal controls. It is also hoped that much more guidance will be given on the particular audit problems of specific industries.[28]

Much of the material contained in the various reports referred to above and also in the new US standards will be incorporated into the relevant chapters throughout the remainder of this text.

3.6 Quality control procedures

This section will deal with some of the attempts which have been made to ensure that auditors comply with their professional standards. Despite their shortcomings, these standards do lay down a minimum level of performance and auditors who do not meet their requirements cannot be regarded as having fulfilled their duty to the shareholders. The need for such measures was highlighted in a most startling manner when the Department of Trade and Industry (DTI) notified the professional accounting bodies that there were some blatant shortcomings in the quality of the work done by some of their members.[29] These included the following:

failure to prepare accounts in the statutory formats as laid down in the Companies Act 1985;

the filing of modified accounts by companies which were not permitted to do so;

accounts filed after the due date;

auditors acting as Company Secretary, despite the fact that officers of the company are barred from acting as auditor, and

failure to provide depreciation on fixed assets, despite the requirements contained in both SSAP 12 and the Companies Act 1985.

There was no indication that these breaches were widespread. The fact that the DTI felt obliged to make this type of complaint would, however, imply that there had been an unacceptable level of default. These errors are, of course, so obvious that they could be revealed by even a cursory glance at the financial statements. This raises the possibility of more serious omissions which remain undetected.

It would appear that the credibility of auditors would be enhanced if there was a mechanism for ensuring that the quality of the work undertaken by individual firms was of an acceptable quality.

3.6.1 *Quality control within firms*

Accounting firms vary in size and in the manner in which they are organised. In general, very few of the smaller firms have any significant involvement in auditing. This means that most audits are conducted by relatively large firms which usually have a hierarchical structure. The titles given to the staff within these firms vary enormously, although the basic structure of any given audit team will generally be as follows:

Partner
The partner is ultimately responsible for the completion of the audit. He will sign the audit report on behalf of the firm. The partner will not be actively involved in the routine audit work.

Manager
The audit manager will be responsible for the overall supervision of the detailed audit testing. He will also liaise between the company's management and the partner. If the firm is auditing the statements of a group of companies, the manager will coordinate the efforts of the various audit teams involved.

Senior
The senior will be directly responsible for the day-to-day supervision of the staff engaged in the collection of evidence. The senior may be a qualified accountant, but could be a trainee who is about to become a member of one of the professional bodies.

Juniors
The junior audit staff will collect audit evidence, working under the supervision of the senior and manager. Juniors may be relatively recent recruits who are training with the firm or, increasingly, could be accounting technicians who are employed to support the qualified staff.

The SAS on quality control[30] suggests that the partner has to satisfy himself of the quality of the audit evidence obtained before signing the audit report. The section devoted to the control of audit work suggests that this can be accomplished by ensuring that the staff engaged on the audit are not given more responsibility than they can cope with and that the work of each member of the team is reviewed. This, in turn, requires that each member of staff should maintain detailed working papers.

The SAS also requires that the quality of the work done throughout the firm as a whole is of an acceptable standard. This covers a number of areas:

1   Each firm should have an established set of procedures. In the context of a large firm, this could mean that there is a standard audit manual which is supported by a series of audit programmes. This will mean that every audit will be conducted in a similar manner.

2   The firm should not accept an appointment unless it is certain that it is both independent and in possession of sufficient staff with the necessary ability to conduct the audit properly.

3   All staff should be aware of the ethical requirements regarding independence and confidentiality. Steps should be taken to resolve any conflicts of interest.

4   The skills and competence of staff should be maintained at the required level, with attention paid to the recruitment of new staff and the training and development of staff within the firm.

5   There should be appropriate consultation on contentious matters. Some firms appoint two partners to certain audits. The engagement partner's duties would be as outlined above. He would, however, be supported by a concurring partner whose task would be to review any major issues which required professional judgement, such as a new accounting policy or a difficulty in obtaining audit evidence.

6   The firm's procedures should be monitored. In large firms, this could mean that staff from an office in one part of the country visit another office and review a number of audit files in order to see whether the firm's standard procedures are being properly applied.[31]

3.6.2 *External enforcement of quality control*

The most effective means of ensuring the quality of audit work is to encourage firms to implement their own internal mechanisms for monitoring quality control. In a number of countries, notably the United States, firms of accountants who wish to practise as auditors must submit their procedures to an external scrutiny.

In the mid-1970s, the US accounting profession was threatened with increased government interference. In response to this, the AICPA made strenuous efforts to increase the level of self-regulation. One step was the creation of a division of practising firms. This division consisted of two sections, the SEC Practice Section (SECPS) and the Private Companies Section. This gave the AICPA the ability to regulate the behaviour of firms, rather than of individual members.

A firm must belong to SECPS if it wishes to audit the financial statements of companies whose shares are publicly traded. These firms must satisfy the AICPA's rules which are intended to ensure that they perform work which is of an acceptable standard and also restrict the extent to which they can provide services other than auditing.[32] A slightly less stringent set of conditions exists for firms which belong to the Private Companies Section. Firms in each of these sections must submit themselves to a peer review at least once every three years.

A peer review is an examination of a firm's overall quality control system. Effectively, it is an audit of the auditor. The review is conducted by either another firm of accountants selected by the firm under review or by a review team from the AICPA.

A survey of the findings of SECPS reviewers has discovered that over 90 per cent of firms received a letter of comment, indicating that there were areas in which some improvement was required, but that well over 80 per cent of the firms received a 'clean' opinion on their initial review. This suggests that most of the comments which were made were not of major importance. The most common type of complaint centred on the quality of supervision within individual audits and also on the overall quality control procedures within firms. The attitude of senior partners towards the technical quality would appear to be the single most important factor.[33]

There was some controversy over the introduction of peer review, partly because of the cost and partly because its effectiveness was questioned. Firms do, however, derive benefits. Their credibility is enhanced, they may be encouraged to adopt more efficient techniques and the risk of litigation is reduced.[34]

The closest equivalent to peer review in the United Kingdom is the Joint Monitoring Unit established by the RSBs to carry out checks on the standards in force at firms authorised to act as auditors. This organisation does not, however, have sufficient resources to enable individual offices to be visited frequently.

3.7 The auditor's legal liability

The auditor may be penalised for failing to apply reasonable care and skill. This could take the form of disciplinary action by a professional body, or civil, or even criminal, proceedings. Again, a serious study of this area is complicated by the fact that very few cases are resolved publicly.

3.7.1 *The auditor's criminal liability*

The auditor could be guilty of a criminal offence under the Theft Act 1968 if he aided or abetted management to publish false statements with intent to defraud shareholders or lenders. The auditor will be guilty under the Financial Services Act 1986 if, either knowingly or recklessly, he associates himself with an invitation to invest in a client company which is inaccurate or misleading. Finally, any person who was party to the carrying on of a business with intent to defraud is guilty of an offence under section 458 of the Companies Act 1985.

Thus, auditors are unlikely to be guilty of a criminal offence unless they deliberately abuse their position by participating in some fraudulent scheme. Quite apart from the possibility of a fine or imprisonment, an accountant who was convicted of such an offence would almost certainly be expelled from his or her professional body.

3.7.2 *The auditor's civil liability*

It is not sufficient in itself to establish that an auditor has been negligent in order to obtain damages from him. Two further conditions must be met:

1   The auditor must have owed a duty of care to the plaintiff.
2   The plaintiff must have suffered a loss as a result of the auditor's negligence.

It is fairly obvious that the auditor owes a duty of care to the shareholders. There is a contract between the audit and the company, the shareholders pay for the audit, and the audit report is addressed to them.

It could, however, be argued that the auditor's duty of care extends beyond those to whom he or she has a contractual relationship. Audited accounts are often used as supporting documents in loan applications, when negotiating for the sale of a private company, and for a host of other purposes. The audited accounts are also filed with the Registrar of Companies and so become a matter of public record. Thus, there are many potential users who could claim to have suffered as a result of an ineffective audit, some of whom could even be completely unknown to the auditor.

It has already been argued that, morally, the auditor has a duty to society as a whole. A moral obligation is not, however, sufficient justification for making the auditor liable for every possible use to which the report could be put. In fact, the extent of the auditor's duty of care to third parties has tended to increase over time. The case of Candler v. Crane Christmas (1951) 2 K.B. 164; (1951) 1 All E.R. 361 appeared to establish that the auditor could not owe any duty of care to a third party, even if it was known that the party was likely to rely on the audited information. Mr Candler had been invited to invest in some companies. The owner of these companies had asked the defendants to prepare some financial statements for the purpose of negotiating this investment. Mr Candler lost his investment when the companies went into liquidation. It was discovered that the auditors had not verified the ownership of some buildings which had been treated as corporate assets. They were, in fact, the personal property of the owner.

The court held that the defendants had not owed a duty of care, despite the fact that the purpose of the statements had been known to them. This case is, however, best remembered for the dissenting comments of one of the judges, Lord Denning, who expressed disquiet at the suggestion that accountants and auditors owed a duty of care to no-one but their clients. He argued that the auditor should be liable to anyone whose use of the accounts was known. Lord Denning's views were upheld in the case of Hedley Byrne and Co Ltd v. Heller and Partners Ltd (1964) A.C. 465, H.L.(E). This case did not involve accountants, but was recognised as having implications for all professionals who provided reports on their clients for the use of third parties. Heller and Partners were bankers to a company with whom Hedley Byrne was planning to do business. Hedley Byrne wished to check the company's financial position and requested a bank reference. The reference which was provided contained an error and the plaintiffs lost their fees and expenses because of this. It was argued that no duty of care was owed because Hedley Byrne were not customers of the bank and also because the reference carried a disclaimer of liability. It was, however, held that the defendents owed a duty of care.

The Hedley Byrne case was considered significant for auditors. It appeared that a duty of care would be owed to a third party provided the auditor had been aware of that person's interest and the use to which it had been intended to put the audited accounts.

The case of Jeb Fasteners Ltd v. Marks, Bloom and Co. (1981) 3 All E.R. 289 applied some of the principles which had been established in other non-accounting cases and extended the auditor's duty of care even further. In this case, the plaintiffs had taken over a company whose financial statements had been audited negligently. It was argued that the overstatement of profit had led to the payment of more than the company was actually worth. The court held that the company in question, BG Fasteners, had been experiencing liquidity problems and it should have been obvious that it would seek financial support. This should have led the auditors to foresee that the company was likely to be taken over. They should also have foreseen that audited accounts were likely to form the basis for the negotiation of the purchase price. Thus, the auditors were found to have a duty of care to the plaintiffs, despite the fact that they had not been aware of Jeb Fasteners' interest in their client.

The Jeb Fasteners decision did not imply that the auditor had a duty of care to every person who used the financial statements. Such a duty would exist only in circumstances in which the use of the statements was reasonably foreseeable. This principle was reaffirmed in the Scottish cases of Twomax Ltd v. Dickson, McFarlane and Robinson 1982 S.C. 113. The plaintiffs had purchased shares in Kintyre Knitwear Ltd. The most recent accounts of this company contained a number of errors and it was found that the auditors had been negligent. A duty of care was established because the auditors were aware that the company was short of capital and also that one of the directors wished to sell his shares. The defendants were ordered to compensate the plaintiffs for their losses on this investment.[35]

This extension of the auditor's liability was brought to an abrupt halt by the case of Caparo Industries plc v. Dickman and Others (1990) (H.L.(E)). The judgement limited the auditor's liability to such an extent that it has, arguably, changed the perceived role of the auditor. During the period from June to October 1984, Caparo Industries had built up a 92 per cent shareholding in Fidelity plc. Caparo started to purchase shares shortly before the publication of Fidelity's annual report. A few months later, Caparo claimed that the annual report had been prepared and audited negligently. They claimed that the auditors owed them a duty of care on two grounds. First, Caparo had been a shareholder when the annual report upon which they had relied was published. Second, it should have been reasonably foreseeable that the company was susceptible to a takeover bid. Its profits had not been as high as projected and its share price had fallen significantly. This meant that the auditor would also have had a duty of care to a potential bidder for the company.

The question of the auditors' negligence was not addressed by the court. In 1987 the judge rejected the case on the grounds that no duty of care had been owed to the plaintiffs. It was stated that there could only be a duty of care if three conditions had been met:

1   There would have to have been a foreseeable economic loss arising from a lack of due care.
2   There would have to have been a close and direct relationship between the defendant and the plaintiff. The plaintiff would have to have been either a person known to the defendant or a limited class of persons who were likely to rely on the statement.
3   The imposition of liability would have to be fair, reasonable and just in the circumstances.

In this case, the crucial factor which prevented a duty of care from arising was the fact that there was no close or direct relationship between Caparo and the auditors. Fidelity was a public company and its shares were constantly being bought and sold. It was also considered unjust to impose a common law liability upon the auditors of public companies which are likely to sell shares, raise loans, or, indeed, be taken over at any time.

The court also held that Caparo's position as a minority shareholder at the time of the publication of the accounts made no difference either. The auditor's duty is owed to shareholders as a class and not to individuals. Caparo appealed against this verdict. The Court of Appeal held that a duty of care was owed to the plaintiffs as shareholders, but not as potential investors. The auditors appealed to the House of Lords. The House of Lords ruled that that the auditor had not owed a duty of care to the plaintiffs. Lord Bridge reviewed a number of precedents involving claims in respect of negligence. He argued that a defendant would owe a duty of care if the following conditions were met:

1   He was fully aware of the nature of the transaction which the plaintiff had in contemplation.
2   He knew that the advice or information would be communicated to the plaintiff, either directly or indirectly.
3   He knew that it was very likely that the plaintiff would rely on that advice or information in deciding whether or not to engage in the transaction in contemplation.

In these circumstances, the defendant could clearly anticipate that the plaintiff would rely on the advice or information. The plaintiff would be entitled to rely on the advice or information, subject to the effect of any disclaimer of responsibility by the defendant.

The situation is entirely different where someone makes a statement which is to be put into general circulation and which may foreseeably be relied upon by strangers for a variety of different purposes. Holding that the maker of the statement could have a duty of care to these strangers would 'subject him, in the classic words of Cardozo C.J. to "liability in an indeterminate amount for an indeterminate time to an indeterminate class": see Ultramares Corporation v. Touche (1931) 174 N.E. 441, 444'. It would also 'confer on the world at large a quite unwarranted entitlement to appropriate for their own purposes the benefit of the expert knowledge or professional expertise attributed to the maker of the statement'.[36]

Lord Bridge examined the auditor's duty of care to the shareholders. It is clear that the shareholders rely upon the audit report as an important part of their review of the directors' financial stewardship. The audit report is addressed to the members. The auditor's fee is paid by the company. These facts establish a relationship between the auditors and the shareholders. Negligence on the part of the auditor could deprive the shareholders of the right to monitor the actions of the directors and the shareholders ought to be entitled to a remedy. He felt that this duty was owed to the shareholders as a class and not as individuals. If the company had suffered a loss, perhaps because the auditor had failed to discover misappropriation of funds, then the claim against the auditor would be made in the company's name.

There were no obvious situations in which an individual shareholder could claim to have suffered a loss which was attributable to negligence on the part of the auditor. A shareholder might claim to have sold shares for less than their true worth because of an accounting error. Lord Bridge did not, however, believe that this loss could be directly attributable to the misleading information contained in the audit report. A shareholder might decide to invest more in the company. This could lead to a loss if the share price had been inflated because of an accounting error. The purchase of additional shares would, however, be an independent transaction which had no connection with the existing shareholding. Thus any duty of care which the auditor had to individual shareholders would not extend to such a transaction.

Lord Oliver agreed that the auditor's function was to protect the company itself from the consequences of accounting errors or wrongdoing and to ensure that the shareholders had reliable information with which to scrutinise the behaviour of the directors. He did not believe that the legislation which imposed the requirement for an audit was intended to protect the public at large, including investors.

The principles established in Caparo were applied in the case of Al Saudi Bank and Others v. Clark Pixley and Another (1990) 2 W.L.R. 344; (1989) 3 All E.R. 361. The bank made a substantial loan to Gallic Credit Ltd. This advance was lost when the company was forced into liquidation. The bank claimed that the company's financial statements had not shown a true and fair view and that the loan would not have been granted if the true position had been known. They also claimed that the auditors had a duty of care because they should have foreseen from the nature of Gallic Credit's business that the company would require to renew its lines of credit with a bank or other lending institution. Thus, even though the auditor had been unaware of the identity of the bank which was about to grant the loan, it should have been obvious that such a transaction was to be negotiated and that the audited accounts would form the basis for the lender's final decision. This argument was rejected on the grounds that there was no direct relationship between the bank and the auditors.

The court stated that the existence of such a relationship could only be decided after a close examination of the facts in each case. In the case under consideration, however, it appeared that the auditor had not sent a copy of the statements to the bank. Nor had the auditor been aware that the financial statements were being sent to the plaintiffs, or to any other bank. The fact that the statements could foreseeably come into the possession of a potential lender was not enough to create the necessary relationship.[37] The lack of a direct relationship led to the rejection of claims against auditors in the cases of McNaughton v. Hicks Anderson and Berg Sons & Co Ltd v. Adams.

Even if a plaintiff can establish a duty of care, he must still prove that he has suffered a loss because of the auditor's actions. In the Jeb Fasteners case, for example, the court held that the company would have been acquired anyway because the plaintiffs wished to acquire the services of two of the directors.

The case of Lloyd Cheyham v. Littlejohn (1985) BCLC helped to clarify the extent to which third parties were entitled to rely upon the audit report. Several aspects of the judgement delivered in this case are worthy of note. First, when deciding upon the auditor's acceptance of the company's accounting policies, the judge relied heavily on SSAP 2. This would appear to give the SSAPs a certain amount of judicial backing. Second, the auditor was able to defend the reasoning behind his report because of the high quality of his working papers and, as a result, managed to establish that he had not been negligent. Third, it was held that plaintiffs in such cases have a responsibility to take reasonable steps to protect their own interests.

Lloyd Cheyham purchased a major interest in Trec Trailers Ltd, a company which hired trailers. Cheyham had relied heavily on the audited accounts of Trec when negotiating the purchase. The auditor, Littlejohn, had been aware of Cheyham's interest. After the completion of the purchase, Cheyham discovered that they had underestimated the maintenance costs of the trailers, particularly the cost of replacing tyres. This problem was so acute that Trec had to cease trading. Cheyham argued that the problem had arisen because Trec had not made an adequate provision for the cost of tyre replacement in their financial statements. The auditor should have been aware of this omission and should have mentioned it in the audit report.

Much of the discussion in the case centred round the treatment of the tyre replacement costs. Eventually, it was decided that the auditor could prove that the need for such a provision had been considered and had been rejected for reasons which could be justified. This meant that he had not been negligent. The judge went on, however, to consider whether the plaintiffs had been justified in placing so much emphasis on the audit report. While it was beyond doubt that the auditor could have a duty of care to a third party in certain circumstances,[38] it was held that the third party could not rely on the auditor's opinion to an unreasonable extent. Cheyham could, and should, have commissioned their own investigation into the affairs of Trec. Such a precaution would have brought the problem to light and would have prevented the loss of the investment.[39]

3.8 Third party liability and the role of the audit

The auditor's basic duty is to lend credibility to the financial statements. The reader of the statements benefits because there is less risk of basing a decision upon misleading information. The audit report cannot, however, protect the reader from any of the other risks inherent in investment, lending, or whatever. This distinction between information risk and business risk is made very forcibly in an article by Pound and Courtis.[40] The authors claim that much of the criticism which is directed at the auditor is a result of confusion over the nature of the two types of risk. This is, in turn, partly because of the expectation gap referred to earlier.

The tendency to blame the auditor is also said to be anomalous. The authors cite studies which suggest that very little attention is paid to the audit report. Given the lack of interest in the auditor's opinion before making the investment, it would appear inconsistent to attribute the blame for any loss sustained to him afterwards. The reason for this would appear to have a great deal to do with the resources at the disposal of most large firms of accountants. In addition to being substantial businesses in their own right, they also tend to protect themselves with professional indemnity insurance. This means that the auditor may be the only party involved with a failed company who is left with sufficient resources to pay damages. This is the so-called 'deep pockets' theory of professional liability.

3.8.1 *The Likierman Report*

In 1988, the Secretary of State appointed three study teams to examine the problems caused by professional liability for auditors, the construction industry and surveyors.[41] The team responsible for the auditing profession examined the extent of the auditor's exposure to claims for damages. It was found that the level of claims was increasing. This was making professional indemnity insurance more expensive. It was also causing other problems. Firms of accountants were, for example, conducting more exhaustive audits and were becoming more selective about their clients.

The study team made four major recommendations:

1 The law of joint and several liability should be changed. The auditor can be sued and forced to bear the entire burden of the plaintiff's loss, even if the directors or other parties were partly to blame. The study team felt that the Law Commission should examine ways in which the liability could be distributed more fairly.

2   Companies should be permitted to pay the premium for insurance of their directors' and officers' liabilities. If the directors were insured then the plaintiffs would not have the same incentive to direct all of the blame at the auditor.

3   The law relating to contributory negligence should be clarified. At present, it is unclear whether a defendant in a case relating to breach of contract can reduce this liability by claiming contributory negligence on the part of the plaintiff.

4   The auditor should be able to agree a contractual limit to any liability. S 310 of the Companies Act 1985 would render such an agreement void.

It would appear unlikely that the first and fourth of these recommendations will be implemented. The changes to the law of joint and several liability could make it much more difficult for an injured party to obtain compensation. The contractual limitation of liability could mean that the damages awarded to the plaintiff would bear no relationship to the amount of the loss suffered. The Companies Act 1989 amended s 310 of the 1985 Act. Companies are now permitted to purchase insurance cover for the liabilities of their directors and auditors.

The confusion over contributory negligence was addressed in a consultation paper published by the Law Commission. It is likely that the law will be changed in the manner suggested by the study team.[42]

3.8.2 *The end of professional liability?*

There can be no doubt that the Caparo decision and the partial implementation of the suggestions made in the Likierman Report are to be welcomed by practising accountants. It is, however, possible that that this apparent respite in the steady increase of the auditor's exposure will prove temporary. Throughout their judgement, the Law Lords in the Caparo case referred to the statutory duties of the auditor and the lack of a clear indication in the Companies Acts that the auditor had a duty of care to individual shareholders. The Caparo decision will almost certainly stimulate debate about the role of the audit. This could act as a catalyst for an extension to the auditor's statutory duties towards the shareholders.

The EC's Fifth Directive is currently trying to change UK law. It is proposed that an auditor who commits a wrongful act then should be obliged to compensate the shareholders or any third parties who suffer loss as a result. There are no strong indications that this proposal will be adopted.[43] The suggestion is, however, ironic in the wake of the Caparo decision. Hatherly considered the effects of an increase in the level of litigation against auditors and suggested how it could change the role of the audit. The natural conclusion would be to impose a statutory requirement on the company to take out a minimum level of insurance cover for third parties in respect of the reliability of its financial statements. This insurance would be provided by the auditor, who would have it underwritten by professional indemnity insurers. This would alter the auditors' responsibility for the collection of audit evidence to support the opinion. Instead, they would collect evidence to the extent that its cost was less than the associated reduction in the insurance premium. Audit reports would not be expressed in terms of opinions on truth and fairness, but would become insurance certificates stating which risks would be borne by the auditor.[44]

Such a bleak view of the possible development of the auditor's role could not be any further removed from the arguments put forward by Flint which were quoted at the beginning of Chapter 2. It would be difficult to make a stronger case for a solution to be found to the expectation gap problem.

3.9 Summary

The auditor has a contractual responsibility towards the shareholders and a moral responsibility towards the other readers of the audit report.

Auditors must conduct their examinations with reasonable care and skill. They cannot be expected to discover every error or misstatement in the financial statements. The professional accounting bodies will determine reasonable care and skill in the light of the SASs. The courts may decide that these requirements are not sufficiently stringent and may demand a higher quality of investigation. The auditor should keep abreast of new auditing techniques and other innovations such as advances in information technology.

The auditors' responsibility for the detection of fraud is not clearly defined. The professional standards have tended to reduce the emphasis on fraud as time has passed and do not appear to require the auditor to look specifically for deliberate misstatement. The courts are, however, likely to apply the test of reasonable care and skill to the detection of fraud in the same manner as for any other type of error.

Research has shown that there is a significant gap between the level of assurance which is expected by the users of the audit report and that which the auditor is actually able to provide. This is damaging to both the user and the auditor. One possible solution to this would be to educate the users. It has, however, been suggested that the onus lies on the accountancy profession to enhance the quality of the audit to meet the public's demands.

The size and complexity of an audit and the need to rely on the judgement of the various members of the audit team have suggested that audit firms should implement quality control procedures to ensure that all of their work is of an appropriate standard. In the United States, these internal quality reviews have been supplemented by imposing an external peer review on practising firms.

The auditors' duty to third parties has led to a number of claims for damages from lenders and investors who claim to have been misled by invalid audit opinions. Most of these cases have been settled out of court. Those judgements which have been made have tended to extend the auditor's liability to third parties, although the recent Caparo and Littlejohn cases have tended to reverse this tendency.

The extent of the litigation threat, combined with the expectation gap, have tended to change the nature of auditing from a professional activity which is designed to add credibility to financial statements to a commercial insurance activity. This is a worrying trend which ought to be addressed by the profession.

REVIEW QUESTIONS

1. Do you believe that the auditor should be responsible to users other than the shareholder?

2. Does the auditor require a codified definition of 'reasonable care and skill', or should this be left to professional judgement?

3. Why should the accountancy profession be unwilling to take full responsibility for the detection of fraud during the annual audit?

4. Discuss the proposition that the expectation gap has arisen because of the public's ignorance and should, therefore, be resolved by the public themselves.

5. Should a system of peer review be introduced in the United Kingdom? What would be the advantages and disadvantages?

6. Why are firms of accountants reluctant to contest charges of negligence in court? Is such an attitude in the best interests of the profession as a whole?

7. Shortly after the House of Lords ruling, the chief executive of Caparo Industries was quoted in the press as saying that investors should be warned not to rely on audited accounts. 'One way would be for them to carry a "health warning" saying the auditor does not accept responsibility for the accounts'. Discuss this statement. Do you believe that it is fair?

EXERCISES

1. The cashier of ABC plc has recently been driving to work in an expensive car. He has also started to take holidays in exotic resorts. The cashier has been an employee of the company for several years. In the past, he has always seemed to enjoy a much more modest lifestyle.

The directors of ABC plc have been discussing the likelihood of the company being taken over by DEF plc, a multinational conglomerate. The directors of DEF have been gathering information and have been in discussions with some of ABC's largest shareholders. ABC's directors do not expect to be retained if the takeover goes ahead.

Assuming that you are the auditor of ABC plc, you are to consider the effect, if any, that each of these pieces of information should have on your approach to the audit.

2. G and Co. are a firm of Chartered Accountants. The firm acts as auditors to HIJ (Cash and Carry) Ltd, a small wholesaling company which imports electronic consumer goods for sale to the retail trade. The company has been owned and managed for many years by Mr Conn. The closing stock figure of HIJ is usually a material amount. G has not attended the count for several years on the grounds that the counting is always well organised by Mr Conn and no problems have ever arisen in this area.

Shortly before the completion of the audit for the year ended 31 December 1996, G and Co. received the following letter:

> Dear Sirs,
>
> We are writing to let you know that we are contemplating making a substantial investment in HIJ (Cash and Carry) Ltd.
>
> We have not commissioned an independent report relating to the financial position of this company.
>
> We will place material reliance upon the audited accounts of the company when making a decision as to whether or not to proceed with such an investment.
>
> Yours faithfully,
>
> LMN plc

G's audit report stated that the financial statements gave a true and fair view, with no qualifications. Shortly after the report was published, LMN announced that it had purchased all of HIJ's share capital.

Two weeks after the takeover, G received another letter from LMN. This claimed that the closing stock figure in HIJ's latest annual report had been grossly overstated. The problem was due to the valuation of some very old and obsolete television sets at cost. These sets would require extensive modification to receive programmes in the United Kingdom and would still be unsellable because of their old-fashioned cabinets. LMN claim that this problem should have been identified by G and Co. especially because the sets have been in HIJ's warehouse for at least three years. LMN's claim was for two specific amounts:

1   The excessive amount paid for the goodwill in HIJ, which was based on latest reported profits.
2   The amount paid for the obsolete stocks. The purchase agreement with Mr Conn stated that stocks would be purchased at their balance sheet valuations.

You are required to consider the following questions:

1   Have G and Co been negligent?
2   Did they owe LMN plc a duty of care?
3   Is LMN's claim likely to succeed?

References and further reading

1. Lee, T.A., *Company Auditing*, Van Nostrand Reinhold, 1986, p. 103.
2. Flint, D., 'The role of the auditor in modern society: an exploratory essay', *Accounting and Business Research*, Autumn 1971, pp. 287–93.

3. s235 (1) and (2) Companies Act 1985.
4. s235 (3) Companies Act 1985. Notice that the auditor is not required to audit the information in the directors' report, merely to ensure that it is not inconsistent with the audited statements.
5. s 237 Companies Act 1985.
6. ICAEW, *'Professional Liability of Accountants and auditors'*, Technical Release 521, 1983. Also published in the January 1984 issue of *Accountancy*, pp. 120–3.
7. Several examples of cases in which the auditor paid substantial damages without admitting liability are listed in Savage, N., 'Auditors: a critical review of their role', *The Company Lawyer*, vol. 4, no. 5, (1983), pp. 187–98. A recent example of such a settlement occurred when Arthur Young (now part of Ernst and Young) paid £24.25m in settlement of legal action over its audit of Johnson Matthey Bank. (See *Accountancy*, December 1988, p. 7 and March 1989, p. 7 for details.) This provoked at least one letter of protest to *Accountancy*, the response to which stated that such a settlement did not necessarily imply guilt. (See 'Desperate remedy', *Accountancy*, May 1989, p. 186.)
8. APC, Auditing Guideline, *Attendance at Stocktaking*, 1983, paragraph 5.
9. Mautz, R.K. and Sharaf, H.A., *The Philosophy of Auditing*, American Accounting Association, 1961, p. 112.
10. See Gwilliam, D., 'Negligence: the legal attitude', *Accountancy*, September 1985, p. 80, for a discussion of some US cases in which professional standards have been found to be deficient. The article did not, however, find a great deal of evidence to suggest that such an attitude would be likely to prevail in the United Kingdom.
11. A detailed description of these techniques is outside the scope of this chapter. Computer auditing will be introduced in Chapter 10. Statistical sampling and the risk-based approach to audit will be introduced in Chapter 11. The application of these techniques will then be developed in subsequent chapters.
12. The declining emphasis on the detection of fraud is chronicled in Brown, R.G., 'Changing audit objectives and techniques', *The Accounting Review*, October 1962, pp. 696–703. This article has been reproduced in Lee, T.A., *The Evolution of Audit Thought and Practice*, Garland Publishing, 1988. It is suggested that the detection of fraud was the principal role of the auditor until 1850. Since then, other objectives such as the detection of clerical error have also been introduced. The expression of an opinion on truth and fairness is now seen as the only major objective.
13. APB, SAS 110, *Fraud and Error*, 1995.
14. The auditor's duty of confidence is described in the *Guide to Professional Ethics*.
15. *Report of the Committee on the Financial Aspects of Corporate Governance*, Gee and Co. Ltd, 1992, pp. 43–4.
16. Gwilliam, D., 'What does reasonable care and skill entail?', *Accountancy*, November 1987, pp. 124–6.
17. Georgen, W.D., *Management Behaviour: An Auditing Horizon*, Touche Ross/University of Kansas Auditing Symposium III, 1976. This paper describes the approach taken by Touche Ross to minimise exposure to the risk of management fraud.
18. Lee, T.A., 'The nature of auditing and its objectives', *Accountancy*, April 1970, pp. 292–6.
19. Beck, G.W., 'The role of the auditor in modern society: an empirical appraisal', *Accounting and Business Research*, Spring 1973, pp. 117–22.
20. The extent of the public's misunderstanding of the nature of an audit investigation is illustrated in a recent study conducted in the United Kingdom. This revealed,

amongst other things, that a substantial percentage of those interviewed believed that the auditor examined most, or even all, of the transactions recorded by the company. See Steen, M., *Audits and Auditors: What the public thinks*, Peat Marwick McLintock, 1989.

21. At least three such publications have been produced by professional bodies. Those which are known to the author are Buckley, R., *What is an Audit?*, APC, 1980, Calpin, M., *Understanding Audits and Audit Reports*, Canadian Institute of Chartered Accountants, 1984, and Shaw, J.C., *The Audit Report: What it says and what it means*, ICAS, 1980. A further attempt to inform the lay reader about the purpose and limitations of an audit can be found in Dunn, J., *'Auditing Explained: A practical guide for managers'*, Kogan Page, 1989.

22. A detailed description of the research study and the hypotheses tested can be found in Arrington, C.E., Hillison, W.A. and Williams, P.F., 'The psychology of expectations gaps: why is there so much dispute about auditor responsibility?', *Accounting and Business Research*, Autumn 1983, pp. 243–50.

    An extension of the analysis of the data collected is available in Arrington, C.E., Bailey, C.D. and Hopwood, W.S., 'An attribution analysis of responsibility assessment for audit performance', *Journal of Accounting Research*, Spring 1985, pp. 1–20.

23. Commission on Auditors' Responsibilities, *Report, Conclusions and Recommendations*, AICPA, 1978. This is often referred to as the 'Cohen Commission Report'.

24. Connor, J.E., 'Enhancing public confidence in the accounting profession', *Journal of Accountancy*, July 1986, pp. 76–83.

25. CICA, *Report of the Commission to Study the Public's Expectations of Audits*, 1988.

26. *ibid*. pp. 12–17.

27. A discussion of the new standards can be found in Guy, D.M., 'The new expectation gap SASs: a view from the US', in *Auditing and the Future*, ICAEW / ICAS, 1989, pp. 125–39. A discussion of these standards and their relevance to the United Kingdom is contained in pages 140–2 of the same publication.

28. Collins, S.H., 'The view after the expectation gap SASs', *Journal of Accountancy*, June 1989, pp. 111–14.

29. The text of the DTI's complaint appeared in several journals. See, for example, *Accountancy*, August 1989, pp. 125–6.

30. APB, SAS 240, *Quality Control for Audit Work*, 1995.

31. The techniques which can be used to monitor the quality of audit procedures are described in Woolf, E., *Risk Management for Auditors*, APC, 1989. This publication, part of the APC's Audit Brief series, also covers the ways in which auditors can insure themselves against these risks.

32. See Arens, A.A. and Loebbecke, J.K., *Auditing: An Integrated Approach*, Prentice Hall International, 1988, pp. 20–2 for a description of quality control in the United States.

33. Evers, C.J. and Pearson, D.B., 'Lessons learned from peer review', *Journal of Accountancy*, April 1989, pp. 96–105.

34. The experiences of three small CPA firms are described in Macklin, M., 'How three firms benefited from peer review', *Journal of Accountancy*, June 1989, pp. 87–90.

35. For a more detailed account of the development of the case law in this area, up to and including the Twomax case, see Keenan, D., 'Professional negligence up to date', *Accountancy*, February 1983, pp. 62–4. A detailed account of the Jeb Fasteners case is contained in Savage, N., 'The auditor's legal responsibility – to strangers?',

The Accountant's Magazine, October 1981, pp. 338–41. The same author has also written an article on the Twomax case, 'Trend for open-ended auditors' liability confirmed by Scottish court', *The Company Lawyer*, vol. 3, no. 4, (1982), pp. 174–5.

36. The full text of the Caparo judgement is reproduced in *The Weekly Law Reports* 23, February 1990, pp. 358–407. This quotation is taken from p. 368.

37. Keenan, D., 'Auditors' duty of care', *Accountancy*, October 1989, pp. 46–8.

38. This statement was, of course, made before the Caparo precedent.

39. A more detailed discussion of the facts of this case can be found in Swinson, C., 'Judicial support comes for auditors' judgement', *Accountancy Age*, 16 January 1986, p. 17. An analysis of its implications for accountants and auditors can be found in Gwilliam, D., 'Setting the standards used by the law', *Accountancy*, April 1986, pp. 17–19.

40. Pound, G.D. and Courtis, J.K., 'The auditor's liability: a myth?', *Accounting and Business Research*, Summer 1980, pp. 299–305.

41. Likierman, A. (Chairman), *Professional Liability: Report of the Study Teams*, HMSO, 1989.

42. The reaction to the Likierman Report is discussed in Lawrence, T., 'Auditors' liability: the Likierman Report and its aftermath', *The Accountant's Magazine*, March 1990, pp. 19–20.

43. The Government stated that it did not feel that the Fifth Directive was the most appropriate forum for a discussion of the role of the auditor. The implications of this Directive are discussed in Department of Trade and Industry, '*Amended Proposal for a Fifth Directive on the Harmonisation of Company Law in the European Community: a consultative document*', 1990.

44. Hatherly, D., 'Audit reports or insurance certificates?', *Accountancy*, May 1989, pp. 27–8.

CHAPTER 4

International comparisons

This chapter will consider the differences which exist between different countries' auditing standards. This is an important area, despite the fact that very little comparative work has been done in this area. The nature and extent of the differences which exist will be illustrated by descriptions of auditing in France and Japan. The attempts to harmonise standards will also be described.

The term 'auditing standards' will be used throughout this chapter to describe all regulations, both professional and statutory. This is to reduce the confusion which might arise because the roles of professional accounting bodies and governments differ from country to country.

By the time you have completed this chapter you should be able to:

- Explain the importance of international comparisons of auditing standards.
- Describe some of the ways in which auditing standards can differ internationally.
- Describe some of the attempts to harmonise standards between countries.

4.1 Why compare auditing standards?

Auditing is often viewed as a mechanical process of checking accounting records. This implies that the audits conducted in other countries are unlikely to differ from those in the United Kingdom. This view may well be strengthened by the fact that there are several major international accounting firms who operate on a worldwide basis. It is, however, misleading and possibly even dangerous to view auditing in such a superficial manner. In financial accounting, for example, all countries use double entry bookkeeping to record transactions and balances. The financial statements which they prepare from these records do, however, differ drastically in terms of disclosure and the accounting policies adopted.[1]

```
┌─────────────────────────┤ ACTIVITY ├─────────────────────────┐
│ Most of the material in early chapters was based on the United Kingdom. │
│ Before you read on, try to list some of the ways in which auditing might differ │
│ between countries. │
└──────────────────────────────────────────────────────────────┘
```

Even a cursory glance through a descriptive text on different countries'
auditing practices[2] reveals that there are major differences between nations with
regard to the following:

1   Extent of audit requirement.
2   Auditor independence.
3   Qualifications required to act as an auditor.
4   Existence and enforcement of professional auditing standards.
5   Reporting standards.

All but the first of these have implications for the credibility provided by the
audit report. The expectation gap problem described in the previous chapter will
be worsened if readers simply assume that professional and statutory auditing
standards are the same in all countries.

4.1.1 *Implications for investors*

Investors who wish to obtain the most attractive combination of risk and return
from their portfolios must diversify as widely as possible, across both industrial
and national boundaries. This means that an investor should hold shares in a
number of foreign companies.[3] Investors could be misled into paying too high
a price for a foreign share if they, or their professional advisers, assume that the
auditing standards applied overseas are of a comparable standard to those at
home. Similarly, investors may be deterred from investing in foreign companies
because of unfounded doubts about the quality of the information provided by
these companies.

4.1.2 *Implications for accountants*

An auditor may have to audit the consolidated financial statements of a
company which has overseas subsidiaries. These subsidiaries may have been
audited by local offices of the same firm or by different firms altogether. This
could pose problems for the auditor, who is obliged to report upon the truth and
fairness of the group accounts regardless of any differences in legislation which
affect the preparation and audit of foreign subsidiaries' statements.[4]

The auditor might ask the subsidiaries' auditors to complete a questionnaire
on the nature of the audit tests carried out, their independence, and their
qualifications. The value of such questionnaires is limited in that there is not
always a direct comparison between different countries' professional and aca-

demic qualifications or between the monitoring of compliance with their professional standards.

The holding company auditor might feel compelled to review some or all of the subsidiary auditor's working papers. The auditor does not have any rights to demand access to a foreign accountant's files. This problem is dealt with by the Companies Act 1985, s 389A (4)[5] which requires the directors of the holding company to make reasonable efforts to obtain whatever information the auditor requires from the subsidiary. It is an offence for the directors to fail to comply with this subsection.

A survey was conducted into the reliance placed upon subsidiary company auditors by the auditors of holding companies.[6] This revealed that 76.6 per cent of the respondents made some attempt to evaluate the quality of the work done to support the subsidiary's audit report. The following techniques were used by these auditors:

1	Questionnaire	76.6 per cent
2	Meeting with subsidiary's auditor	62.0 per cent
3	Review of subsidiary auditor's working papers	60.4 per cent
4	Review of subsidiary auditor's planning memorandum	50.4 per cent

This survey was not restricted to audits of multinationals. Those respondents who had to deal with foreign accounting firms did, however, perceive differences between the standards of different geographical regions. Thus, auditors from Canada appear to be regarded in the same light as their UK counterparts while more extensive reviews would be conducted of the work done by Latin American firms.

A survey in the United States suggested that companies with substantial foreign operations are more likely to employ one of the large international accounting firms which claim to have an international network of offices.[7] This would appear to solve the problem in that international firms can adopt the same audit approach throughout their many offices and, in theory, an audit conducted by any of the firm's offices will be of the same standard. However, the international firms are not always organised in such a manner as to ensure that uniform standards can be enforced.[8]

4.1.3 *Implications for individual countries*

Differences between audit requirements might be seen to be undesirable, particularly within economic groupings such as the EU. The identification of these differences is a vital first step towards the harmonisation of practices. This topic will be developed in a later section.

An analysis of the factors which have shaped auditing standards might also be useful to standard-setters in developing countries. It might be possible to identify systems in force in other countries which could be modified to suit their needs. In general, many innovations might usefully be copied. Enforcement of standards, for example, may prove difficult. Professional bodies might find it difficult to monitor compliance and impose sanctions. Government agencies have greater resources and more effective sanctions at their disposal. Their involvement in standard-setting could, however, make the process bureaucratic and inflexible. This dilemma has been resolved in Canada by a statutory requirement that auditors must adhere to the standards contained in the CICA handbook.

4.2 The extent of the differences

This section will discuss the extent to which auditing standards differ between countries. There has been relatively little research in this area, despite its importance. There is, however, a wealth of descriptive material. Books by Stamp and Moonitz,[9] Campbell[10] and Needles[11] each contain useful summaries of auditing standards in several countries. Further information is contained in a series of books published by the ICAEW.[12] Finally, a number of international accounting firms have series of booklets on business practices in the various countries in which they operate.

The nature of the differences which can arise in respect of various important elements of the auditing standards will be discussed in general terms. This will be followed by descriptions of auditing standards in France and Japan.

4.2.1 *Extent of audit requirement*

All but the smallest active companies in the United Kingdom are required to have an audit. This is unusual in that company law in most other countries tends to restrict the requirement to companies which are quoted on a stock exchange or which exceed a certain size. In the United States, for example, Securities and Exchange legislation requires companies which are quoted on a national stock exchange or whose shares are traded 'over-the-counter'[13] to have an audit. Private companies which have more than 500 shareholders and assets of more that $5 million must also publish audited accounts. Smaller, unquoted companies are not subject to any mandatory audit requirement. Many companies in the United States do, however, undergo an audit on a voluntary basis because most banks insist on having audited financial statements before granting a loan.

In some countries, shareholders of small companies can elect to dispense with the audit requirement. Canadian legislation imposes an audit requirement on all companies. Those companies whose shares are not offered to the public and whose assets and gross revenues are less than $5 million and $2.5 million respectively may be exempt, but only if every shareholder consents to this in writing on an annual basis. Private companies in Australia are also exempt from a mandatory audit, but again this is subject to annual confirmation by all of the shareholders. Private companies cannot have more than fifty members.

The South African government has created a new type of corporate entity in order to relieve small businesses from some of the burdens imposed by company law. These 'close corporations' do not have to have an audit. They are, however, required to appoint an 'accounting officer', who must be a qualified accountant, to take charge of the preparation of the financial statements. The statements must also be approved and signed by all of the members. These corporations cannot have more than ten members. .

Some countries extend the audit requirement beyond the limited company. The audit requirements in Sweden extend to limited companies, branches of foreign corporations, unlimited partnerships and sole proprietorships which exceed certain size criteria, and unlimited partnerships. A number of countries require the appointment of a 'shareholder' or 'statutory' auditor. The role of such auditors tends to be rather more restricted than that usually attributed to an external auditor. In Spain, every company is required to have at least two auditors appointed from the shareholders. There are no professional or academic qualifications for this post. The 'auditors' cannot be directors. These representatives are required to sign the financial statements before they are presented to the shareholders. This does not involve any liability to third parties. At best, such an auditor might conduct a review of the financial statements. It is unlikely that any audit evidence would have been collected to support the opinion.

4.2.2 *Auditor independence*

The need for auditor independence and the regulations in force in the United Kingdom to protect it were described in Chapter 2. Some of the rules in force in other countries show that the problems described in that chapter are not insurmountable. The problem of auditors providing their clients with other services has been overcome in Belgium and Italy by prohibiting such additional appointments. While this might reduce the possibility of conflict of interest it would be disruptive to introduce such a regulation in countries such as the United Kingdom and the United States where it is common for auditors to have other duties.

The need for an annual reappointment can make the auditor dependent upon the goodwill of the directors. Belgian auditors are appointed for a three-year term. This appointment can then be renewed for an indefinite number of further three-year appointments. The auditor cannot resign or be removed from office without good reason. Italian auditors are also appointed for three-year terms. This appointment can be renewed only twice, which means that the maximum length of a firm's association with any given company is only nine years. Three-year appointments reduce the risk of interference by management. The upper limit on the number of reappointments also reduces the extent to which the auditor will become dependent on any given client company.

Italian companies which are quoted on the stock exchange come under the jurisdiction of the Commissione Nazionale per la Società e la Borsa (CONSOB). This body must examine the auditor's proposal, including the projected time and fees, and give permission for the firm to act. This review will help to ensure the auditor's investigative independence.

The rules relating to auditor independence are rather lax in some countries. Auditors are appointed by the directors in Brazil and Venezuela, which would appear to conflict with the concept of independence.

4.2.3 Qualifications required to act as an auditor

There is a surprising range of requirements relating to the academic, professional and experience requirements for auditors in different countries.[14] It is possible to become a Chartered Accountant in the United Kingdom before one is 25. It is virtually impossible to obtain an equivalent qualification before the age of 30 in many other European countries. The professional bodies in the United Kingdom have slightly different membership requirements. Broadly, trainee accountants must either have a university degree or, in the case of ACCA, have passed the relevant foundation examinations. This first qualification must then be supplemented by a period of study combined with practical experience. Students must pass examinations set by the bodies themselves before qualifying.

In some countries, such as Germany, the state is much more directly involved in the administration of the profession. An auditor must have a degree, which need not be in accountancy. This is followed by a period of five years' business experience, four of which must be in public accounting, with at least two years in a firm of accountants. Finally, the auditor must pass a difficult set of examinations, both written and oral. These are conducted by the state rather than by an independent professional body.

Danish auditors must have a Bachelor's degree and then go on to take a Master's degree in auditing. The second degree is obtained by a combination of examination and dissertation and is taught at four universities. These courses are usually followed on a part-time basis and usually take seven or eight years to complete. Students must then obtain three years' relevant experience before sitting yet another set of examinations controlled by a board of the Ministry of Industry.

It is not always necessary to complete a set of 'professional' examinations. There are two routes to membership of the professional accounting body whose members conduct audits in the Netherlands. One of these involves taking a combination of Bachelor's and Master's degrees at university, the first taking roughly five years, the second taking two or three years.

It is not always necessary to have practical experience. In the Netherlands, students work for their Master's degree on a part-time basis and are usually employed by accounting firms during this period. They are not, however, obliged to have any relevant experience before qualifying. It is also possible to become an auditor in Italy by a combination of a university course followed immediately by an examination set by the state.

4.2.4 *Existence and enforcement of codified auditing standards*

Codified auditing standards should enable the readers of audit reports to evaluate the quality of the work done to support the opinion. The United Kingdom has had such standards since 1980. Other countries, such as the United States, have been issuing auditing standards for much longer. Most countries have, or are in the process of creating, a series of professional standards.

The standards of some countries are more detailed than others. This does not necessarily imply that the work done is any more rigorous. Auditors in the United States have standards requiring that debtors' balances are tested by direct communication with the customers and that audit staff attend stock counts. No such standards exist in the Netherlands. Many Dutch auditors do, however, attend stock counts anyway and the practice of circularising debtors is growing.

The enforcement of these standards may be by the profession or by the state. UK auditing standards are enforced by the professional bodies. The quality of audit work in the United States is monitored by the SEC. It is virtually impossible to evaluate the effectiveness of the enforcement of auditing standards. The auditor's work is unlikely to be subjected to detailed scrutiny unless something disastrous, such as the collapse of the company, happens after the report has been signed. This does, of course, make it difficult for a foreign investor or auditor to place any confidence in a review of the codified standards.

4.2.5 *Reporting standards*

Audit reporting will be covered in detail in Chapters 5 and 6. This section will simply consider some of the matters which may be included in an audit report. The wordings of audit reports can differ significantly. A study of reports in twenty-seven countries managed to identify five distinct groupings of report types.[15] Such differences are, however, often superficial. The wording of a UK audit report is significantly different from its US equivalent and yet the nature of the tests conducted and the meaning of the reports are very similar.

Some auditors are required to pay much more attention to the possibility of fraud or mismanagement by the company directors. This is the case in Sweden, where the auditor is required to report on any breaches of company law by management. The auditor must also consider whether any acts or omissions by the directors could lead to a claim for restitution against the company. Any such problems should be reported.

Some countries require their auditors to produce detailed 'long form' audit reports for the management of the company. The long form report in Germany provides management with further analysis and explanation of certain figures in the financial statements. This is often regarded as a report on management's efficiency. This report is not published. A potential lender could, however, request a copy as a condition for granting a loan.

4.2.6 *Auditing standards in France*

All companies in France are required to have an audit although, as with the United Kingdom, there are exemptions for companies which fall below a certain size as measured in terms of total assets, turnover and employees.

The auditor has a number of statutory duties. Since the implementation of the Fourth Directive, the objective of the financial statements is to portray a true and fair view (*image fidèle*). The auditor must report on the truth and fairness of the accounts, although the term true and fair is not interpreted in quite the same way as it is in, say, the United Kingdom. The auditor must also prepare a special report which deals with any contracts or agreements between the company and the directors.

The auditor's statutory duties extend beyond the truth and fairness of the financial statements. In particular, he is required to report any illegal act which he discovers in the course of his audit work to the public prosecutor. Failure to make such a report is a criminal offence. There is also a statutory requirement that companies produce certain annual and semi-annual forecasts of cash flow, profit and liquidity. The auditor is obliged to review these forecasts and to warn the directors if they reveal any risks that the company may cease to be a going concern. In certain circumstances, he may also be obliged to warn the shareholders at the general meeting.

Independence requirements are strict. The statutory auditor (*Commissaire aux Comptes*) is not permitted to receive any remuneration from the company, apart, of course, from the audit fee. The auditor is appointed by the shareholders for a six-year period, which can be renewed for an indefinite number of six-year terms in the future. The replacement of the *Commissaire* during an appointment requires court action. The professional body has laid down a formula for the calculation of the number of hours to be spent on the audit of smaller companies. This helps to protect the auditor's investigative independence.

There is a separate professional body for auditors, the Compagnie Nationale des Commissaires aux Comptes (CNCC). This body is supervised by the Ministry of Justice. Membership of the Compagnie is open to graduates who must then pass a professional examination, although there are exemptions granted to members of the Ordre des Experts Comptables, the professional body which supervises the activities of public accountants. Members must also have completed at least two years' practical professional training. There is a minimum age requirement of 25.

Codified auditing standards are evolving. French companies are required to maintain their bookkeeping records in a form specified by government. The Compagnie has taken advantage of this standardisation to develop some standardised audit manuals. The quality of audit work done on quoted companies is monitored by the Stock Exchange Commission (COB). A number of 'incapable' auditors have been removed from practice as a result of COB investigations.

The auditor is required to submit three reports, two of which are published.

The matters which should be stated in the general report to the shareholders include the following:

- An opinion on the accuracy of the information in the financial statements and its compliance with the law.
- Reasons for any qualifications of the opinion.
- Details of any changes in accounting policies and disclosure practices.
- Details of any irregularities or illegal acts discovered.

The special report, which is also made to the shareholders, relates to any contracts or agreements between the directors and the company and must state whether the contracts were approved in advance by the board and how the company is affected by them.

Finally, the auditor is obliged to present a report to the directors. This report gives details of the audit tests carried out, describes any irregularities or inaccuracies uncovered by the audit, lists any amendments which must be made to the financial accounts, gives a commentary on the results for the year, and comments on the auditor's review of the management forecasts of the company's future.

4.2.7 Auditing standards in Japan

Accounting in Japan has been influenced by a rather confusing amalgam of influences from different sources. Historically, Japan was heavily influenced by Germany. More recently, America has exercised a much greater degree of influence. These factors have also affected Japanese auditing standards.

Japan follows the practice adopted in a number of continental countries of having two sets of audit requirements. All but the smallest businesses are required by the Commercial Code to appoint a 'statutory' auditor (a *Kansayaku*). In addition, Securities and Exchange Law requires listed companies and other large corporations to appoint an 'account' auditor whose role corresponds to that of an external auditor in Britain.

The duties of the statutory auditor are contained within the Commercial Code. The basic role of the statutory auditor is to act as an agent on behalf of the shareholders to evaluate the stewardship of the directors. In the case of medium-sized companies, the statutory auditor must report on a number of matters, including whether the financial statements comply with the law and the company's articles. This report should also state whether any fraudulent entries have been discovered in the accounting records, whether the directors have failed to perform any of their duties, whether the law or the company's articles have been violated, and whether any proposed distribution is improper. In large companies the statutory auditor is also obliged to report on whether the account auditor's opinion is qualified and whether that opinion is appropriate.

The statutory auditor need not be professionally qualified, although he is supposed to be independent. Once the statutory auditor has been appointed by the shareholders he will normally work on a full-time basis for that company and is, therefore, to all intents and purposes an employee.

The role of the account auditor is much closer to that of the external auditor in the United Kingdom. His basic duties are to form an opinion on the truth and fairness of the financial statements and their compliance with relevant legislation. Rules regarding the independence of the account auditor are slightly more reassuring. The account auditor is appointed by the shareholders. He must not be an employee, although it is permitted to hold a small number of shares or have a small debtor or creditor balance. Any interests in the company must be disclosed in the audit report. He is forbidden to provide tax services or management advisory services to management.

Account auditors must be members of the Japanese Institute of Certified Public Accountants. Membership of this body requires some extremely demanding examinations to be taken which are set by the Japanese government. The first level is designed as a test of the candidate's literacy. The pass rates for the second and third levels were only 6.3 per cent and 33.5 per cent respectively during the period from 1980 to 1984. Members must also complete one year's training as a junior accountant and have two years' practical audit experience with a CPA.[16] Auditing standards are set by the Business Accounting Deliberation Council, a governmental body.[17]

4.3 Harmonisation of auditing standards

It has already been suggested that the differences between auditing standards create difficulties for the users of audited financial statements. It would, therefore, be desirable to harmonise auditing standards and so reduce, or even eradicate, these differences.

ACTIVITY

Try to suggest why standards are still different, despite the perceived benefits of bringing them into line. Some suggestions will be put forward in section 4.3.1.

4.3.1 *Barriers to harmonisation*

Nobes identified four main barriers to the harmonisation of accounting standards.[18] These are the size of differences, the lack of a strong accountancy profession in some countries, nationalism, and the economic consequences of change.

The previous section described a variety of major differences in auditing standards. The sheer number of changes which would have to be made in order to achieve comparability would, in itself, be a major undertaking. There could also be good reasons for the differences. French auditors are required to pay more attention to the manner in which the business is run and to ensuring that the directors are complying with the law than their counterparts in Britain. This could, however, have a great deal to do with the fact that accounting statements in France tend to be used more for economic planning than for making investment decisions. Thus harmonisation could lead to unnecessary work for UK auditors or could make the work of French auditors less relevant.

The lack of a strong accountancy profession can make it difficult to exert influence in some countries. Japanese auditing standards are set by a government agency. Any attempt to introduce new standards through the professional body would be hampered by its relative lack of influence. Similarly, standards are often set by professional bodies, thus making it difficult to achieve harmonisation at a governmental level.

Nationalism could also be difficult to overcome. It exists partly at an emotional level, with standard-setters feeling reluctant to adopt foreign techniques and approaches. There could also be practical problems associated with the adoption of a standardised approach. It could be difficult to have a set of internationally agreed standards modified in response to a change in local circumstances. A commitment to harmonisation could render auditing standards inflexible.

There could also be a number of economic consequences associated with the adoption of new standards. It was, for example, argued that the rotation of audit appointments and the prohibition of auditors acting in other capacities for the same companies could have proved unduly disruptive in Britain. The introduction of independence standards similar to those in Italy would have proved expensive for UK auditors and, perhaps, their clients.

There is a further barrier which does not apply to the same extent in respect of accounting. It has been argued that auditing is a much newer discipline than financial accounting and that developments in auditing tend to lag behind those which apply to accounting in general.[19] It may be that auditing standards simply enjoy a lower profile than those which relate to the preparation of financial statements and that improvements will take some time because of this.

4.3.2 *International auditing standards*

In 1978, Stamp and Moonitz published an influential book which argued for the establishment of a programme for the setting of international auditing standards.[20] This was because the various standard-setting organisations across the world were unlikely to develop standards which were either complete or compatible with one another. These standards would have to cover the following areas:

- Independence, integrity and objectivity.
- Expertise and competence.
- Evidence.

- Communication.
- Enforcement.

Stamp and Moonitz also identified nine 'vital' countries whose support would be crucial to the establishment of these standards. These were:

- United States
- Britain
- Australia
- Canada
- France
- Japan
- West Germany
- The Netherlands
- Brazil

Each of these countries had a role to play because of its economic importance, its influence on the development of accounting or its geographical location. Brazil, for example, was seen as a link between the developed and the developing nations.

It was suggested that an international auditing standards committee should be formed to develop standards and encourage their adoption. This committee should include each of the vital countries. Standards would then be ratified by member nations.

The International Federation of Accountants (IFAC) was formed in 1977. Its broad objectives are 'the development and enhancement of a coordinated world-wide accountancy profession with harmonised standards'.[21] Membership of IFAC stands at more than 100 national professional accounting bodies drawn from over eighty countries. IFAC has a number of standing committees, including the International Auditing Practices Committee (IAPC). The IAPC publishes 'International Standards on Auditing' (ISAs). These are intended to promote best practice around the world and are, indeed, recognised as acceptable by a number of stock exchanges as being an acceptable alternative to national standards. The ISAs are broadly similar to those of the United Kingdom. This is hardly surprising because the exposures drafts upon which they were based were themselves the basis for the British draft SASs.[22]

ISAs cannot override national auditing standards. IFAC members are, however, expected to comply with them whenever possible and to encourage their adoption at a national level. This happens to a varying extent from country to country. The United Kingdom, for example, has tended to develop its own standards and has not always adapted to new international standards. Other countries, particularly developing nations, have tended to adopt international standards as an alternative to producing their own.

Stamp and Moonitz updated their arguments in the light of IFAC's first few years of existence.[23] They argued that IFAC should concentrate on the enforcement of standards and auditor independence. These were seen as crucial to the credibility of the audit and yet they were also the areas in which there was the greatest diversity of standards. IFAC should monitor the performance of the national bodies and expose those which were unsatisfactory.

The EU has been responsible for a number of changes which have been designed to harmonise standards throughout Europe. The Eighth Directive has had the greatest impact on audit by attempting to bring educational and independence requirements into line. The provisions of this directive were enacted into UK law by the Companies Act 1989.[24]

4.4 Summary

Business and investment are becoming increasingly international. This means that it is becoming more and more necessary to rely upon the work done by auditors from other countries. Differences between auditing standards can be confusing and even quite misleading.

A number of major differences have been discovered between standards relating to the extent of the audit requirement, independence, qualifications, the existence of codified standards, and reporting. These were illustrated by an examination of standards in France and Japan.

The IAPC publishes International Auditing Guidelines in order to assist in the process of harmonisation. The accounting bodies which belong to IFAC, the IAPC's parent body, should encourage their members to comply with IAGs whenever they carry out an audit.

Harmonisation within the EC has been helped by the introduction of the Eighth Directive.

—————————— REVIEW QUESTIONS ——————————

1. Substantial expectation gaps arise within countries. How is the problem likely to be affected by the increasing use of audited financial statements by foreign nationals?

2. Should the auditor of a group of companies be allowed to state the names and nationalities of the auditors of those group members which have been audited by overseas firms in the audit report? How would this affect the reader of the report?

3. Many countries do not require small companies to appoint an independent accountant as auditor but demand that one or more shareholders be appointed to conduct a review of the statements. Should this practice be adopted in Britain?

4. In some countries the audit requirement extends to partnerships and even sole proprietorships which exceed a certain size. Should similar regulations be implemented in Britain?

5. What economic consequences would arise if auditors in Britain were

required to report on the possibility of claims against the company because of acts or omissions by the directors, as is the case in Sweden?

6. Is there any point in the IAPC issuing IAGs if it cannot monitor compliance?

EXERCISES

1. You are the auditor of International Conglomerates plc. The company has several major overseas subsidiaries. Describe the matters which should be covered in a questionnaire for the auditors of these subsidiaries. Should this questionnaire be sent only to those auditors who do not belong to your firm's international network or should a copy go to every subsidiary auditor?

2. Compare and contrast the auditing standards of France and Japan with those of the United Kingdom. What differences appear to exist in the fundamental role of the auditor in each of these countries?

References and further reading

1. The field of international accounting has attracted a great deal of attention. Readers who wish to obtain an insight into the nature and extent of the differences which can exist should refer to Nobes, C.W., and Parker, R.H., *Comparative International Accounting*, Prentice Hall, 1995. Chapters 8 to 14 consist of country studies and Chapter 4 reviews some of the attempts to classify the different practices. The same authors have written a companion volume *Issues in Multinational Accounting*, Philip Allan, 1988. Chapters 2 and 3 cover the causes and nature of the differences which exist between countries.
2. See, for example, *Legal and Regulatory Financial Reporting Requirements: Worldwide*, Arthur Andersen and Co., 1984. This consists of forty-five brief descriptions of financial reporting and auditing requirements. Other descriptive publications cover a smaller number of countries in greater depth. These will be referred to below.
3. This assertion assumes the validity of the efficient markets hypothesis. A readable discussion of this theory is contained in Keane, S.M., *Stock Market Efficiency*, Philip Allan, 1983. The need to diversify internationally is described in Chapter 7.
4. The procedures which should be undertaken in respect of the work done by other accounting firms are described in APB, SAS 510, *The Relationship Between Principal Auditors and Other Auditors*, 1995 and Campbell, L.G., *International Auditing*, Macmillan, 1985, Chapter 12.
5. A similar provision was included in s 392 of the Companies Act 1985 prior to the revision of the Act by the Companies Act 1989.
6. Moizer, P., Turley, S. and Walker, D., 'Reliance on other auditors: a UK study', *Accounting and Business Research*, Autumn 1986, pp. 343–52.

7. Eichenseher, J.W., 'The effects of foreign operations on domestic auditor selection', *Journal of Accounting, Auditing and Finance*, Spring 1985, pp. 195–209.

8. Five different models for the organisation of international firms are identified in Weinstein, A.K., Corsini, L. and Pawliczek, R., 'The Big Eight in Europe', *The International Journal of Accounting*, Spring 1978, pp. 57–71. At one extreme, every partner is a member of a global firm. At the opposite extreme, some of the offices which operate under the firm's international name are merely correspondents. They are, effectively, agents of the firm and, as such, they are not under its direct control.

   The manner in which one firm, Arthur Andersen, manages to ensure a consistent standard throughout its worldwide network of offices is described in Hanson, J.D., 'Internationalisation of the accounting firm', in Hopwood, A.G. (ed.), *International Pressures for Accounting Change*, Prentice Hall, 1989. The author suggests that the structure of some of his competitors prevents the global approach described.

9. Stamp, E. and Moonitz, M., *International Auditing Standards*, Prentice Hall, 1978. This includes surveys of Britain, the United States, Australia, Canada, The Netherlands, France, West Germany, Japan, and Brazil.

10. Campbell, L.G., *International Auditing*, Macmillan, 1985. This includes surveys of Australia, Canada, France, West Germany, Japan, The Netherlands, Britain, and the United States. All of these countries are also covered by Stamp and Moonitz. The Campbell text is, however, more recent.

11. Needles, B.E., *Comparative International Auditing Standards*, American Accounting Association, 1985. This surveys standards in France, The Netherlands, Switzerland, Britain, Jordan, Kuwait, Japan, Canada, Mexico, and the United States. Unlike Campbell and Stamp and Moonitz, the surveys contained in this text have been written by academics from the respective countries.

12. The ICAEW has collaborated in the publication of a series of country studies. See, for example, Dijksma, J. and Hoogendoorn, M., *European Financial Reporting*, The Netherlands, Routledge, 1993.

13. This is equivalent to the Unlisted Securities Market in the United Kingdom and should not be confused with the British over-the-counter market.

14. The different educational and experience requirements of many of the professional bodies across the world are reviewed in Heaston, P.H., 'Qualification requirements for public accounting in selected foreign countries: a comparison with the United States', *The International Journal of Accounting*, Fall 1984, pp. 71–94.

15. Hussein, M.E.A., Bavishi, V.B. and Gangolly, J.S., 'International similarities and differences in the auditor's report', *Auditing: A Journal of Practice and Theory*, Fall 1986, pp. 124–33.

16. Choi, F.D.S. and Hiramatsu, K. *Accounting and Financial Reporting in Japan*, Van Nostrand Reinhold, 1987, pp. 187–9.

17. Further information about Japanese auditing standards can be found in *Corporate Disclosure in Japan: Auditing*, part of a series published by the Japanese Institute of Certified Public Accountants in 1987.

18. Nobes, C.W., 'Harmonisation of financial reporting', in Nobes, C.W. and Parker, R.H., *Comparative International Accounting*, Philip Allan, 1985.

19. Pomeranz, F., 'Prospects for international accounting and auditing standards: the transnationals in governmental regulations', *International Journal of Accounting*, Fall 1981, pp. 7–17.

20. Stamp and Moonitz, *op. cit.*

21. Preface to *International Auditing Guidelines and Statements on Auditing of the International Federation of Accountants*, IFAC Handbook, 1989.
22. See Dove, R., 'A facelift for international auditing', *Accountancy*, October 1994, p. 133 for further details of the ISAs and their similarities to UK standards.
23. Stamp, E. and Moonitz, M., 'International auditing standards', *The CPA Journal*, June 1982, pp. 24–32 and July 1982, pp. 48–53.
24. A summary of the provisions of the Eighth Directive is contained in Oldham, K.M., *Accounting Systems and Practice in Europe*, Gower, 1987, pp. 319–21. The implications for individual member states are outlined on pp. 104–5.

PART II

AUDIT REPORTING

The whole point of the external audit of a set of financial statements is to enable the auditor to report an opinion to the users of the financial statements. This section of the book follows on from Part I by describing the end product of the process in rather more detail than has been possible so far. It also provides a basis for the material in Part III, which describes the processes which lead up to the audit report.

Chapter 5 describes the basic audit unqualified report which is applied in the vast majority of cases. It deals with the content and meaning of this short document. It also discusses the difficult topic of truth and fairness, a simple phrase which accountants frequently find almost impossible to define.

Chapter 6 looks at the effects of uncertainty and disagreement on the standard audit report. It explains how the report may have to be modified in response to these problems and also discusses some of the implications of having a qualified audit report for the companies concerned.

CHAPTER 5

The audit report

Reporting is, by definition, a fundamental element of an audit. It is important, therefore, that the report is clear, unambiguous, and expressed in terms which can be understood by those to whom it is addressed. This chapter will discuss the content and meaning of the standard audit report. The difficulties associated with its interpretation will be explored, as will some of the suggestions for its improvement.

By the time you have completed this chapter, you should be able to:

- Explain the content of the standard UK audit report.
- Explain the problems associated with the definition of truth and fairness.
- Discuss the importance of the precise wording used in the standard audit report.

5.1 Audit reports in the United Kingdom

The audit report of a limited company must be laid out in the following standard format:

AUDITOR'S REPORT TO THE MEMBERS OF XYZ LIMITED
We have audited the financial statements on pages . . . to . . . which have been prepared under the historical cost convention and the accounting policies set out on page . . .

Respective responsibilities of directors and auditors
As described on page . . . the company's directors are responsible for the preparation of financial statements. It is our responsibility to form an independent opinion, based on our audit, on those statements and to report our opinion to you.

Basis of opinion
We conducted our audit in accordance with Auditing Standards issued by the Auditing Practices Board. An audit includes examination, on a test basis, of

evidence relevant to the amounts and disclosures in the financial statements. It also includes an assessment of the significant estimates and judgements made by the directors in the preparation of the financial statements, and of whether the accounting policies are appropriate to the company's circumstances, consistently applied and adequately disclosed.

We planned and performed our audit so as to obtain all the information and explanations which we considered necessary in order to provide us with sufficient evidence to give reasonable assurance that the financial statements are free from material misstatement, whether caused by fraud or other irregularity or error. In forming our opinion we also evaluated the overall adequacy of the presentation of information in the financial statements.

Opinion
In our opinion the financial statements give a true and fair view of the state of the company's affairs at 31 December 19.. and of its profit for the year then ended and have been properly prepared in accordance with the Companies Act 1985.

Signed (Auditor's name, qualification, address)

Date.[1]

It may not be possible to report in these terms. Auditors could, for example, be unable to obtain sufficient audit evidence to support such an opinion or the directors could have insisted on adopting a misleading accounting policy. The effects of such problems on the report will be dealt with in Chapter 6.

5.1.1 *The content of the report*

The basic audit report consists of seven main elements:

1 The title.
2 A paragraph identifying the financial statements audited.
3 A statement of the respective responsibilities of the directors (or their equivalents) and the auditors.
4 The basis of the auditors' opinion.
5 The auditors' opinion.
6 The auditors' signature.
7 The date of the auditors' report.

ACTIVITY

(a) Read through the specimen audit report again and see how each of the elements listed above is represented.
(b) Try to think why each of these elements is necessary.

These issues will be discussed though the remainder of section 5.1.1.

The title of the report should identify those to whom it is addressed. In the case of a company, the report will be addressed to the members. While the auditor may also have a responsibility to the other readers of the report, the report should contain a warning that the audit was conducted with the shareholders' needs in mind and that the truth and fairness of the financial statements have been considered from the shareholders' point of view. An audit conducted for, say, the creditors would, for example, place much greater emphasis on the ownership and valuation of the assets which are to be pledged as security.

Most annual reports contain a great deal of voluntary disclosure, which need not be audited. The auditor should restrict the report to those pages which have been examined so that readers are aware of this when they are reading the additional information.

The statement of the respective responsibilities of the auditors and the directors merely states the legal positions of both parties. In that sense, the statement does not contain any real information. The statement does, however, ensure that the readers are not misled about the extent of the auditors' involvement in the accounting process. Essentially, the audit report is a response to the statements as prepared by the directors. This means that the auditors are merely forming an opinion on whether the treatment adopted is acceptable. A set of statements prepared by a disinterested accountant acting on behalf of the shareholders might have been significantly different from a set produced by the board of directors.

The basis of opinion is also unlikely to contain any real information because it merely states the auditors' 'official' duties which are laid down in the Companies Act and SAS requirements anyway. It does, however, ensure that readers are aware of these requirements and could provide a subtle warning about the extent to which it is reasonable to assume that the statements are free from error. This could, therefore, go some way towards reducing the expectation gap. It is also possible that the auditor will be unable to achieve the standards laid down because of some limitation imposed on the scope of the audit work.

The report should contain an explicit statement of the auditors' opinion on the truth and fairness of the financial statements. In the case of a limited company, the auditors should declare whether the statements show a true and fair view and whether they have been properly prepared in accordance with the Companies Act 1985.

Auditors must sign and date the audit report. The signature provides evidence that the auditor accepts responsibility for the report. The date is necessary because auditors have an active duty to check for post-balance sheet events up to the date on which the report is signed. After this date the auditors have only passive duties to respond to events which come to their attention.[2] Auditors can minimise this responsibility by dating reports as quickly as possible after the financial statements have been finalised and approved by the directors.

In addition to the explicit statements referred to above, auditors may have to make further statements by default. Section 237 of the Companies Act 1985 requires the auditor of a limited company to form an opinion on whether:

- The company has kept proper accounting records.
- The profit and loss account and balance sheet are in agreement with the accounting records and returns.
- All the information and explanations which he considers necessary for the purposes of the audit have been obtained and adequate returns for their audit have been received from branches not visited.
- Full disclosure has been made of the directors' emoluments and other benefits.

The auditor is not required to make an explicit statement regarding any of these matters unless he has some reservation about them.

5.1.2 *The directors' report*

The auditors' opinion is normally restricted to the profit statement, the balance sheet and their related notes. They do, however, have some responsibility for the other information which is published by the company. Auditors have a statutory responsibility under s 235(3) of the Companies Act 1985 to consider whether the information in the directors' report is consistent with the audited accounts. Dividend payments, for example, are described in both the profit and loss account and in the directors' report. The auditor does not have to verify the information in the directors' report itself. His only duty is to consider whether the information which is contained in both the directors' report and the other statements is consistent. Much of the information in the directors' report is not disclosed elsewhere in the annual report and the auditor has no statutory duty to form an opinion on the accuracy of this.

The auditor should, however, review all of the information which the directors propose to publish in the directors' report and elsewhere in the annual report. If any of this proves to be misleading, it may be felt that the credibility of the financial statements as a whole will be undermined. The matter should be discussed with the directors and they should be asked to correct the facts. If the directors refuse, then the auditor's responsibilities are, unfortunately, rather unclear.[3]

5.2 A true and fair view

The Companies Act 1985 requires that the annual accounts give a true and fair view (s 226 (2)). The auditor is also required to form an opinion on truth and fairness and must state this opinion in his report. The Companies Act does not, however, define the term 'true and fair'.

ACTIVITY

Try to write down a definition of truth and fairness in your own words. Look at your definition. How useful would it be if, say, you were arguing with a company's finance director over whether a particular accounting treatment was acceptable?

Do not worry if you found this exercise rather difficult. The accountancy profession has not actually managed to define the concept of truth and fairness in such a manner as to make it easy to resolve arguments over whether a particular set of statements actually gives a true and fair view or whether one alternative is better than another in this respect.

5.2.1 *Companies Act requirements*

The accounts will not present a true and fair view if they have been prepared in accordance with misleading accounting policies. The statements must also disclose all of the information which is necessary to obtain a full understanding of the company.

Schedule 4 of the Companies Act 1985 contains almost forty pages of detailed rules regarding disclosure and valuation. It is, however, acknowledged that the application of these rules will not, in itself, lead to a true and fair view. This is demonstrated in s 226 (5) of the Act itself, which states that the requirement to give a true and fair view overrides the requirements of Schedule 4 and all of the Act's other accounting requirements.[4] The disclosure requirements are also supplemented by s 226 (4) which requires the company to disclose any additional information which is necessary to give a true and fair view.

The flexibility inherent in the Companies Act enables the directors and the auditors to use their knowledge of the company to devise the most appropriate accounting policies for their type of business. Prescriptive rules would make the financial statements more uniform, but could also make them less informative. The flexibility also enables accountants to react quickly to changes in the business environment without having to wait for changes in accounting regulations.[5]

5.2.2 *Professional requirements*

During the 1960s the accountancy profession's credibility was damaged by a number of scandals which had been caused by the lack of consistency in accounting. The professional bodies responded by establishing the Accounting Standards Steering Committee (subsequently the Accounting Standards Committee or ASC). Prior to its replacement by the Accounting Standards Board, this body had published standards (SSAPs) on over twenty topics. Every member of each of the six professional bodies[6] which are involved in the standard-setting process is obliged to observe accounting standards when preparing or auditing financial statements which are intended to give a true and fair view.[7]

The standard-setting system was open to criticism. The ASC was under-funded. Its committee members were part-time and had very little technical support. The system was also cumbersome. The councils of each of the professional bodies had to agree to the adoption of a proposed standard, thus giving each of several additional committees an effective right to veto the introduction of new SSAPs.

The ASC was replaced in September 1990 by a new body which has the power to issue its own standards. The members of this body, the Accounting Standards Board (ASB), are employed on a full-time basis and are supported by professional staff. The ASB is supervised by the new Financial Reporting Council (FRC), whose chairman is appointed by the Department of Trade and Industry and the Bank of England. These changes were intended to increase the quality of accounting standards and the speed with which they are issued in response to new problems in accounting.

The Companies Act 1989 introduced a number of changes which were intended to support this new standard-setting body. A new section, 36A, was inserted into Schedule 4 of the Companies Act 1985. This requires that the company must state whether the accounts have been prepared in accordance with applicable accounting standards. The company must give particulars of any material departure from those standards and the reasons for it. Previously, the standards had no direct statutory backing.

Section 12 of the Companies Act 1989 inserted some new provisions into the 1985 Act to provide for the revision of defective accounts. S 245 enables this to be done on a voluntary basis if the directors decide that the original version did not comply with the requirements of the Companies Act 1985. If the Secretary of State suspects that the accounts do not comply with the requirements of the Act then s 245A empowers him to request that the directors either provide an explanation of their accounting treatment or revise the statements. If necessary, the Secretary of State can apply to the court to have changes made to the statements or their audit. The Secretary of State can also authorise other persons to make this type of application to the court. The Financial Reporting Council has established a review panel which will investigate and take action against those companies which appear to be in breach of the rules.[8]

The question of whether a company's financial statements give a true and fair view is, ultimately, a matter for the courts to decide. There is no guarantee that the courts will agree with the logic underlying the SSAPs or other accounting standards. It could, however, be argued that a reader would expect the financial statements to be prepared in accordance with the standards enforced by the preparer's professional body. If this is so, it could then be argued that the statements will not give a true and fair view if the standards are ignored.

Mautz and Sharaf point out, however, that the auditor should always evaluate the relevance of accounting principles to the company and should be prepared to reject the policies laid down in the professional standards if it is felt that they are inappropriate or misleading.[9] The ASB permits the adoption of accounting policies other than those laid down in the FRSs and SSAPs, provided this is done because the rigid application of a standard would be misleading. Any such deviation must, however, be disclosed in the notes to the accounts. If the auditors agree with the policy, then they need do nothing. They must, however, be prepared to justify their acceptance of the company's treatment.[10]

5.2.3 *The conceptual framework*

One of the greatest problems faced by the preparers and auditors of accounts is the lack of a proper conceptual framework for accounting. A conceptual framework has been defined by the US Financial Accounting Standards Board as 'a constitution, a coherent system of interrelated objectives and fundamentals that can lead to consistent standards and that prescribes the nature, function and limits of financial accounting and financial statements'.[11] This definition may make the conceptual framework project sound like a rather dull, academic exercise. This could not, however, be further from the truth. In order to give a true and fair view, one must establish the needs and objectives of the viewer. This will, in turn, lead to the definition of the purpose of the financial statements and of their fundamental elements. Unless these is substantial agreement about these matters, accounting standards will always be set in a piecemeal manner, with the possibility of inconsistencies between standards and differences of opinion over their interpretation. Furthermore, the development of new standards often becomes protracted because of arguments about the fundamental issues at stake.

Off-balance sheet financing is a classic example of the problems created by the lack of a conceptual framework. This is a generic term which describes the deliberate structuring of legal agreements in such a way that they have the effect of granting a loan without having to be shown as such in the recipient's balance sheet. For example, a whisky distiller would sell its stock to a bank. At the same time, it would grant the bank an option to sell the stock back for a price equivalent to the original selling price plus interest during the intervening period. The stock stayed on the distiller's premises. Legally, the distiller does not owe the bank anything until the option is exercised. Effectively, the bank has granted a loan secured on the distiller's stock. It has taken the accountancy profession many years to publish an accounting standard on this.[12] This is partly because of problems of defining such basic items as assets and liabilities in the absence of an agreed conceptual framework for financial accounting.

The extent to which there are weaknesses in the rules governing accounting can be gauged by the fact that there are a number of books in print on the subject of 'creative accounting'.[13] Creative accounting is the deliberate abuse of the subjectivity inherent in accounting and also the exploitation of loopholes in the rules to achieve a more acceptable profit and loss account or balance sheet. While such an approach to accounting may be immoral, it is not illegal and is, therefore, difficult for the auditor to prevent.

In the absence of a comprehensive conceptual framework, the only real test of 'truth and fairness' is a comparison of the accounting policies adopted with the codified requirements as laid down by the Companies Act 1985 and the SSAPs and FRSs published by the ASB.[14] The collapse of Polly Peck International brought this issue into focus when it was revealed that the group's profit had been inflated by the effects of SSAP 20. The company had raised cash by borrowing in hard currencies – on which a low rate of interest was payable – and had made deposits denominated in soft currencies – which attracted a high rate of interest. This gave the company a substantial amount of net interest receivable, which bolstered profits considerably. Unfortunately, the capital value of its debt was appreciating rapidly while the value of its soft currency deposits was dwindling. These losses more than offset the net interest receivable. SSAP 20 did not require these capital losses to flow through the profit statement. Instead, they were debited straight to reserves in the balance sheet. The company's auditors accepted that the financial statements gave a true and fair view, despite the fact that a large loss had been omitted from the profit and loss account and that this could only have been spotted by a reasonably sophisticated reader.[15]

5.2.4 *Capital market studies*

In recent years, a great deal of work has been done on the reaction of the capital markets to accounting information. This would appear to suggest that there is very little point in attempting to distort the figures by means of accounting policies because the stock market seems to be able to correct for this when setting share prices.

It would appear that analysts pay so much attention to the annual report, and interpret the figures which it contains with so much care, that any attempt to manipulate the figures by means of accounting policies will almost certainly fail. The company must publish details of its accounting policies and must also disclose a great deal of detailed information in the notes to the accounts. This means that a skilled reader can adjust the figures to make them more directly comparable with those of similar companies.[16]

These studies do not diminish the role of the auditor. If the company publishes false information or does not disclose important information then even the most skilled analyst would be unable to make the necessary corrections.

5.3 The wording of the report

It was suggested in Chapter 3 that the role of the audit is often misunderstood and that users expect much more assurance than the auditor actually provides. Perhaps this is partly due to the wording of the auditor's report. The Commission on Auditors' Responsibilities (CAR) made the following criticisms of the standard report which was used in the US at that time:

1 It uses standardised language. This reduces the report to a symbolic document, rather than a means of communication between the auditor and the reader.

2 There is no explicit statement of several important points. In particular, the facts that the financial statements are representations of management and that there is a great deal of subjective judgement in the process of forming an audit opinion are omitted.

3 Technical terminology is used. This is regarded as unclear or ambiguous to average readers.

4 There is no indication of the extent to which the auditor's responsibilities have been expanded and clarified since the standard report was drafted.[17]

A great deal of research has been done on the extent to which the audit report is read and understood by the various groups of potential users. In general, it would appear that the audit report commands less attention than any other section of the annual report and is misinterpreted by many of its readers.[18]

ACTIVITY

Read through the standard UK audit report at the beginning of this chapter. To what extent do you believe the criticisms listed by CAR could be directed at the UK report?

HINT: try to read the report from the point of view of a user who has no real background in accountancy.

Arguably, many of the criticisms would apply to the standard, even though it appears to have been written in a manner which makes it simple for non-accountants to understand. Indeed, the absence of accounting 'jargon' might make the report even more confusing for the readers.

The report certainly does use a standardised language. In the vast majority of cases, audit reports will be identical apart from obvious items such as names and dates.

Non-accountants may fail to appreciate the very subtle warnings implicit in the statement of the directors' reponsibilities. Non-accountants may not realise that this could imply some bias in the financial statements.

There is a considerable amount of technical terminology. The most obvious example is 'true and fair view'. It is unlikely that many non-accountants will understand the problems associated with interpreting this phrase. Similarly, the phrase 'reasonable assurance' may mean different things to non-accountants and auditors.

There is certainly no explicit warning of the extent of the auditor's responsibilities to the shareholders and other readers. It is, for example, unlikely that many non-members will appreciate that the reference to the members in the title is meant to exclude them.

5.3.1 *Developments in audit reporting in the United States*

In 1980, the Auditing Standards Board (ASB) in the United States issued a draft Statement on Auditing Standards on audit reporting. This was in response to the criticisms voiced by CAR. The changes were intended to clarify, rather than alter, the auditor's responsibilities. Perhaps surprisingly, the draft provoked such a hostile reaction that it was withdrawn.

At that time, the standard audit report was as follows:

> AUDITOR'S REPORT
>
> We have examined the balance sheet of X Company as of December 31, 19XX and the related statements of income, retained earnings and changes in financial position for the year then ended. Our examination was made in accordance with generally accepted auditing standards and, accordingly, included such tests of the accounting records and such other auditing procedures as we considered necessary in the circumstances.
>
> In our opinion, the financial statements referred to above present fairly the financial position of X Company as of December 31, 19XX and the results of its operations and the changes in its financial position for the year then ended, in conformity with generally accepted accounting principles applied on a basis consistent with that of the previous year.

The draft SAS suggested the following changes:

- Add the word 'independent' to the report title.
- State that the financial statements 'are the representations of management'.
- State that 'an audit is intended to provide reasonable, but not absolute, assurance as to whether financial statements taken as a whole are free of material error'.
- Replace 'examined' with 'audited' in the scope paragraph.
- State in the scope paragraph that the 'application of (generally accepted auditing standards) requires judgement in determining the nature, timing, and extent of tests and other procedures and in evaluating the results of those procedures'.
- Change 'present fairly' to 'present'.
- Delete the reference to 'consistent application of GAAP'.

Broadly, professional accountants supported the proposals. Responses from industrial and financial institutions tended to be hostile. The greatest divergence of views was over the statement that an audit gave 'reasonable but not absolute assurance' and over the increased emphasis on management's responsibilities.[19]

Despite the problems described above, the ASB issued a new standard report in

1988. This differed from the previous standard report in that it stated the relative responsibilities of the auditor and management, the fact that the auditor could not provide total assurance, and the nature of the audit process.[20] The new report reads as follows:

> INDEPENDENT AUDITOR'S REPORT
>
> We have audited the accompanying balance sheet of X Company as of December 31, 19XX and the related statements of income, retained earnings and cash flows for the year then ended. These financial statements are the responsibility of the Company's management. Our responsibility is to express an opinion on these financial statements based on our audit.
>
> We conducted our audit in accordance with generally accepted auditing standards. Those standards require that we plan and perform the audit to obtain reasonable assurance about whether the financial statements are free of material misstatement. An audit involves examining, on a test basis, evidence supporting the amounts and disclosures in the financial statements. An audit also includes assessing the accounting principles used and significant estimates made by management, as well as evaluating the overall financial statement presentation. We believe that our audit provides a reasonable basis for our opinion.
>
> In our opinion, the financial statements referred to above present fairly, in all material respects, the financial position of X Company as at December 31, 19XX, and the results of its operations and its cash flows for the year then ended in conformity with generally accepted accounting principles.
>
> (signature)
>
> (date)[21]

5.3.2 Symbolism in the audit report

It is debatable whether the precise wording of the audit report is of any great significance. It is, of course, desirable that the reader understands the auditor's responsibilities. Readers can, however, educate themselves by obtaining copies of the professional standards and guidelines and referring to text books. It is unlikely that the auditor's obligations could be changed by the rewording of the report. The auditor's duties are, after all, laid down in legislation.

These sentiments are echoed by Mautz and Sharaf who point out that '... even professional readers may have difficulty in distinguishing niceties of expression which the auditor relies on to absolve himself of certain legal responsibilities'. They go on to argue that the principal objectives of the audit report are that it should state the nature of the underlying examination in a clear and unequivocal manner and that it should express the auditor's judgement in straightforward terms.[22]

This argument has been taken a stage further by a suggestion that readers tend to view the audit report as a symbol. The standardised wording encourages readers to do little more than glance at it to see whether the auditor has expressed any reservations about the figures. The users of the report will have an implicit understanding of the underlying message contained in the report and will not, therefore, be particularly interested in its precise wording. If this is so, then there is very little point in making minor adjustments to the content of the standard report. Users are unlikely to alter their perceptions of its meaning unless there is a major revision.[23]

The idea that the audit report is merely a symbol which represents the auditor's examination and judgement is applied to great effect in the standard opinion paragraph recommended by the Mexican Institute of Public Accountants:

> In my opinion, based on the examination which I carried out, the accompanying financial statements, prepared by the management of the company, present the financial position of Mexican Company, S.A. at December 31, 19XX and the results of its operations for the year then ended.

Thus, the report makes no explicit mention of auditing standards, accounting principles, or truth and fairness. All of these are implied.[24]

5.4 Summary

The report is an integral and important part of the audit. The auditor must satisfy the requirements of the SAS on audit reporting. This lays down the form and content of the report. The Companies Act 1985 also contains certain items which must be dealt with in the report.

One of the most difficult problems facing the auditors is the fact that they must state an opinion on the truth and fairness of the financial statements. There is, however, no agreed definition of truth and fairness. Some guidance is given in Schedule 4 of the Companies Act and also in the accounting standards. The preparation and audit of financial information are complicated by the fact that there is no cohesive theoretical framework for accounting.

The wording of the audit report has received a great deal of attention over a number of years. There is, however, some doubt as to whether the precise wording of the report is of any great relevance.

───────────────── **REVIEW QUESTIONS** ─────────────────

1. It would appear that capital markets can adjust for the effects of different accounting practices. If this is so, is there any need for the main financial statements to give a true and fair view, provided they are accompanied with detailed notes of accounting policies and other supporting information so that readers can adjust the figures for themselves? How would this affect the role of the auditor?

2. There is a great deal of flexibility inherent in the interpretation of the statutory and professional rules relating to accounting. To what extent does this create dangers for the auditor?

3. It has been suggested that more attention would be paid to the audit report if the standard presentation was abandoned and auditors were encouraged to vary their format and wording. Discuss the advantages and disadvantages of this.

EXERCISES

1. The following audit report has been drafted by one of your juniors:

> AUDIT REPORT ON THE FINANCIAL STATEMENTS OF B LTD.
>
> We have audited the financial statements of B Ltd in accordance with our standard audit procedures. We encountered the following problems in the course of our audit:
>
> The company manufactures high-technology electronic products. In order to determine whether stocks had been counted and valued correctly, we were obliged to rely on the advice of an independent firm of electronic engineers. Our examination of the contents of the petty cash box revealed that the amount of cash in hand had been overstated by £3.
>
> We are, however, satisfied that the accounts give a true and fair view. The company has also complied with the disclosure requirements of the Companies Act 1985 and has also kept proper accounting records.
>
> G and Company,
>
> Chartered Accountants.

List the errors in the form and content of this report.

2. In the absence of a more coherent test, truth and fairness can only really be measured by using the formal requirements contained in the Companies Act 1985 and the FRSs and SSAPs as a series of checklists. Select one or more of the accounting standards and read through it thoroughly. Try to identify at least one way in which it could be deliberately misinterpreted by an unscrupulous preparer of financial statements who wanted to manipulate the financial statements without actually breaking any of the rules. What insight does this exercise provide into the problems faced by auditors in deciding whether a set of financial statements give a true and fair view? How might the auditors be left open to criticism?

3. Before the publication of SAS 600, the standard audit report read as follows:

> AUDITOR'S REPORT TO THE MEMBERS OF XYZ LIMITED
>
> We have audited the financial statements on pages . . . to . . . in accordance with Auditing Standards.
>
> In our opinion the financial statements give a true and fair view of the state of the company's affairs at 31 December 19.. and of its profit and source and application of funds for the year then ended and have been properly prepared in accordance with the Companies Act 1985.
>
> Signed (Auditor's name, qualification, address)
>
> Date.[25]

Compare and contrast this report with the current version. Do you consider the differences to be significant? Which version do you prefer?

References and further reading

1. APB, SAS 600, *Auditors' Reports on Financial Statements*, 1993.
2. See APB, SAS 150, *Subsequent Events*, 1995, for details of the procedures which auditors would carry out and for further information about their reponsibilities in this area.
3. This problem is discussed in greater depth in the APB, SAS 160, *Other Information in Documents Containing Audited Financial Statements*, 1995.
4. A good example of this arose when the introduction of the Companies Act 1981 altered the rules regarding the valuation of long-term work in progress. The new rules were in direct conflict with those which had been imposed by the accountancy profession. Many companies simply ignored the new regulations and cited the requirements of the relevant accounting standard as justification. A fuller description of this can be found in Walton, D., 'Companies prefer SSAP 9 to ED 40', *Accountancy*, June 1987, pp. 35–6.
5. These arguments are discussed at greater length in Chapter 1 of Flint, D., *A True and Fair View in Company Accounts*, The Institute of Chartered Accountants of Scotland, 1982.
6. ACCA, ICAEW, ICAS, ICAI, The Chartered Institute of Management Accountants, and the Chartered Institute of Public Finance and Accountancy.
7. ASC, *Explanatory Foreword*, 1975.
8. Some of the cases which have been dealt with by the Review Panel are described in Singleton-Green, B., 'Fear stalks the world of financial reporting', *Accountancy*, December 1992, p. 117 and Ghosh, J., 'Conflicts, resolutions and enforcement', *Accountancy*, April 1993, p. 90.
9. Mautz, R.K. and Sharaf, H.A., *The Philosophy of Auditing*, American Accounting Association, 1961, p. 160.
10. ASB, *Foreword to Accounting Standards*, 1993.
11. FASB, *Scope and Implications of the Conceptual Framework Project*, 1976, p. 2.
12. ASB, FRS 5, *Reporting the Substance of Transactions*, 1994. This standard would now require the transaction between the distiller and the bank to be disclosed as a loan on the face of the balance sheet.
13. The most famous is Smith, T., *Accounting for Growth*, Century, 1992, but see also Griffiths, I., *Creative Accounting: How to make your profits what you want them to be*, Unwin Hyman, 1986, and Jameson, M., *A Practical Guide to Creative Accounting*, Kogan Page, 1988.
14. There is a helpful discussion of the legal arguments in this area in McGee, A., 'The "true and fair view" debate: a study in the legal regulation of accounting', *The Modern Law Review*, November 1991, pp. 874–88.
15. See Gwilliam, D. and Russell, T., 'Polly Peck: where were the analysts?', *Accountancy*, January 1991, pp. 25–6 and 'Compliance with the letter but not the spirit', *Accountancy*, April 1991, p. 35.
16. Much of the evidence to support this theory is summarised in Watts, R.L. and

Zimmerman, J.L., *Positive Accounting Theory*, Prentice Hall, 1986, Chapter 4. The implications of this for financial reporting are described in Keane, S.M., *Stock Market Efficiency*, Philip Allan, 1983, Chapter 9.

17. Commission on Auditors' Responsibilities, *Report, Conclusions, and Recommendations*, AICPA, 1978, pp. 72–5.

18. A very thorough review of this branch of the literature can be found in Estes, R., *The Auditor's Report and Investor Behavior*, Lexington Books, 1982, Chapter 2.

19. The responses of public accounting firms, industrial firms and financial institutions are compared in Dillard, J.F. and Jensen, D.L., 'The auditor's report: an analysis of opinion', *The Accounting Review*, October 1983, pp. 787–98.

20. For an analysis of the changes brought about by the new standard see Roussey, R.S., Ten Eyck, E.L. and Blanco-Best, M., 'Three new SASs: closing the communications gap', *Journal of Accountancy*, December 1988, pp. 44–52.

21. AICPA Statement on Auditing Standards 58, *Reports on Audited Financial Statements*, 1988.

22. Mautz, R.K. and Sharaf, H.A., *op. cit.*, p. 202.

23. An excellent discussion of the concept of the audit report as a symbol is contained in Seidler, L.J., 'Symbolism and communication in the auditor's report', Auditing Symposium III, Touche Ross / University of Kansas, 1976. This essay also uses the concept to discuss the results of some of the empirical research conducted on the use of the audit report.

24. Translation of Bulletin Number 36, dated 1975, of the Instituto Mexicano de Contadores Publicos, contained in *Doing Business in Mexico*, Price Waterhouse, 1984.

25. APC Auditing Standard, *The Audit Report*, 1989.

CHAPTER 6

Qualified audit reports

The auditor may be unable to state that the financial statements show a true and fair view. He may have been unable to obtain sufficient evidence to support such an opinion, or he may disagree with the manner in which the statements have been prepared. If the auditor has any such reservations then he should say so in his report.

The auditing standard on audit reports[1] describes the circumstances in which the auditor should express a qualified opinion and also provides guidance on the manner in which the report should be modified. This chapter will describe the content of a qualified audit and the difficulties of reporting on the financial statements of a small company and will discuss the problems of evaluating the implications of such reports for the company.

By the time you have completed this chapter, you should be able to:

- Explain what is meant by a qualified audit report and the reasons for which a qualification might be necessary.
- Explain the problems associated with determining whether a reservation is material.
- Describe the different forms of qualification and state when each would be appropriate.
- Explain what effects a qualified audit report might have for the company concerned.

6.1 Reasons for qualifications

An audit report is said to be 'qualified' if the auditor has some reservation about the truth and fairness of the financial statements.

ACTIVITY

Look back at the example of the unqualified audit report in Chapter 5. Try to list the possible reasons which would prevent auditors from expressing an opinion in these terms.

Broadly, a qualified audit report may be required in two sets of circumstances:

- The auditors may be uncertain about the truth and fairness of the statements, or
- They may have formed the opinion that they do not give a true and fair view.

Both of these circumstances could be rather more complicated than they appear at first glance.

6.1.1 *Uncertainty*

In the context of audit reporting, uncertainty can take three forms:

Inherent uncertainty
'An uncertainty whose resolution is dependent upon uncertain future events outside the control of the reporting entity's directors at the date the financial statements are approved.'[2]

Fundamental uncertainty
'An inherent uncertainty is fundamental when the magnitude of its potential impact is so great that, without clear disclosure of the nature and implications of the uncertainty, the view given by the financial statements would be seriously misleading.'[3]

Limitation of audit scope
Arises where the auditors are unable to obtain audit evidence which may reasonably be expected to be available. This could be because access to evidence has been withheld or because of some event which was beyond the control of either the directors or the auditors.[4]

Any of the above could prevent the auditors from forming an opinion on the truth and fairness of the financial statements. Each will, however, be dealt with differently in the audit report. This will be illustrated in section 6.3 below.

Inherent uncertainties are extremely common. Many of the figures which the auditors must examine are based upon assumptions and estimates made by management. Thus, the valuation of stocks, debtors and fixed assets are all subject to uncertainty. The company could also be subject to litigation or be faced with financial difficulties which threaten its future. The outcome of such problems may be difficult to predict and so it may be impossible to collect sufficient evidence to support an opinion.

It is unlikely that the directors would restrict the scope of the audit. The auditors have a statutory right of access to all of the records and also to any explanations which they require for the purpose of their audit. The Companies Act 1985 requires the auditors to describe any lack of cooperation in the audit report. This would, therefore, lead to two qualifications, one due to uncertainty about the figures and the other due to the failure to provide the auditors with the necessary assistance.

6.1.2 Disagreement

The auditors may not agree that the financial statements give a true and fair view. This could be because they do not comply with FRSs and SSAPs or because their description of certain facts is incorrect. The statements could also be misleading because important information has been omitted. Finally, the statements may not comply with the Companies Act or other relevant legislation.

6.1.3 Resolving reservations

There is no reason why the auditors should not attempt to avoid a qualification in the audit report. Quite apart from the risk of displeasing the directors, a qualified report could reduce the credibility of the information in the financial statements and make them less useful to the shareholders.

The auditors cannot, of course, ignore a problem which should result in a qualified report. They can, however, avoid qualifying on the grounds of disagreement by persuading the directors to alter the draft statements so that they show a true and fair view. The directors can also rectify a limitation of the scope of the audit work by making the necessary information available. This could involve making a special print-out of a computer file, or the recreation of lost records.

6.2 Materiality

The subjectivity involved in accounting means that the auditor will always be uncertain to some extent about the truth and fairness of the financial statements. It is also unlikely that any two accountants will ever be in complete agreement about the choice of accounting policies, the precise meaning of a SSAP, and so on. This would seem to suggest that almost every audit report should be qualified on the grounds of both uncertainty and disagreement. This is not, in fact, the case.

The ICAEW conducts an annual survey of the audit reports of 300 listed and large unlisted companies. Typically, only two or three per cent receive qualified reports. The Auditing Standard on reporting states that the auditor should have regard to the concept of materiality when forming his opinion. This is because it would be misleading to report on trivial uncertainties or disagreements.[5]

Unfortunately, there is no clear definition of materiality. The APB defines materiality as

> an expression of the relative significance or importance of a particular matter in the context of financial statements as a whole. A matter is material if its omission or misstatement would reasonably influence the decisions of an addressee of the auditors' report. . . . Materiality . . . has both qualitative and quantitative aspects.[6]

ACTIVITY
Materiality is probably one of the most important concepts in auditing. Read through the definition provided above and list some of the problems which you would anticipate in putting this concept into practice.

The lack of a conceptual framework for financial reporting means that there is no clear agreement on the reasons for which the members of the annual report are expected to read the annual report and make decisions. They might be expected to make investment decisions, or it could be argued that the report is published only for stewardship purposes.

It is also difficult to tell how a piece of information might affect the behaviour of the readers. Readers will differ in terms of accounting knowledge, attitude to risk, and so on. Any given piece of information might affect some readers and not others.

In any dispute between the auditors and the directors, the directors will be able to use any ambiguity about the interpretation of this definition as an argument for treating the matter as immaterial.

Materiality can be affected by both the amount and nature of the item. The amount involved should be considered in terms of its effect on the statements themselves, on individual account balances and on the relationships between the figures. An item which is insignificant in terms of its size can, however, be material because of some other factor. Directors' salaries, for example, are always material because of the statutory disclosure requirements in respect of these and also because of the interest shown by the shareholders. The nature of the business could also affect the materiality of the item. If, for example, a food manufacturer had been charged with hygiene offences, the contingent liability in respect of the possible fine could be negligible. The possible effect of the adverse publicity on future sales could, however, make it necessary to disclose the matter.[7]

The materiality decision is an important one which relies heavily upon professional judgement. This creates the possibility of inconsistencies between the materiality thresholds of different auditors. At least one study has managed to model materiality decisions using publicly available information and has concluded that there are differences between accounting firms.[8] It would, however, be impossible to devise a rigid set of rules which could be used to arrive at sensible materiality decisions in every set of circumstances.

6.3 The wording of a qualified audit report

It is important that the auditors' opinion is expressed in clear terms which enable its readers to understand the report's implications. SAS 600 contains a number of decision rules to ensure that this is the case.

6.3.1 *Inherent uncertainties*

The logic underlying the rules with respect to uncertainty seems to be that it could be potentially misleading to make any unnecessary reference to an inherent uncertainty. Doing so might tend to attach a greater significance to them than they really merit.

   Any material uncertainty need not be mentioned in the audit report provided it is (a) not fundamental and (b) adequately disclosed in the financial state-

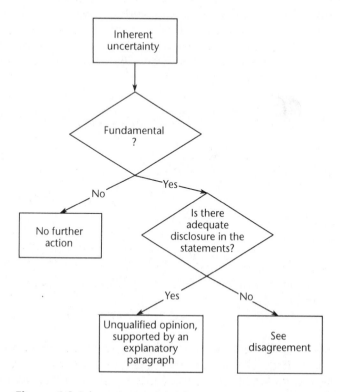

Figure 6.1 Inherent uncertainty.

ments. If the uncertainty is not adequately disclosed then this constitutes a disagreement over the company's accounting policy and is dealt with under a different set of rules which are discussed later. If, for example, there was a material uncertainty over the outcome of a damages claim against the company then the auditors would review the disclosures in the financial statements, including the notes. If there was sufficient information for the members to appreciate the nature of the problem then the auditors could reasonably conclude that the financial statements give a true and fair view (see Figure 6.1).

If the uncertainty is fundamental then the auditors should not rely completely on the shareholders reading the statements in sufficient detail to spot the matter. Instead, the auditors should highlight the disclosure by referring to it in the audit report. This is done by adding a paragraph to the section of the report which deals with the basis of the auditors' opinion. Thus, the audit report might appear as follows:

AUDITOR'S REPORT TO THE MEMBERS OF XYZ LIMITED

We have audited the financial statements on pages . . . to . . . which have been prepared under the historical cost convention and the accounting policies set out on page . . .

Respective responsibilities of directors and auditors

As described on page . . . the company's directors are responsible for the preparation of financial statements. It is our responsibility to form an independent opinion, based on our audit, on those statements and to report our opinion to you.

Basis of opinion

We conducted our audit in accordance with Auditing Standards issued by the Auditing Practices Board. An audit includes examination, on a test basis, of evidence relevant to the amounts and disclosures in the financial statements. It also includes an assessment of the significant estimates and judgements made by the directors in the preparation of the financial statements, and of whether the accounting policies are appropriate to the company's circumstances, consistently applied and adequately disclosed.

We planned and performed our audit so as to obtain all the information and explanations which we considered necessary in order to provide us with sufficient evidence to give reasonable assurance that the financial statements are free from material misstatement, whether caused by fraud or other irregularity or error. In forming our opinion we also evaluated the overall adequacy of the presentation of information in the financial statements.

Fundamental uncertainty

In forming our opinion, we have considered the adequacy of the disclosures made in the financial statements concerning the possible outcome of a damages claim against the company. The future settlement of this claim could result in additional liabilities of £. . . . Details of the circumstances relating to this fundamental uncertainty are described in note . . . . Our opinion is not qualified in this respect.

Opinion
In our opinion the financial statements give a true and fair view of the state of the company's affairs at 31 December 19.. and of its profit for the year then ended and have been properly prepared in accordance with the Companies Act 1985.

Signed (Auditor's name, qualification, address)

Date

In this case, the auditor has decided that the size of the claim is sufficient to warrant highlighting it in the audit report. This would be appropriate if the extent of the exposure could threaten the company's future or force it to raise further finance to meet any settlement. While this note does not actually add anything to the information which was already available in the statements, it does enable the auditors to claim that they have done everything possible to ensure that the members paid appropriate attention to this disclosure.

The need for this form of explanatory paragraph was highlighted in the aftermath of the collapse of the Bank of Credit and Commerce International (BCCI).[9] The final set of financial statements carried an unqualified audit report, despite the auditors having become aware of the uncertainty associated with the bank's future. The bank's future was dependent on a rescue package which had been promised by the government of Abu Dhabi. These arrangements were described briefly in one of the notes to the financial statements. Under the International Auditing Guidelines in force at that time, auditors were not required to refer to inherent uncertainty provided it was disclosed in the financial statements. Price Waterhouse was, therefore, able to deal with the fact that the bank's future was dependent on government support simply by drawing attention to the note which described the arrangements. A Parliamentary committee agreed that Price Waterhouse had complied with the relevant auditing standards, but expressed concern that those rules seemed to mask the truth from the bank's depositors: 'The interests of depositors were not well served by the inadequate disclosures in the BCCI 1989 accounts.'[10] The SAS does not actually require any form of qualification in respect of inherent uncertainty as such. It does, however, require any inadequate disclosure to be treated as a disagreement (see section 6.3.3 below).

6.3.2 Qualifications due to limitation of scope

Any material limitation of scope will result in a qualified report (see Figure 6.2). If the audit work is restricted by a limitation and this cannot be resolved by, for example, obtaining evidence from some alternative form of testing, then the auditors will be forced to qualify. This would normally take the form of an 'except for' report:

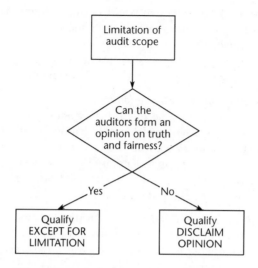

Figure 6.2 Limitation of audit scope.

AUDITOR'S REPORT TO THE MEMBERS OF UVW LIMITED

We have audited the financial statements on pages . . . to . . . which have been prepared under the historical cost convention and the accounting policies set out on page . . .

Respective responsibilities of directors and auditors

As described on page . . . the company's directors are responsible for the preparation of financial statements. It is our responsibility to form an independent opinion, based on our audit, on those statements and to report our opinion to you.

Basis of opinion

We conducted our audit in accordance with Auditing Standards issued by the Auditing Practices Board, except that the scope of our work was limited as explained below.

An audit includes examination, on a test basis, of evidence relevant to the amounts and disclosures in the financial statements. It also includes an assessment of the significant estimates and judgements made by the directors in the preparation of the financial statements, and of whether the accounting policies are appropriate to the company's circumstances, consistently applied and adequately disclosed.

We planned and performed our audit so as to obtain all the information and explanations which we considered necessary in order to provide us with sufficient evidence to give reasonable assurance that the financial statements are free from material misstatement, whether caused by fraud or other irregularity or error. However, the evidence available to us in respect of closing stock was limited because stock sheets in respect of £. . . of the company's recorded stock were accidentally lost before we could examine them. There were no other satisfactory audit procedures that we could adopt to confirm that closing stock was properly valued.

In forming our opinion we also evaluated the overall adequacy of the presentation of information in the financial statements.

Qualified opinion arising from limitation in audit scope
Except for any adjustments that might have been found to be necessary had we been able to obtain sufficient evidence concerning closing stocks, in our opinion the financial statements give a true and fair view of the state of the company's affairs at 31 December 19.. and of its profit for the year then ended and have been properly prepared in accordance with the Companies Act 1985.

In respect alone of the limitation on our work relating to closing stocks:

- We have not obtained all the information and explanations that we considered necessary for the purpose of our audit.
- We were unable to determine whether proper accounting records had been maintained.

Signed (Auditor's name, qualification, address)

Date

In this case, the value of the stock must have been material, otherwise the matter could have been ignored, but not so great that the auditors were unable to form an opinion about the truth and fairness of the financial statements. Assuming the same facts as in the previous example, except that the stocks involved were worth so much in relation to profit and net assets that the auditors could not decide whether the statements gave a true and fair view:

Other paragraphs as before

Opinion: disclaimer on view given by financial statements
Because of the possible effect of the limitation in evidence available to us, we are unable to form an opinion as to whether the financial statements give a true and fair view of the state of the company's affairs as at 31 December 19.. and of its profit for the year then ended. In all other respects, in our opinion the financial statements have been properly prepared in accordance with the Companies Act 1985.

In respect alone of the limitation on our work relating to closing stocks:

- We have not obtained all the information and explanations that we considered necessary for the purpose of our audit.
- We were unable to determine whether proper accounting records had been maintained.

Signed (Auditor's name, qualification, address)

Date

The disclaimer is obviously a rather extreme form of qualification. The auditors are withholding their opinion on the truth and fairness of the financial statements. In that sense, the members may feel that the report cannot be said to add any credibility to the financial statements and is, therefore, unsatisfactory. It does, however, provide the members with some warning about this problem and also quantifies the extent of the auditor's uncertainty.

The auditor would have been forced to qualify in respect of all material reservations. The fact that the disclaimer was in respect of stock suggests that all other areas have been examined without any serious problems.

6.3.3 Qualifications due to disagreement

If the auditors disagree with some aspect of the calculation or disclosure of the information in the financial statements, then they will go through the following process (see Figure 6.3).

If, for example, the directors of XYZ Ltd had decided to exclude the damages claim from the financial statements and the related notes, the auditors would probably report in the following terms:

Figure 6.3 Disagreement.

Other paragraphs as before

Qualified opinion arising from disagreement about accounting treatment
No provision has been made in the financial statements in respect of an action against the company. If this is decided against the company it could result in the payment of damages of £. . . . In our opinion the company should have treated this claim as a contingent liability in accordance with the provisions of SSAP 18.

Except for the absence of this contingent liability, in our opinion the financial statements give a true and fair view of the state of the company's affairs at 31 December 19.. and of its profit for the year then ended and have been properly prepared in accordance with the Companies Act 1985.

Signed (Auditor's name, qualification, address)

Date

If the value of the claim was so serious as to, say, threaten the company's ability to continue as a going concern then the auditors would be forced to express an adverse opinion:

Other paragraphs as before

Adverse opinion
No provision has been made in the financial statements in respect of an action against the company. If this is decided against the company it could result in the payment of damages of £. . . . In our opinion the company should have treated this claim as a contingent liability in accordance with the provisions of SSAP 18.

In view of the effect of the failure to provide for the contingent liability referred to above, in our opinion the financial statements do not give a true and fair view of the state of the company's affairs at 31 December 19.. and of its profit for the year then ended. In all other respects, in our opinion the financial statements have been properly prepared in accordance with the Companies Act 1985.

Signed (Auditor's name, qualification, address)

Date

The second form of qualification is again the more serious. In this case the auditors are saying that the financial statements do not give a true and fair view.

In both cases the readers are better equipped to make intelligent use of the financial statements. Both forms of report quantify the auditors' reservations and, therefore, provide the members with two sets of figures: those disclosed by the company and those which would have been preferred by the auditors.

6.4 Effects of qualifications

In the United States, a qualified audit report can have serious consequences for a company. Every year, the company must file its annual report with the Securities and Exchange Commission (SEC). The SEC will refuse to accept the return if the audit report contains certain types of qualification, effectively suspending dealing in the company's shares. There are no equivalent penalties in the United Kingdom. A qualified report could, however, affect the attitudes of the users of the financial statements. This could have more serious implications for the company.

There have been many attempts to study the effect of qualified audit reports on the behaviour of users. Some have tried to isolate the effects of qualifications on share prices.[11] Other studies have made use of questionnaires to obtain an insight into the effect of a qualified report on the attitudes of specific readers.[12]

While it would be useful to know exactly what the consequences of a qualification were, it would appear that very little confidence can be placed in the results of some of the studies which have been conducted. In a review of this branch of the literature, Craswell[13] indicates that many of the results which have been obtained are contradictory. Furthermore, the validity of both the market based and the questionnaire type approaches is open to question. In order to examine the effects of an audit qualification on share price, Craswell points out that the researcher would have to solve the following problems:

- The actual date of announcement of the qualification is difficult to determine, particularly because the market can often measure the probability of a qualified report from the delay in the publication of the financial statements.
- The researcher would have to be able to predict which qualifications would be perceived by the market as containing 'good' as opposed to those which contained 'bad' news.
- Firms receive qualifications because of the conscious decisions of managers and auditors. Certain types of firm could be more likely to receive a qualified report. The researcher could confuse the effects of the qualified report with those of the other factors which were common to such firms.
- Audit reports are published in conjunction with other information. It is difficult to isolate the reaction to the audit report from that of the market's reaction to the other disclosures.

Questionnaire type studies are also difficult to design. It is particularly important that the information given in the case is as realistic as possible. It is also difficult to draw general conclusions from a study which indicates that one particular sample of users, such as a group of bank lending officers, reacted in some way to a certain type of qualification. There is no guarantee that such a result would have any general application.

6.4.1 *The going concern qualification*

SSAP 2 and the Companies Act 1985 require that the financial statements should be prepared under the assumption that the company is a going concern. In other words, it should be assumed that the company will continue to operate into the foreseeable future. If there is reason to believe that the company will be unable to continue, then the fixed assets and stock will have to be valued at their estimated open-market values.

The auditor's duties in respect of the going concern concept are outlined in an SAS.[14] This suggests that it is the responsibility of the directors to assure themselves that the going concern basis is appropriate.[15] The auditors should ensure that the directors have made adequate enquiries when discharging this obligation.

This review is a key part of the audit. Auditors' failure to provide warnings about company collapse is one of the key components of the expectations gap discussed in Chapter 3. In addition to reviewing the directors' investigations, the auditors should consider the effects of any matters which could threaten the company's ability to continue as a going concern. This should not be too onerous a requirement because modern auditing techniques tend to stress the importance of a detailed knowledge of the business so as to appreciate the areas where the risk of material misstatement is highest. The review could, for example, concentrate on cash flow and profit forecasts and budgets. If any problems are anticipated then the auditors would ask management to explain how they intend to overcome them.

If there are any serious doubts about going concern then the auditors would have to consider the implications of this for the truth and fairness of the financial statements. If the auditors are of the opinion that there is a fundamental uncertainty about the validity of the going concern basis then they should check that the cause of this uncertainty is adequately disclosed in the financial statements. If it is, then they should issue an unqualified audit report with an explanatory paragraph. If the auditors disagree with the company's decision with regard to the going concern basis then they should issue an adverse opinion.

It is interesting to consider the impact of a qualification on the grounds that the company cannot be considered a going concern. Conventional wisdom would have it that such an opinion could be a self-fulfilling prophecy. The fact that the company's auditors did not believe that the company could survive would deter creditors and other lenders from providing finance and the company would collapse as a result. This is reinforced by the fact that the auditors would not qualify their opinion in this way unless there was very good reason for doing so. A going concern qualification is likely to have an immediate effect on their fee income. The company will either be forced out of business as a result or its directors will be antagonised and will find other auditors.

The effects of the going concern qualification have been analysed at length by Taffler and Tseung.[16] As part of this study, the authors identified a total of forty companies which had received a going concern qualification. The vast majority of these had not failed. One conclusion which could be drawn from this is that no attention was paid to the qualification. This would be rather surprising given that the auditor is a trained professional with unrestricted access to information about the company and its management. It would seem unwise to ignore such a warning about the company's stability.

One has, however, to be careful in interpreting this statistic. As Taffler and Tseung point out, a going concern qualification could be the very signal which warns the directors of impending disaster and which forces them to take appropriate action. Thus, the fact that companies can receive a going concern qualification and still manage to continue can be interpreted as evidence either that the audit is ignored or that it is read and acted upon. This illustrates the problem of measuring the impact of the report on its readers.

6.5 Summary

If the auditor is uncertain about the truth and fairness of the financial statements or disagrees with the figures then he may have to qualify his opinion. The auditor need not qualify if he is satisfied that his reservations are not material. Materiality is, however, defined in terms of the effect of the matter on the decisions made by users and is, therefore, difficult to determine.

There are three forms of qualification: except for, disclaimer and adverse. The except for form of qualification is used in most cases of uncertainty and disagreement. The others are extreme qualifications which should be used only where the auditor cannot state that the financial statements give a true and fair view.

It is difficult to design tests or experiments which provide reliable evidence about the effects of a qualified report. This can be illustrated by looking at the problem of the going concern qualification. Even if the company could resolve the difficulties which had led to the qualification, one would expect the company to collapse because lenders and suppliers would withdraw their support. This does not, however, appear to be the case. Very few of the companies whose accounts are qualified in this manner are, in fact, liquidated. Such findings can support arguments both for and against the usefulness of qualified reports.

──────────────── **REVIEW QUESTIONS** ────────────────

1. If auditors are always uncertain about the validity of their opinions, does this undermine the value of audit reports?

2. Discuss the relationship between the materiality decision and the auditor's perceived duty of care to third parties.

3. If the auditor is forced to disclaim opinion, should the shareholders regard the audit fee as a waste of money?

4. Given the variety of different problems that the auditor could encounter, should he be limited to such a short list of standard forms of qualification?

5. Before the publication of SAS 600, auditors were required to qualify their opinions in respect of all material uncertainty whether or not there was adequate disclosure in the financial statements. Discuss the possible advantages and disadvantages of doing so.

6. How could the relationship between the auditor and management change if conclusive proof emerged that a qualified audit report had adverse implications?

7. Many investors rely on highlights from the annual report as provided by on-line and CD-ROM-based information services and do not read the reports themselves. These services do not contain the text of the audit report and frequently do not even flag any qualifications in the report. What are the implications of this for the investors and the auditors?

EXERCISES

1. Read the standard audit reports in this chapter and re-read the report shown at the beginning of Chapter 5. List the ways in which SAS 600 attempts to ensure that the audit report is clear and understood by its readers.

2. You are the external auditor of ZYX plc. The company has a year end of 31 December 1988. On reading the minutes of board meetings, you discovered the following:

(a)   On 26 June 1988, an employee was seriously injured by a defective piece of machinery. The fault in this machine had been brought to the company's attention long before the accident, but had been ignored. It is expected that the employee will sue the company for several hundred thousand pounds.

(b)   On 12 January 1989, one of the company's major customers went into liquidation, owing ZYX plc £80,000. Unsecured creditors were not expected to receive any payment.

You approach the managing director of the company to ask why there is no mention of either of these matters in the draft accounts. The managing director replied that the claim in respect of the accident cannot be provided for because the amounts involved have not been finalised and, anyway, the matter would probably be settled out of court. The bad debt need not be disclosed because the liquidation occurred after the balance sheet date. He went on to suggest that you have no interest in these matters because your appointment as an auditor extends to an examination of the accounting records only and not to the board minutes.

According to ZYX's draft accounts, turnover for the year was £8m and net profit before tax was £750,000.

(a) Bearing in mind the provisions of SSAP 18 on Accounting for Contingencies and SSAP 17 on Accounting for Post Balance Sheet Events, draft an audit report for ZYX plc. You should assume that the company refused to alter the statements.

(b) How would you respond to the managing director's assertion that your investigation should be restricted to the accounting records only?

References and further reading

1. APB, SAS 600, *Auditors' Reports on Financial Statements*, 1993.
2. APB, *Glossary of Terms*, 1995.
3. *ibid.*
4. SAS 600, *op. cit.*, paragraphs 68–9.
5. For example, see Skerratt, L. and Tonkin, D.J., *Financial Reporting 1993–94: A Survey of UK Reporting Practice*, ICAEW, 1994.
6. APB, *Glossary of Terms*, 1995.
7. The topic of materiality is discussed at greater length in Lee, T.A., *Materiality: A Review and Analysis of its Reporting Significance and Auditing Implications*, APC, 1984.
8. Morris, M.H. and Nichols, W.D., 'Consistency exceptions: materiality judgements and firm structure', *The Accounting Review*, April 1988, pp. 237–54.
9. See Kochan, N. and Whittington, B., *Bankrupt: The BCCI Fraud*, Victor Gollancz Ltd, 1991 for a detailed account of this case.
10. Treasury and Civil Service Committee, Fourth Report, *Banking Supervision and BCCI: International and National Regulation*, House of Commons, 4 March 1992.
11. See, for example, Firth, M., 'Qualified audit reports: their impact on investment decisions', *The Accounting Review*, July 1978, pp. 642–50. This study compared the share price behaviour of companies whose audit reports had been qualified with those which had not. It was suggested that the market did react to a qualification. Furthermore, the type of qualification would appear to have an effect on the extent of the market's reaction.
12. See, for example, Estes, R. and Reimer, M., 'An experimental study of the differential effect of standard and qualified auditors' opinions on investors' price decisions', *Accounting and Business Research*, Spring 1979, pp. 157–62. The authors provided two groups of investment analysts with identical sets of financial statements. The statements given to one group had an unqualified audit report. The audit reports given to the other group had been qualified on the grounds of disagreement because the company had not complied with an accounting standard on the treatment of an investment. The analysts who received the statements with the qualified report tended to place a lower value on the company's shares.
13. Craswell, A.T., 'Studies of the information content of qualified audit reports', *Journal of Business Finance and Accounting*, Spring 1985, pp. 93–115. The difficulties of conducting this type of research are also discussed in Bailey, W.T., 'An appraisal of research designs used to investigate the information content of audit reports', *The Accounting Review*, January 1987, pp. 141–6.
14. APB, SAS 130, *The Going Concern Basis in Financial Statements*, 1994. This standard

contains an appendix which outlines the accounting requirements in respect of going concern as laid down by the Companies Act and the accounting standards.

15. This is supported by guidance from the Committee on the Financial Aspects of Corporate Governance (Cadbury Committee) in its *Going Concern and Financial Reporting*, 1994.

16. Taffler, R.J., and Tseung, M., 'The audit going concern qualification in practice: exploding some myths', *The Accountant's Magazine*, July 1984, pp. 263–9.

PART III

THE COLLECTION OF EVIDENCE

This section deals with the material which most non-accountants will tend to associate most strongly with audit – the detailed testing of the figures which make up the financial statements. Rather than getting bogged down in the detailed content of the tests themselves, this section is structured around the framework which lies at the heart of modern auditing techniques.

Chapter 7 outlines the risk-based approach and explains why it is regarded as the most cost-effective. Chapter 8 discusses the topic of audit evidence in more detail and describes the problems of evaluating the quality of evidence from different sources. Chapter 9 deals with the ways in which organisations can reduce the risk of fraud and error by implementing sound internal controls in both manual and computerised systems. It also explains how the auditor can exploit the controls which are built into the system.

Chapter 10 highlights some of the opportunities and problems which computers can create for auditors. It is, however, assumed that virtually all audits are computer audits and so this material is expanded upon in later chapters. Chapter 11 discusses the important topic of audit sampling. Rather than going into the mathematical and statistical background, this chapter concentrates on the implications for audit of basing opinions on sample results.

Chapters 12, 13 and 14 put the methods described in earlier chapters into the context of the testing of the sales cycle, purchases cycle and balance sheet respectively.

CHAPTER 7

The conduct of an audit

This chapter will consider the manner in which an accounting firm conducts an audit. While different firms will have slightly different procedures, all are subject to the same legal and professional obligations and will also wish to use the most efficient procedures available. This will tend to encourage the adoption of similar approaches.

By the time you have completed this chapter, you should be able to:

- Explain the factors which are shaping the development of the audit approach.
- Explain what is meant by the risk-based approach to an audit and describe the various elements of the risk-based model.
- Describe the various stages in an audit.
- Explain how audit work is organised and recorded: during the initial stages of the audit, during the final stages.
- Outline the alternatives to the risk-based approach.

7.1 Factors shaping the development of the audit approach

The approach taken to an audit is influenced by two sets of factors. First, and most importantly, the auditor must satisfy the various statutory and professional obligations. Second, the audit must always be seen in its commercial context. The auditor provides a service with the intention of making a profit.

ACTIVITY

Try to think why the auditor's statutory and professional obligations with respect to the conduct of detailed audit work might be:

(a)   in conflict with, or
(b)   consistent with

the auditor's commercial interests.

The auditor's principal duty is to add credibility to the financial statements by reporting on their truth and fairness. Discharging this duty requires the collection of audit evidence which will be expensive in terms of staff time for the auditor. Audit testing may also prove disruptive for the company being audited and could have an adverse effect on the auditor's relationship with management. This means that the auditor could be tempted to reduce the extent of audit testing because of commercial considerations.

While it might be possible to increase profits in the short term if the auditor cut corners on audit work, such an approach could prove unwise in the longer term. If the auditor is found to be reckless or negligent in the conduct of an audit then this could undermine the firm's credibility. This could lead to the loss of business because there is little point in paying for an audit from a firm which is not respected by the readers of financial statements. Furthermore, allegations of negligence could lead to the payment of damages and an increase in the cost of professional indemnity insurance.

7.1.1 *Professional and legal influences*

The principal regulation governing the approach taken to the audit is Statement of Auditing Standards 100. SAS 100.1 requires that auditors should 'carry out procedures designed to obtain sufficient appropriate evidence, in accordance with Auditing Standards contained in SASs, to determine with reasonable confidence whether the financial statements are free of material misstatement'.[1] This standard is supported by an SAS devoted to the topic of audit evidence.[2] Amongst other things, this requires auditors to 'obtain sufficient appropriate audit evidence to be able to draw reasonable conclusions on which to base an audit opinion'.

While these requirements are extremely clear and are obviously necessary in order to ensure that the audit report expresses a credible opinion, they do leave a great many questions unanswered:

- How much evidence is 'sufficient'?
- What degree of assurance is implied by 'reasonable confidence'?
- How is a 'material' misstatement to be distinguished from one which is immaterial?

While these questions are of fundamental importance, it is impossible to produce a set of prescriptive rules to resolve them. Thus, they have effectively been left to the professional judgement of individual auditors.

The full extent of the auditor's duties have not been clearly defined. It was suggested in Chapter 3 that most complaints against auditors tend to be settled out of court and so there is a dearth of recent case law in this area. It has also been suggested that the definition of reasonable care and skill in the conduct of an audit can change with the passage of time. The auditor could be required to provide a higher quality of assurance in response to changes in the business environment and the development of new auditing techniques.

7.1.2 *Commercial influences*

Auditors operate within rigid commercial constraints. A firm could not retain its clients if it charged excessive audit fees or if its audit approach was unduly disruptive. Professional staff within firms are usually required to keep detailed records of the time spent on each audit. Individual partners and managers are held responsible for the staff hours spent on each of the assignments within their portfolios. The hourly rates are calculated on an absorption costing basis. The fees recovered from each assignment will then be compared with the notional cost of staff time to ensure that a 'profit' has been made.

The auditor may, therefore, appear to have an incentive to collect a lower amount of evidence in order to reduce the fee and ensure that the audit appears to be profitable to more senior members of the firm. This would, however, leave the firm open to a charge of negligence. It is unlikely that an audit partner would risk the possible payment of damages and loss of reputation which would follow such an accusation.

7.1.3 *The firms' response*

The various problems described above have led to the development of the so-called 'risk-based' approach to an audit. This reconciles the needs for increased assurance and reduced fees by tailoring the amount of evidence collected in accordance with the nature of the business under examination and by concentrating effort on those figures which are most likely to be incorrect. This is done by quantifying various factors which can affect the likelihood of material errors.

By deciding upon the extent of testing in a formal manner, the auditor should be able to justify the amount of work done on each item in the profit and loss account and balance sheet. It should, therefore, be easier to demonstrate that professional obligations have been met. The risk-based approach should also cost less because less work will be done on figures which are unlikely to be materially wrong.

One further advantage of this approach is that it forces the auditor to examine the commercial environment in which the company operates. This provides an insight which could make it easier to provide the company with constructive advice about business problems, either as an additional service, for which an additional fee can be charged, or as a means of securing reappointment in future years.

7.2 The risk-based approach

Audit risk has been defined as 'the risk that auditors may give an inappropriate audit opinion on financial statements'.[3]

7.2.1 *Audit risk*

It is rarely possible for the auditor to test every entry in the accounting records and so there is always some doubt as to whether the financial statements give a true and fair view. This is acceptable, provided that the level of risk accepted by the auditor is kept within reasonable limits. The starting point for the risk-based approach is to determine the overall level of risk which the auditor is prepared to accept when forming an audit opinion.

The quantification of audit risk is, to some extent, a mixed blessing. If the auditor's opinion is ever challenged, it could be argued that a confidence level of, say, 95 per cent was inadequate and that a higher degree of assurance should have been obtained. Such an argument would, however, be put forward by someone who had an obvious vested interest in discrediting the auditor. It would almost certainly be easier to defend a decision to accept a risk of error of, say, 5 per cent in forming an opinion than it would be to justify the acceptance of an unquantified level of risk.

There is, unfortunately, no 'correct' level for acceptable audit risk. The auditor must display reasonable skill and care and so only a relatively small level of risk can be accepted. Many firms appear to work towards a 95 per cent level, if only because this is a round figure which can be achieved without resorting to an uneconomic amount of detailed testing.

Once the acceptable level of audit risk has been identified, the next step is to separate it into its constituent elements. Most models classify audit risks as follows:

Audit risk = $IR \times CR \times DR$
where:
IR equals 'inherent risk',
CR equals 'control risk', and
DR equals 'detection risk'.

Detection risk is sometimes broken down into two further factors: 'analytical risk' (AR) and 'substantive risk' (SR), thus modifying the formula to:

Audit risk = $IR \times CR \times AR \times SR$.

Each of these risks corresponds to a different type of review or examination conducted during the audit. The auditor attempts to discover material misstatements in the figures by means of reviews of inherent and control risks and by analytical procedures and substantive testing. The inherent risk factor corresponds to the likelihood of material misstatement occurring in the figures. The other factors relate to the probability that the related procedure will fail to detect a material irregularity. By multiplying the four probabilities, it is possible to calculate the overall probability that an error will not be discovered. The auditor must ensure that this overall probability does not exceed the acceptable level.

The auditor has very little control over the levels of inherent, control and analytical risk. The auditor will be unable to reduce them in the short term, although it may be possible to make suggestions to management which would lead to their reduction in future years. This means that the auditor must quantify each of these three sources of risk in turn, calculate their combined value and then calculate the level of substantive risk which can be accepted if the overall amount of audit risk is to be achieved.

Suppose, for example, that the auditor of XY plc was prepared to accept an audit risk of 5 per cent. The inherent risk was valued at 80 per cent. Control risks were quantified at 50 per cent and analytical review risk was 90 per cent. If the auditor relied on these three reviews without any further testing, this would leave a 36 per cent risk (i.e. 80 per cent × 50 per cent × 90 per cent) of the statements containing a material error. This could be reduced to the acceptable level by conducting sufficient substantive testing to give a substantive risk of 14 per cent. Thus, the overall risk would be reduced to:

$$80\% \times 50\% \times 90\% \times 14\% = 5\%.$$

The links between the various types of risk can be seen in Figure 7.1. This portrays the various elements of the risk model as 'filters'. The auditor uses the review of inherent risk to establish the likelihood of material error assuming that there were no controls or audit evidence. This probability is then adjusted to take into account the possibility that the errors will be missed by the company's control systems (80% × 50% = 40%), then the probability that it would not be detected by the auditor's analytical review (40% × 90% = 36%), and finally the probability that it would be missed by substantive testing (36% × 14% = 5%).

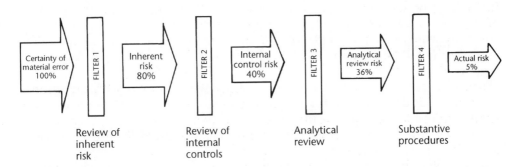

Figure 7.1 Links between various types of risks.

ACTIVITY

Try to think about how each of these 'filters' might work in practice.
HINT: think about what the various auditing terms might actually mean in 'common sense' terms.
The answer to this activity is dealt with by the remainder of section 7.2.

7.2.2 *Inherent risk*

Inherent risk is 'the susceptibility of an account balance or class of transactions to material misstatement, either individually or when aggregated with misstatements in other balances or classes, irrespective of related internal controls'.[4] The evaluation of inherent risk is the most demanding aspect of audit planning. There is always a risk that the statements are incorrect. There are, however, circumstances which can increase this risk considerably. The auditor must investigate the business's environment, its financial position and the motives of its management and consider whether the directors are under undue pressure to distort the truth and fairness of the financial statements.[5] It would be impossible to draft a comprehensive checklist of warning signs; the auditor must simply be alert to the possibility of such risk and react to any indications of it as they become available.

Inherent risks can arise because of agency problems. If, for example, the directors are paid bonuses which are related to the reported profit figure, then the auditor would be suspicious of any attempts to improve the reported results. An attempted takeover bid could have a similar effect on management's attitude towards the financial statements. The directors could face dismissal if the bidder is successful. They could be tempted to manipulate the financial statements in order to convince the shareholders that the company is worth more than has been offered.

Inherent risk can also arise because the directors are afraid that truthful reporting could harm the company. Some businesses could be subject to political interference if their profit figures are too high. A large company which had relatively few competitors could be afraid of accusations of over-pricing. This could lead to attempts to reduce the reported profit figure. Conversely, a company which was in financial difficulties would be reluctant to deter lenders and even potential customers by admitting that it was in danger of collapsing.[6]

Inherent risk is not merely a function of managerial motives. Unintentional errors and fraudulent recording of transactions by clerical staff can also affect the truth and fairness of the financial statements. This is one reason for the reference to the nature of individual account balances in the definition quoted above.

The auditor must consider the possibility of a higher than normal risk of errors. A high incidence of errors could be associated with, for example, rapid staff turnover. New staff are likely to make mistakes because of their lack of experience. A major modification to computer software could have a similar effect. The new program coding could be incorrect, thus leading to errors every time it is run. Furthermore, the staff who operate the system may take some time to become familiar with the changes.

The auditor should also consider the risk of fraud associated with each of the figures in the financial statements. Any aspect of the accounting system which involves the receipt or payment of cash is particularly vulnerable. An employee could, for example, generate a bogus creditor's balance in order to claim the resultant payment. This would lead to the overstatement of the purchases figure for the year. If this was repeated often enough, the profit figure would be materially understated. Similarly, the existence of high value stocks creates the threat of fraudulent entries in the stock records, with a consequent over-statement of the cost of sales figure.

Despite the importance attached to the assessment of risk, there is very little guidance available on the quantification of its effect on audit testing. This is an area where specific guidance is urgently required. There has, however, been some empirical research into the incidence of errors[7] and the importance attached to various characteristics of audit clients by auditors.[8] It would appear, for example, that management motives can have an effect upon the nature and frequency of errors. It is also apparent that the turnover of accounting staff can have an effect on the quality of the record-keeping. There is not yet, however, an agreed basis for the measurement of such factors.[9]

7.2.3 Control risk

Management will usually introduce controls into the accounting system so that fraud and error can be either prevented or detected. These controls can take many forms, but include the supervision and checking of the records by staff independent of those who made the entries. Control risk is 'the risk that a [material] misstatement . . . would not be prevented, or detected and corrected on a timely basis, by the accounting and internal control systems'.[10] Whereas the evaluation of inherent risk as a formal part of the collection of evidence is a relatively recent phenomenon, auditors have been relying on internal controls to prevent or detect material errors for many years.

To some extent, internal controls are likely to offset some of the inherent risks discussed in the previous section. If, for example, an aspect of the system is used to record cash transactions, there will probably be an appropriate level of control to prevent fraud. Similarly, one would expect to find a higher level of supervision in a department which had been forced to take on a large number of new staff. It is, however, impossible to design a set of controls which is totally effective. Checks can fail for a number of reasons; in particular they will not constrain the behaviour of senior management.

The collection of audit evidence from internal control is a major topic. It will be covered in depth in Chapter 9.

7.2.4 *Detection risk*

Detection risk is 'the risk that auditors' substantive procedures . . . do not detect a [material] misstatement that exists in an account balance or class of transactions'.[11] The auditor's 'procedures' can usefully be classified into two categories: analytical review and other substantive testing. Analytical review is a term used to describe a host of different techniques, all of which are designed to identify figures which appear unreasonable in the light of related items or the auditor's experience. These can be as simple as the comparison of each figure in the statements with those published in the previous year or can be so sophisticated that a computer package must be used to perform the necessary calculations.

Substantive procedures include analytical review but they also include 'tests to obtain audit evidence . . . such as tests of details of transactions and balances, review of minutes of directors' meetings and enquiry'.[12] These 'other' substantive procedures are, therefore, the detailed tests of the transactions and balances which are often associated with auditors.

It is useful to distinguish between analytical review and substantive testing. Analytical review is likely to be used throughout the audit and will yield a fixed amount of assurance. The auditor will place a greater amount of reliance on it if the figures appear reasonable, but cannot influence the amount of assurance obtained. The other types of substantive test normally involve the detailed testing of individual entries or balances in the accounting records. The auditor can increase the amount of evidence obtained from such testing simply by examining a greater number of items.

It is expensive to obtain evidence from detailed testing because it is much more time-consuming than the reviews of inherent and control risks and analytical review. This is one reason why the substantive testing risk is usually the residual figure in the overall audit risk equation. It is more cost-effective to concentrate substantive testing on those figures which have a higher risk of being incorrect.

Another reason for evaluating the other risks before designing a programme of substantive tests is the fact that the auditor must respond to different types of inherent, control and analytical risks in an appropriate manner. If, for example, the auditor suspects that management wishes to deliberately overstate the profit figure, substantive testing would be concentrated on those figures which could most easily be distorted in order to achieve this objective. Thus, the auditor would concentrate much more heavily on those estimates and provisions which affect the profit and loss account, particularly those where management would appear to have been optimistic. It would also be necessary to allocate more of the audit partner's time to the consideration of any proposed changes in accounting policies, disagreements over contentious adjustments, and so on. Alternatively, the discovery of a loophole in the system of controls would be dealt with by conducting an investigation in order to see whether the opportunity for fraud had been exploited.

Analytical review will be covered in greater detail in section 7.4.4. The design of substantive tests will be dealt with in Chapter 8.

| **ACTIVITY** |

Detailed substantive testing is the final item in the formula for the risk model, implying that it is the residual percentage. Try to suggest why this may be so.

HINT: think in terms of the cost of each source of evidence and also the factors which determine the reliability of each.

The auditor would want to rely as heavily as possible on the other sources of evidence because detailed substantive testing is very labour-intensive and is, therefore, relatively expensive. It is possible to conduct analytical reviews and reviews of inherent risks relatively quickly while planning the audit and reviewing the audit files. Their marginal costs are, therefore, quite low. A great deal of the work required on internal controls can be brought forward and updated from the previous year's audit files. The alternatives to detailed testing are, therefore, cost-effective.

The auditor will always have to collect some evidence from detailed testing because there is usually an upper limit on the amount of assurance which can be obtained from each of the alternatives (e.g. systems of internal control may be reasonably reliable, but they can never be regarded as 100 per cent effective). It is rarely possible to collect sufficient evidence from these without supplementing them with detailed tests. The amount of evidence obtained from detailed testing is a function of the number of items tested. It is, therefore, possible to increase the amount of assurance from detailed testing simply by increasing sample sizes.

Detailed tests are also less prone to yielding misleading results. The auditor could, for example, be lulled into a false sense of security by a review of inherent risks.

7.3 The chronology of an audit

The basic steps involved in the conduct of an audit can be shown in Table 7.1. The numbers in brackets refer to sections or subsections within this text. In addition, Chapters 12 to 14 deal with the audit of specific items in the profit and loss account and balance sheet. The reviews of inherent and control risk and the application of analytical and substantive procedures will be demonstrated for each major figure in the statements.

While it is helpful to represent the audit as a series of discrete steps, it is also rather unrealistic. Planning, for example, is an ongoing activity which continues throughout the audit. Similarly, the review for inherent risk and analyt-

Table 7.1 Stages in an audit

	Initial stages	Interim stages	Final stages
Auditor appointed (1.3.1)	*		
Engagement accepted and defined in writing (7.4.2)	*		
Audit planning commences (7.4.3)	*		
Initial review of inherent risks (7.2.2)	*		
Initial analytical review (7.4.4)	*		
Initial review of accounting system (9.4.2)			
Operation of controls identified during initial review confirmed (9.4.3)		*	*
Substantive testing (8.5)		*	*
Review of evidence collected during testing (7.5)			*
Review of truth and fairness of financial statements (7.5)			*
Letter of representation (7.5.1)			*
Audit report signed (5.1)			*
Management informed of internal control problems encountered during the audit (9.6)			*

ical review must continue right up until the audit report is signed. There is, however, a logical progression running through the outline approach suggested above in that it suggests a means by which various risks can be assessed and substantive testing can be concentrated on the areas where it is most necessary. It also covers various important administrative aspects of the audit.

During the initial stages of the audit, senior members of the audit team will discuss the manner in which the audit is to be conducted and will agree a timetable with the directors of the company. Once the initial plans have been agreed, the audit team can begin to collect audit evidence. There are several reasons why testing will be conducted during the year. It enables the auditor to observe the system as it actually operated during the period under review. It saves time after the year end because the auditor will already have checked the recording of a significant proportion of the year's transactions by then. Finally, many companies have their financial years ending on 31 December or 31 March. Accounting firms would have tremendous peaks and troughs in their workload if all audit testing had to be concentrated into the period immediately after each company's year end.

During the final stages of the audit, which usually begin just before the year end itself and do not conclude until the audit report has been signed, the auditor must go through the process of actually forming an opinion on the truth and fairness of the statements.

7.4 The initial stages of the audit

A number of vital decisions must be taken at the planning stage of the audit, some of which must be discussed with the management of the company. Otherwise, the auditor may not be able to form a valid opinion on the financial statements. A badly planned audit may also create unnecessary cost or inconvenience for the company and could, therefore, damage the auditor's reputation.

7.4.1 *Acceptance of the audit*

It has already been pointed out that the auditor is likely to be reappointed from year to year on an almost automatic basis. This does not, however, mean that the auditor should always accept the directors' nomination without careful thought. An accounting firm may have been associated with a company for many years. During this time, the company could have grown to such a size that the firm is unable to conduct a satisfactory audit. This could be because the audit fee has come to represent such a significant proportion of gross recurring income that the firm is no longer independent. Alternatively, the firm may be unable to offer the necessary skills required for the audit. The company could, for example, have replaced its computer system with a more sophisticated one which required specialised knowledge to audit. Unless the auditor had an employee with appropriate qualifications it would be better to suggest that another firm take over the audit.[13]

It is also possible that the audit will no longer be commercially attractive. A high risk audit could, for example, increase the firm's premium for professional indemnity cover. This could make the audit unprofitable unless the company was prepared to bear the additional cost in the form of a higher fee.

7.4.2 *The engagement letter*

It is important that the directors of the company fully understand the extent of the auditor's responsibilities, particularly with regard to possible contentious areas such as the detection of fraud. The most effective means of doing this is to issue the board with a letter which contains a detailed description of the scope and purpose of the audit. This letter would also warn the directors of their responsibilities with regard to ensuring the truth and fairness of the statements and also providing the auditor with information. The letter would describe the basis upon which fees would be charged.

The APB recommends that every company should receive such a letter, mainly to prevent the friction which could arise because of any misunderstanding between the auditor and the directors.[14] Normally, this letter should be issued at the commencement of the auditor's professional relationship with the company and its content discussed with the directors at that stage. There is no need to issue a new letter each year, unless there is a substantial change in the nature of the services which the auditor is providing.

7.4.3 *Planning*

It is misleading to think of audit planning as a single, distinct phase of the audit. A great deal of planning will usually have been done even before the auditor has been appointed. Most firms of accountants have their own standard audit manuals which prescribe the precise manner in which that firm's staff should conduct an audit. This manual will be constantly updated. Thus, certain important decisions, such as the acceptable level of audit risk, are not left to the individual partner in charge of the audit but will have been taken by experts within the firm's technical department. This is not intended to constrain professional judgement, but is intended to ensure that all audits are conducted to the same standards throughout the firm.[15]

Once the firm has decided to accept the audit, it is important to decide upon the strategy which is to be adopted. It may, for example, be necessary to ensure that specialist staff within the firm are available at certain key times during the year to assist the audit staff. The audit team may require advice about information technology, actuarial calculations for the audit of the company's pension scheme, tax advice for the audit of the corporation tax provision and so on. If experts are not available within the firm then arrangements will have to be made for the appointment of independent advisers.[16]

A timetable has to be drafted to ensure that the audit is completed on time and that various important deadlines are noted. If the company has a provisional date for the annual general meeting, it will be necessary to work backwards from this to allow time for the statements to be typeset, printed and posted to the shareholders. This means that a number of secondary deadlines will have to be established for the completion of audit testing, the agreement of the statements with management, and so on. The timetable would also include such key events as the date of the company stock count and the date when the finance director expects draft accounts to be ready.

The time budget is another important document which would be produced at this stage. This gives an estimate of the number of hours which should be spent on each figure in the statements. These estimates are usually based upon the actual hours recorded during the previous year's audit. One function of this budget is to motivate the audit team to complete the audit as quickly as possible. This can, however, lead staff to under-report the number of hours spent on a task, perhaps by working unpaid overtime.[17] Such behaviour can, of course, make it difficult to plan future audits and may even cost the firm money. If the partner knew exactly how many hours the audit had taken, it could be possible to justify a higher fee. Despite the motivational problems associated with time budgets, one advantage of presenting the audit team with this detailed breakdown of the anticipated chargeable hours is that additional time can be allocated to items with a higher inherent risk.

The audit partner will also have to make a variety of strategic decisions at this time. If a statistical sampling scheme is to be used, certain parameters will have to be established. The partner may decide to make increased use of computer packages. The company may wish to reduce the audit fee and so may wish to second staff to the auditor to assist in the collection and filing of documents and so on, thus reducing the number of hours charged to the audit.

Planning does not cease after the initial stages of the audit. Plans will have to be updated if assumptions about the levels of inherent risk or the quality of internal controls within the system turn out to be incorrect. The audit senior in charge of the audit team will also have to make plans about the allocation of duties to staff within the audit team and about the manner in which the partner's instructions are actually going to be implemented.[18]

7.4.4 *Analytical review*

Analytical review is a collective term which is used to describe a host of techniques which are used to identify anomalous figures in the financial statements. The auditor examines the figures, looking for plausible relationships between items. If these relationships do not exist then there is an increased risk that the figures are incorrect and the reasons for the anomalies must be discovered.

All analytical review techniques consist of three basic steps. First, the auditor must acquire some information or data about a figure or group of figures in the financial statements. Second, the relationship between this information and the item or items under investigation should be predicted and a range of acceptable outcomes established. Finally, the auditor should compare the predicted and actual relationship and take appropriate action. If the actual relationship is in line with expectations, the auditor may react by reducing the amount of detailed testing in this area. If the actual relationships are significantly different from expectations, the auditor will seek an explanation from management. If a plausible explanation is obtained, the auditor will seek evidence to substantiate it. In the absence of an explanation, the auditor will be forced to conduct more extensive detailed testing.

The simplest form of analytical review is the comparison of the current year's figures with those of the previous year. If the amounts are similar or have changed in line with such factors as the Retail Price Index then there is unlikely to be a great need for more extensive substantive testing.

Ratio analysis is also a very useful means of dealing with relationships within the financial statements. If, for example, the gross profit percentage is significantly lower than that of the previous year, the auditor should consider the possibility that the figures for either sales or cost of sales are incorrect. It could be that fraud or error has led to the understatement of sales, the inclusion of fictitious expenses in the cost of sales, or the miscalculation of the closing stock figure. The actual explanation could, of course, have no real audit significance. The decrease in the percentage could be due, for example, to a deliberate reduction in unit selling prices in order to undercut competitors. Similarly, an increase in the average number of days taken by debtors to settle their debts could imply that the debtors figure had been overstated by a failure to write off bad debts. Alternatively, management could simply have decided to relax credit control in order to encourage sales.

It is also useful to compare the actual figures with any forecasts or budgets prepared by management. One advantage of this is that the budgets would have been prepared with the benefit of inside knowledge. Furthermore, any significant variances will probably have been fully investigated and explained as part of the budgetary control system.

At a more sophisticated level, a number of statistical regression models have been developed which can compare trends in a formal manner. These can also make use of external information published by similar companies and by government and industry bodies. Given the proliferation of microcomputers, particularly portable machines which can be taken out to clients' offices, it is possible to provide audit teams with powerful software packages which make these models relatively easy to apply.

Analytical review can be used during audit planning to identify figures for detailed investigation, during the interim and final stages as a means of substantive testing, and at the final stage of the audit as part of the final audit review.[19]

The most effective analytical procedure for substantive testing is proof in total. Certain expenses, for example, can be easily related to factors which are relatively simple to check. The most obvious example of this is debenture interest. The auditor can avoid testing samples of the individual payments made to the large numbers of debenture holders by multiplying the total value of debenture loans by the relevant rate of interest. The total cost of the interest should not be significantly different from the amount predicted.

The auditor may also be able to conduct substantive tests by comparing financial and non-financial data. If, for example, a steel stockholder sold various types of steel plates, but priced all products at a standard price per tonne, the auditor could calculate the total tonnage sold according to the shipping records and multiply this by the standard selling price. This figure should be similar to the recorded turnover.

On a more detailed level, computer files can be interrogated to identify anomalous items. A program could be written to divide each employee's gross wage according to the payroll by the number of hours worked. Anyone being paid more than, say, £20 per hour or claiming more than, say, 50 hours per week could be identified on a print-out for investigation.

At the conclusion of the audit, it is important that the auditor takes time to review the figures to make sure that the relationships appear reasonable in the light of information gained during the audit. If, for example, the auditor had gained the impression that the company was heavily constrained by poor cash flow, this should be reflected in the balance sheet. The auditor would be suspicious if the working capital section of the company's balance sheet appeared healthy.[20]

There have been a number of attempts to investigate the extent to which analytical review procedures can be relied upon. A survey of the causes of accounting errors and their detection revealed that 27 per cent of the sample items had been discovered by analytical review techniques.[21] Some doubts have been expressed about the reliability of the techniques which rely upon subjective judgement. An experiment by Biggs and Wild revealed that auditors tended to bias their expectations of certain figures towards the actual results according to the draft statements.[22] This result is disturbing in that auditors may be blinkered in their review of trends and may not always conduct extended investigations because of this.

A review of the effectiveness of statistical regression packages has revealed that these techniques can increase the effectiveness of the audit and also reduce the overall amount of testing which is required. This is particularly true if the auditor uses monthly, rather than annual, figures in the model and places some reliance on the model so that detailed testing is concentrated more heavily on those months which are more likely to be incorrect.[23]

7.5 Final audit review

At the conclusion of the audit, it is important that the auditor takes time to consider the truth and fairness of the financial statements. This may appear to be obvious, given that this has been the purpose of the entire audit exercise. Unfortunately, it is easy for audit staff to become so engrossed in their detailed examination of the figures that they fail to discover some glaring error, such as an unacceptable accounting policy or incomplete disclosure.

During the final review, the audit partner or manager should examine the financial statements. It has already been suggested that analytical review techniques could be applied at this stage in order to evaluate the impression given by the figures in the draft accounts. The review should, however, include much more than this. The auditor would, for example, complete checklists to ensure that the reporting requirements of the Companies Act and the FRSs and SSAPs have been complied with. The overall quality of the evidence obtained to date would also be examined to ensure that it provided a satisfactory basis for the expression of an opinion.[24]

7.5.1 The letter of representation

The auditor must review the quality of the evidence obtained before signing the report. Inevitably, there will be certain items which cannot be proved correct, leaving the auditor with a certain amount of uncertainty. The report will have to be qualified if there is material uncertainty. This would, however, be a rather extreme reaction to certain types of reservation which are common to virtually all audits. These would include the slight possibility that the directors have concealed major contingent liabilities, capital commitments, or loans from the auditor. It would be difficult, but not impossible, to do so. Management could also have made important estimates or forecasts, such as the estimated useful lives of fixed assets, in a reckless manner or may have deliberately biased them in order to manipulate the profit figure.

One of the ways in which the auditor can ensure that these matters have been dealt with properly is to ask the directors of the company to provide a written assurance that full and adequate disclosure has been made in the statements. This is done by means of a 'letter of representation'. The auditor's understanding of any questionable items will be written out in the form of a letter from the company's board to the auditor. This letter would also confirm any verbal assurances which have been made by management. This letter would then be signed by two directors acting on behalf of the board. The letter of representation does not absolve the auditor of any of the duty to form an opinion or collect evidence. The auditor should try to verify the information in the letter, even if only by attempting to disprove the statements contained within it. If, for example, the directors claim that there is no outstanding litigation against the company, the auditor should still ask the company's legal advisers to confirm this fact. Such confirmation would not prove that there were no outstanding cases because the lawyer may not necessarily be aware of all possible claims. The response to this request would, however, show that the auditor had attempted to corroborate the board's assurances.

The auditor should be suspicious of any refusal to sign a letter of representation. The need for such assurance would usually have been described in the engagement letter. The reasons for any refusal to provide written confirmation should be established. It would be difficult for the auditor to state that the accounts give a true and fair view if the directors are unwilling to do so.[25]

7.6 Working papers

The auditor is required to keep detailed audit working papers which document all aspects of the planning and completion of the audit work and also of the conclusions formed during the audit. The working papers should also record all matters of judgement in some detail.

ACTIVITY

Why should the audit work be recorded in this level of detail?

The maintenance of detailed working papers will help the auditor in a number of ways. It will ensure that the audit staff are working in a methodical manner and will enable more senior members of the team to review their work. These working papers will then be available to assist in the planning of the following year's audit.

Detailed files may also be of immense importance if the auditor is ever criticised or accused of negligence. Disputes are likely to involve issues where the auditor has exercised some professional judgement. If the working papers contain details of everything that was known to the auditor at the time of the decision then it will be much easier to defend against any criticism arising once the outcome is known.

There are usually two categories of working papers: permanent and current. The permanent files contain information which is of continuing relevance to the auditor, including notes about the company's systems, details of its management structure, copies of the engagement letter, and so on. It is a slight misnomer to refer to such records as 'permanent' because it is important that they are kept up to date at all times.

The current files are used to record the evidence collected to support the audit opinion for any given year. These files do not have any ongoing relevance, although the audit team may find it helpful to refer to the previous year's files in order to see what problems have arisen and how they have been overcome. It is, in fact, common practice to record suggestions for the improvement of the audit in the files, marked for the attention of the next year's team. Older current files will usually be stored for several years in case of a complaint that a recurring problem has been missed by the auditor.[26]

7.7 Other audit approaches

The risk-based approach will be the most efficient and effective means of collecting audit evidence in most circumstances. It is not, however, the only approach which can be taken. Before the introduction of the risk-based approach, most large accounting firms used the systems-based approach. This differed from the approach described in this chapter in that all assurance was drawn from a combination of the review of internal controls and substantive testing. Auditors still reviewed the levels of inherent risk and conducted analytical review. They did not usually reduce the extent of detailed testing in response to such reviews. Instead, high inherent risks or anomalies identified during analytical review would be dealt with by extending detailed testing.

The vouching approach is likely to be even less efficient. The auditor obtains all audit evidence from detailed testing and none from reviews of the system, inherent risk or analytical review. This approach may, however, be forced upon the auditor in certain high risk audits, particularly the audits of small companies.

7.8 Summary

The auditor must conduct the audit in such a way that sufficient evidence is obtained to satisfy all professional requirements, notably the Auditor's Operational Standard, and all duties imposed by statute and case law. It is also necessary to meet the constraints of time and cost imposed by the commercial nature of the service provided.

The risk-based approach would appear to be the most effective means of achieving these various objectives. This involves evaluating the extent of inherent risk, internal control risk and analytical review risk. Each of these three reviews yields a probability of a material error remaining undetected. The auditor must then conduct sufficient detailed testing to reduce the overall risk that the statements do not give a true and fair view to an acceptable level. The principal advantage of the risk-based approach is that detailed testing is concentrated in those areas where an error is most likely.

While each accounting firm will have its own audit approach and every audit undertaken by any given firm will differ slightly, it is possible to draft an outline approach to an audit which suggests how the various stages in the process of forming an opinion are related. This gives an insight into the various steps in planning an audit, collecting evidence, and forming an overall conclusion about the truth and fairness of the financial statements.

REVIEW QUESTIONS

1. Discuss the extent to which it is desirable for all accounting firms to adopt similar audit approaches. Does this simply restrict the company's freedom to choose an appropriate type of audit?

2. Auditors have been aware of the concept of inherent risk for many years and have also made heavy use of analytical review for quite some time. The reduction of detailed testing in response to these reviews is, however, a relatively recent development. Is the 'risk-based' approach simply an excuse to conduct a more superficial audit?

3. A textbook on auditing defines audit risk as 'the chance of *damage to the audit firm* as a result of giving an audit opinion that is wrong in some particular' (emphasis added). This definition would appear to suggest that risk is not merely related to the possibility of expressing an invalid opinion, but is also a function of the probability of the discovery of the auditor's negligence. If, for example, a company was taken over after the audit, the new owners would be able to conduct their own review of accounting policies and could even replicate some of the tests which an auditor might undertake.

   Discuss the extent to which an auditor should modify or increase the extent of audit testing simply because his work is likely to come under greater scrutiny.

4. If the inherent risks associated with a company's audit have been considered lower than normal in previous years, would an auditor be justified in assuming that the inherent risks continue to be low without any further review?

5. If an audit is a means of lending credibility to statements prepared by company directors by means of an independent examination, discuss the proposition that a letter of representation is a worthless document.

6. The directors of a company are of the opinion that their auditor's current files might contain a great deal of useful management information. They

write to the auditor after the conclusion of the audit and ask for access to the files. How should the auditor respond?

EXERCISES

1. Sunburst Plc is a quoted company. The company has appointed Reeder and Co. as auditors for the first time, the previous firm having been considered unsatisfactory because of the delay in the completion of the previous year's audit.

Sunburst has two autonomous divisions. The head office and the contract division are located at Northtown, four miles from Reeder's offices. This division manufactures and installs heating systems in offices, factories and so on. All work is done to customers' specifications. The retail division is based at Southtown, 250 miles from the head office. This division manufactures electric heaters for sale through retail outlets.

Each division employs its own accountant on a full-time basis. The profit and loss accounts and balance sheets of each division are prepared locally and then consolidated at head office to produce the draft financial statements for the company. In recent years, the contract division has been highly profitable, but the results from the retail division have been disappointing. The directors of the company have made it known that they are looking for a buyer for the Southtown factory. If none can be found, the division will be closed down and the workforce made redundant.

The managers of Sunburst have achieved a high reputation for their professionalism and knowledge of the industry. The company's main shareholder, an institutional investor with a 20 per cent holding in the company, has been approached by a large conglomerate which is interested in purchasing Sunburst as a going concern with a view to merging it with a subsidiary which has similar interests. Sunburst's directors have been informed of this approach and have expressed dismay at the prospect of losing their autonomy.

The directors of Sunburst wish to impress the stock market by announcing their results before any of their competitors. They wish to publish their statements within four weeks of the year end instead of the eight weeks taken in the previous year. They are so confident of their success that they have already told several business journalists that they expect the profit to exceed the previous year's by at least 30 per cent.

List the various indicators of inherent risk in the foregoing case and suggest how they might be overcome.

2. Potter and Company have audited the financial statements of Grower Ltd for many years. The partner in charge of the audit has never felt any great need to pester the management and staff of Grower with too much detailed testing. After all, he said, 'an auditor is a watchdog and not a bloodhound'. On his retirement, the staff of Potter and Company presented the partner with a carriage clock, on the case of which had been engraved his favourite saying 'My word is my bond'.

The Grower audit was taken over by another partner. She noted that the audit had always commenced three weeks prior to the year end and usually took approximately five weeks to complete. Following this approach, an audit team was despatched at the usual stage of the year and told to audit the statements in accordance with the firm's standard policy.

Shortly before the reporting deadline, the partner received a phone call from the managing director of Grower stating that:

(a)   He was most upset that the audit was far from complete. Furthermore, the accounts section of the company was in disarray. The auditors had spent so much time 'pestering' the staff for explanations and demanding documents that had been filed away months ago that they had hardly been able to continue with their normal duties.

(b)   The audit senior was demanding the use of a special computer program to review the nominal ledger files. This hardly seemed necessary given that such a procedure has never been conducted in the past and the audit report was overdue as it was.

(c)   He had been asked to sign a 'letter of representation'. This appeared to insinuate that many of the statements made to the auditor were now suspect. He had dealt with Potter and Company for several years and had never been so insulted in all his life. He had no intention of signing this letter.

The partner asked about the engagement letter and was told that no such document existed.

(a)   Suggest why this year's audit would appear to have been badly planned (ignore the problems which would appear to have arisen in the past).

(b)   Suggest why it is unfortunate that Potter and Company had not provided Grower Ltd's managing director with an engagement letter well before the commencement of this year's audit.

3.   The managing director of Skimp Ltd wishes to reduce his audit fee by seconding staff to the auditor. He has suggested that chargeable hours could be reduced in the following ways:

(a)   The audit staff appear to spend a great deal of time fetching and replacing documents. This time could be saved in one of three ways:

   (i)   the audit team could be allocated a clerk who would locate these files on request, or

   (ii)   the audit team could give the clerk a list of the documents which they required at the beginning of each audit visit and these could be located and brought to the audit team 'as soon as was convenient', but certainly within two weeks at the most, or

   (iii)   given that many of the tests were of a routine nature, the clerk could do most of the testing and provide the audit team with the results.

(b)   The auditor's computer specialist had a very high chargeout rate. Rather than waste three days of his very expensive time each year, the company's programming staff could assist the audit team with the implementation of their audit software. Indeed, given their familiarity with the system, they could write the simple routines employed by the auditor more quickly than an outsider ever could.

Discuss the managing director's proposals and state which, if any, should be adopted.

The exercises in Chapters 12, 13 and 14 will provide a further opportunity to put the content of this chapter into practice.

References and further reading

1. APB, SAS 100, *Objective and General Principles Governing an Audit of Financial Statements*, 1995.
2. APB, SAS 400, *Audit Evidence*, 1995.
3. APB, *Glossary of Terms*, 1995.
4. *ibid.*
5. The importance of this is underlined by the fact that the APB has issued SAS 210, *Knowledge of the Business*, 1995.
6. Despite the caveats about the limitations of a standard list of business risk factors, such a list has been included in Brumfield, C.A., Elliott, R.K. and Jacobson, P.D., 'Business risk and the audit process', *Journal of Accountancy*, April 1983, pp. 60–8. This table can also be found, in a slightly amended form, in Adams, R., 'Accepting new audits can be a risky business', *Accountancy Age*, 12 November 1987, p. 28 and in Adams, R., 'Risk: a model approach', *Accountancy*, May 1989, pp. 120–2. Further discussions of the factors which could induce management to deliberately distort the statements can be found in Georgen, W.D., *Management Behaviour: An Auditing Horizon*, Touche Ross/University of Kansas Auditing Symposium III, 1976; Romney, M.B., Albrecht, W.S. and Cherrington, D.J., 'Auditors and the detection of fraud', *Journal of Accountancy*, May 1980, pp. 63–9; Albrecht, W.S. and Romney, M.B., *Auditing Implications Derived from a Review of Cases and Articles Relating to Fraud*, Touche Ross / University of Kansas Auditing Symposium V, 1980.
7. A useful overview of this branch of the literature is contained in Johnson, R.N., 'Auditor detected errors and related client traits: a study of inherent and control risks in a sample of U.K. audits', *Journal of Business Finance and Accounting*, Spring 1987, pp. 39–64. The same author summarised his findings in 'Evaluating audit risk components', *Accountancy*, February 1987, pp. 124–5.
8. See, for example, Colbert, J.L., 'Inherent risk: an investigation of auditors' judgements', *Accounting, Organisations and Society*, vol. 13, no. 2, pp. 111–21, 1988.
9. Accounting firms base their evaluation of inherent risk upon checklists and questionnaires. These are, however, regarded as commercially sensitive documents and are not, therefore, published. There is a description of a system of risk indices, which could be adapted for use by external auditors, in Chapters 17 and 18 of Chambers, A.D., Selim, G.M. and Vinten, G., *Internal Auditing*, Pitman, 1987.
10. APB, SAS 300, *Accounting and Internal Control Systems and Audit Risk Assessments*, 1995, paragraph 5.
11. *ibid*, paragraph 6.
12. APB, *Glossary of Terms*, 1995.
13. These points are developed to some extent in APB, SAS 240, *Quality Control for Audit Work*, 1995.
14. APB, SAS 140, *Engagement Letters*, 1995. This standard includes a specimen engagement letter.
15. A number of firms have published their audit manuals. These include: Coopers & Lybrand, Gee and Co, 1992; Stoy Hayward, Butterworth, 1991; and Grant Thornton, Longman, 1990.
16. The use of independent experts' advice is covered in APB, SAS 520, *Using the Work of an Expert*, 1995.
17. See Lightner, S.M., Leisenring, J.J. and Winters, A.J., 'Underreporting chargeable time', *Journal of Accountancy*, January 1983, pp. 52–7. Questionnaire responses from

972 accountants working in professional firms revealed that 67 per cent had under-reported chargeable time. Some 51 per cent of those who did so were of the opinion that they would be unable to meet their budgets if they reported honestly.

A review of some of the studies into the effects of tight time budgets and their potential implications for firms is contained in Kelley, T. and Seiler, R.E., 'Auditor stress and time budgets', *The CPA Journal*, December 1982, pp. 24–34.

18. Further details about the more mechanical aspects of audit planning can be found in APB, SAS 200, *Planning*, 1995.

19. The application of analytical review techniques is discussed in APB, SAS 410, *Analytical Procedures*, 1995.

20. Analytical procedures are not the only techniques which should be used at the conclusion of the audit. For more details, see APB, SAS 470, *Overall Review of Financial Statements*, 1995.

21. Hylas, R.E. and Ashton, R.H., 'Audit detection of financial statement errors', *The Accounting Review*, October 1982, pp. 751–65.

22. Biggs, S.F. and Wild, J.J., 'An investigation of auditor judgement in analytical review', *The Accounting Review*, October 1985, pp. 607–33.

23. Knechel, W.R., 'The effectiveness of statistical analytical review as a substantive auditing procedure: a simulation analysis', *The Accounting Review*, January 1988, pp. 74–95.

    A detailed case study of the application of one of these packages to the audit of a manufacturing company can be found in Campbell, R.J. and Rankin, L.J., 'Regression analysis in planning and testing', *The CPA Journal*, May 1986, pp. 50–9.

24. See APB, SAS 470, *op. cit.*, for further details.

25. APB, SAS 440, *Management Representations*, 1995, contains a specimen letter of representation.

26. Further information about the completion and review of audit working papers can be found in APB, SAS 240, *op. cit.*, paragraphs 11–14. See the APC Auditing Guideline, *Review of Financial Statements*, 1980, for more details.

CHAPTER 8

Audit evidence and testing

Chapter 7 outlined the approach which would be taken to an audit. This chapter will develop the sections which dealt with the collection of evidence to support the audit opinion. This chapter also develops the idea introduced in Chapter 3 where it was stated that the auditor should apply reasonable skill and care in forming an audit opinion.

By the time you have completed this chapter, you should be able to:

- Explain why it is necessary to collect audit evidence.
- Describe the various types of evidential material.
- Explain how the quality of audit evidence can be evaluated.
- Describe the audit evidence process.
- Explain the rules used by auditors in the design of audit tests.

8.1 Why collect evidence?

The audit report is intended to reassure the readers that the accounting statements are a credible source of information about the company. The shareholders will not be prepared to accept the auditor's opinion on the truth and fairness of the financial statements unless he has collected sufficient evidence to be reasonably certain that the figures have not been materially misstated.

The collection of audit evidence lies at the heart of the audit. Mautz and Sharaf claim that 'Auditing in its entirety is made up of two functions, both closely concerned with evidence. The first is the evidence-gathering function; the second is that of evidence evaluation.'[1] Audit evidence is simply 'the information auditors obtain in arriving at the conclusions on which their report is based'.[2]

The Companies Act 1985 contains an implicit requirement for auditors to collect evidence in that it specifies that auditors form an opinion on whether they have received all of the information and explanations which they need when they draft the audit report. The courts have also made it clear that auditors must support their opinions with evidence.

The SASs lay down some fairly onerous requirements regarding the collection of audit evidence. SAS 400.1, for example, states that 'Auditors should obtain sufficient appropriate audit evidence to be able to draw reasonable conclusions on which to base the audit opinion.'[3] Unfortunately, the Standard does not go on to define the attributes of relevance and reliability or the quantity of evidence which must be obtained in order to satisfy this requirement.

8.2 Types of evidential material

Lee identified eight types of evidential material,[4] subdivided between that which is immediately available and that which must be created by the auditor:

1 Immediately available:
   (a) Documentation.
   (b) Accounting records.
   (c) Other records.
   (d) Physical existence.
2 Created material:
   (a) Explanations.
   (b) Questionnaires.
   (c) Third party confirmations.
   (d) Subsequent events.

The distinction between immediately available and created evidence is not particularly important. In practice, the auditor will identify the most suitable source for each item in the statements.

ACTIVITY

Try to suggest an example of each of these types of evidential material. These will be described in the remainder of section 8.2.

8.2.1 *Documentation*

Documentation consists of any forms or papers which can be used to verify the company's basic accounting data. These include invoices, order forms, clock cards, and so on.

8.2.2 *Accounting records*

Businesses record transactions in a series of accounting records. The information extracted from these is then used to produce the accounting statements. The nominal ledger is the most important of these records. This is supported by other records such as sales and purchase day books and debtors' and creditors' ledgers. The auditor must examine these records in order to ensure that the transactions which have occurred during the year have been properly recorded.

8.2.3 *Other records*

The auditor has the right of access at all times to whatever records he requires for the purpose of his audit, whether or not these are directly related to the preparation of the statements. The auditor can use payroll records, the company's asset registers or any of a number of other records to support the figures in the statements. He will also wish to read through the minutes of board meetings in case any of the matters discussed, such as a possible takeover attempt or a claim for damages, have any audit significance.

8.2.4 *Physical existence*

The existence of a number of assets can be proved by means of physical inspection. This is often necessary in the case of stocks, tangible fixed assets, cash, share certificates and so on.

8.2.5 *Explanations*

The auditor should ask for an explanation of any matters about which he is unsure. This will often happen if a transaction appears to have been recorded in an unusual way. The auditor will also ask for explanations of any major assumptions which have been made, such as estimates of asset lives or of the net realisable values of stocks.

The fact that a credible explanation exists is not, of course, conclusive evidence that a matter has been dealt with correctly. It may be, however, that the explanation can be corroborated in some way. If there is no other evidence to substantiate the matter then, as we have already seen, the auditor will have to include it in the letter of representation.

8.2.6 *Questionnaires*

The controls built into the system are often a major source of audit evidence. Questionnaires can be used to collect information about the system and to arrange it in such a way that the key controls are identified. Each accounting firm will usually have its own standardised package of questionnaires dealing with the desirable features which should exist in each major area within the accounting system.

8.2.7 *Third party confirmations*

It is often cheaper and more effective to check a balance by writing to the third party concerned. It is common practice to write to debtors and creditors, asking for confirmation of the amounts shown in the company's records. This approach is also used to ensure that the client's bank balance has been correctly stated.

8.2.8 Subsequent events

Many uncertainties can be resolved by examining information which comes to light after the year end. If, for example, an overdue debtor's balance was paid after the end of the year then there is no need to worry about the need for a provision.

8.2.9 Deductive reasoning

Flint extended the list by pointing out that the auditor can use his common sense to create evidence which was, in some ways, more likely to highlight errors and irregularities than the items just listed. He suggested that '[d]eductive reasoning is by far the most important and also the most difficult source of audit evidence'.[5] He argued that many types of audit testing involve deductive reasoning, including analytical review, the evaluation of the results of samples and the assessment of the subjective estimates made by management.

8.3 The evaluation of sources of evidence

The auditor will often be faced with a range of possible sources of evidence. He must have some means of deciding which is most appropriate to any given objective. Some assistance is provided by SAS 400, which suggests the following:

1   Audit evidence from external sources is more reliable than that obtained from the entity's records.
2   Audit evidence obtained from the entity's records is more reliable when the related accounting and internal control system operates effectively.
3   Evidence obtained by auditors is more reliable than that obtained by or from the entity.
4   Evidence in the form of documents and written representations is more reliable than oral representations.
5   Original documents are more reliable than photocopies, telexes or facsimiles.

ACTIVITY

Read through each of these arguments and suggest why each may be true. Is this advice particularly helpful?

Evidence which has come from a third party (e.g. a purchase invoice) will be more difficult for the entity or its employees to falsify. It should, however, be borne in mind that high-resolution scanners, computerised drawing packages and colour printers have now made it relatively easy to make an extremely realistic copy of any document, which can then be duplicated or modified at will.

If the company's control systems are operating properly then it will be more difficult for documents to be falsified or altered. Such activities might require widespread collusion within the organisation – which could be difficult to coordinate.

The company's staff cannot interfere with evidence generated by the auditor. This does, however, assume that the auditor is able to produce such evidence independently. An accountant might not, for example, be capable of identifying specialised items of stock or fixed assets without risk of being misled.

Written evidence is less likely to be falsified because it can be referred back to. Spoken statements can be withdrawn or altered at a later stage. Originals are more difficult to falsify than copies, although the point made above about copying and printing technology may tend to contradict this.

While these guidelines are helpful when it comes to evaluating the quality of evidence collected, it is unlikely that the auditor will be offered a choice between the various types of evidence. In the audit of sales, for example, almost all of the evidence will be copies of documents prepared internally by the company. The quality of the underlying control systems will be determined by the management and may be unsatisfactory.

8.3.1 *The auditor's reaction to poor quality evidence*

In a sense, the auditor need not be concerned about a lack of audit evidence. If he cannot obtain sufficient evidence about a matter which is material, then he can satisfy his statutory and professional obligations by qualifying his audit report on the grounds of uncertainty. Having said so, it is unusual for a company to be unable to provide adequate evidence to support each of the balances in the accounts.

The auditor has at least a moral obligation to make the best possible use of the available evidence in order to avoid a qualification wherever possible. The auditor would also lay himself open to calls for his replacement if he chose to publish a qualified audit report rather than collect sufficient evidence.

8.3.2 *Upgrading evidence*

There is a synergistic relationship which can be used to enhance the quality of relatively poor evidence. The SAS on audit evidence states that 'audit evidence is more persuasive when items of evidence from different sources or of a different nature are consistent'.[6] This relationship can be illustrated by comparing the checking of a purchase transaction with that of a sale. When auditing purchases, the auditor would tend to take the existence of a purchase invoice as fairly conclusive proof that the transaction is valid. This is because the document has been prepared by a third party and could not have been easily falsified.

A sales invoice is not very persuasive because it has been prepared by the company's own staff. Having said so, the auditor can check the quantity and the description of the items sold according to the invoice by examining a copy of the despatch note and the customer's order, the prices charged by referring to the company's official price list, the discount allowed by looking at the custom-er's file and so on. With the exception of the customer's order, all of these documents have been prepared internally by the client's staff. The fact that different people, working in different departments, are involved does, however, mean that there is a degree of independence between the preparation of the various documents and this means that the evidence obtained from each one is enhanced.

8.3.3 *Unnecessary evidence*

While the auditor must be careful to ensure that he has obtained sufficient evidence of an appropriate quality, he must keep this task in its proper perspective. The audit report is, after all, only an opinion on the truth and fairness of the statements and not a guarantee of accuracy. Mautz and Sharaf warn that 'time may not permit the auditor to take the necessary steps to obtain compelling evidence', and continue, '[a]uditing works within a framework of economic usefulness that requires the balancing of cost with benefit derived'.[7]

The collection of too much evidence can be as harmful to the auditor as the collection of too little. The collection of evidence takes time and costs money. If the auditor insists on too high a level of assurance before he signs his audit report then he will reduce the risk of expressing an incorrect opinion. Unfortu-nately, he will also be forced to charge the company a higher fee than would have been necessary. Ultimately, this cost will have to be borne by the share-holders. Gathering the additional evidence could also delay the publication of the audit report. An excessive degree of caution could cost the auditor the possibility of reappointment.

8.4 The audit evidence process

Hatherly has suggested that the collection of evidence involves a logical sequence of steps.[8] He presented these under the following headings:

1   Detailed audit objective
2   Knowledge of business
3   Population statistics
4   Interrelated accounts
5   Analytical review

6   Accounting system and its internal controls
7   Compliance evidence
8   Detailed substantive tests.

While he was not writing specifically about the risk-based approach described in Chapter 7, Hatherly's framework provides a useful starting point for the design of an audit approach to a specific figure in the statements.

Each of the steps, apart from the last, provides information which is of use in the planning of subsequent stages. Hatherly suggests that there is a change in emphasis as one works through the process with earlier steps being primarily concerned with the collection of information for planning purposes, and later steps being more concerned with the collection of evidence.

8.4.1 Detailed audit assertions

The detailed audit assertions are listed in the SAS on evidence as follows:[9]

1   Existence: an asset or a liability exists at a given date.
2   Rights and obligations: an asset or a liability pertains to the entity at a given date.
3   Occurrence: a transaction or event took place which pertains to the entity during the relevant period.
4   Completeness: there are no unrecorded assets, liabilities, transactions or events, or undisclosed items.
5   Valuation: an asset or liability is recorded at an appropriate carrying value.
6   Measurement: a transaction or event is recorded at the proper amount and revenue or expense is allocated to the proper period.
7   Presentation and disclosure: an item is disclosed, classified and described in accordance with the applicable reporting framework.

These questions have to be asked in respect of each of the items which appears in the profit and loss account and balance sheet. The auditor also has to consider whether the omission of certain items, such as contingent liabilities, is justified.

The above list is rather long and involved. It would also be very inefficient to answer each of the questions in the manner in which they are raised in the standard. Fortunately, there is a pattern running through them which can be exploited both as an *aide mémoire* and as a means of reducing the amount of audit testing. This is discussed in section 8.5.

8.4.2 Knowledge of the business

It was pointed out in the previous chapter that the auditor requires a detailed knowledge of the business in order to plan the audit. It is important that the auditor should not restrict this information gathering exercise to the planning stage of the audit. As new information comes to light, the auditor should amend and adapt his plans as necessary. Furthermore, the auditor should always be trying to deepen his understanding of the motives of the company's directors. If they appear to be under pressure to distort the truth and fairness of the published accounts, then the auditor will have to take a much more sceptical approach to the audit work in general and to management assurances in particular.

8.4.3 *Population statistics*

Many of the figures which the auditor must test will consist of a large number of individual transactions or balances. The auditor must be aware of the numbers of items within each major population and their distribution in terms of the size of items or their ages. This information will assist the auditor in the design of his audit tests. It may be, for example, that a population will have to be stratified and a separate sample taken from each stratum. If the auditor was not aware of the composition of a population, there could be a danger of him placing reliance upon a sample which is not representative.

8.4.4 *Related accounts*

The simple mechanics of double entry bookkeeping mean that there must be interrelationships between certain account balances. If, for example, an accounting error has led to the incorrect recording of transactions in the sales account, the balance on the related account of debtors will have been similarly affected. The auditor must be aware of these relationships. Audits tend to be conducted by teams of audit staff. Each member of the team must be trained to recognise the implications of the effect of an error in one account for the balance on another. Errors could be overlooked if the team members are allowed to work in isolation. The interrelationships between account balances can be exploited by the auditor in order to simplify the design of audit tests.

8.4.5 *Analytical review*

Analytical review is an important source of evidence. It was discussed in detail in section 7.4.4 of Chapter 7. The steps in the audit evidence process are meant to interact. The population statistics collected at an earlier stage could be a very valuable source of data for the auditor's analytical review. An aged analysis of stock, for example, could be used to assess the adequacy for the provision for obsolete stock.

8.4.6 *Internal controls and compliance testing*

These two steps are closely linked. Auditors can obtain evidence by reviewing the system and identifying specific controls which would prevent the figures from being distorted by fraud or error. Auditors must, however, prove that these

detailed examination of individual items in the financial statements, it is possible to understand the purpose of each of the procedures described – thus making it easier to remember them. This logic can also be used to answer examination questions on audit testing – as a prompt to memory, as a structure for answers and as a means of deriving a sensible programme of tests for any awkward items which may not have been encountered before.

8.5.1 *The rules*

There are four basic rules of thumb which can be applied to the design of audit objectives:[12]

1. Debit balances are tested for validity. Credit balances are tested for completeness.
2. In general, profit statement balances are tested by the examination of a sample of transactions taken from those recorded during the year. Balance sheet items are tested as at the year end.
3. Many transactions can lead to potential liabilities, which should be tested for completeness.
4. Particular care should be taken over high risk items.

8.5.2 *Directional testing*

The first rule is often referred to as 'directional testing'. It relies on the fact that there has to be a debit entry in the nominal ledger for every credit and vice versa if the trial balance is to square.

If the auditor has tested all of the debit balances to ensure that they do not contain any invalid items then, by implication, he can be certain that there are no invalid items contained in the credit balances. This can best be illustrated by an example. Suppose that the sales figure had been overstated by the posting of invalid transactions to the sales account; there would have to have been an equivalent overstatement in the figure for, say, debtors or bank in order to maintain double entry. Thus, in proving that there has been no material overstatement of the debtors and bank balances, the auditor is, effectively, proving the same thing for sales. The principle of tests on one balance having implications for the audit of another is known as 'corollary testing'.

The argument is equally valid for the tests of the completeness of the credit balances. If, for example, there had been an omission from creditors, there would also have been an omission from purchases. Thus, in testing creditors' balances for completeness, one is also testing purchases.

There are no real exceptions to the rule of directional testing, although it has to be remembered that those adjustments which are recorded by means of a journal entry at the year end consist of both a debit and a credit entry. These must be tested for both validity and completeness. This applies to stock and depreciation as well as provisions, accruals and prepayments.

Tests of the validity of recorded transactions and balances are known as 'overstatement tests'. Tests of completeness are known as 'understatement tests'. The concept of directional testing applies to each of the risk factors introduced in Chapter 7. If, for example, the auditor was collecting evidence on the purchases figure, the first step would be to evaluate the inherent risk of purchases being invalid items being recorded, perhaps in order to conceal fraud. The review of the system would concentrate on the identification of controls which were intended to prevent the recording of invalid items in the purchases account. Analytical review would concentrate upon indications that the figure had been overstated.

In designing detailed substantive tests, tests for overstatement start with a sample of items selected from the relevant account in the nominal ledger. Tests for understatement are intended to ensure that nothing has been omitted and so they will start with a sample of items which ought to have been recorded. These are then traced into the relevant account, making sure that they have been valued correctly.

It is relatively easy to design overstatement tests. The items are drawn from a well-defined population. Thus, in testing purchases, one would select from the entries in the purchases account. These might have to be broken down by sub-sampling from the purchase day book to provide a sample of purchase invoices for checking against related documentation, such as the purchase order and goods received note.

Understatement tests are more difficult to design. The starting point is the population of potential items which could have resulted in an entry to the account under review. The population from which the items are selected is known as the 'reciprocal population'. For example, a sample of potential sales could be selected from the records of goods despatched during the year. Those selected despatches which did, in fact, result in sales would be posted to the

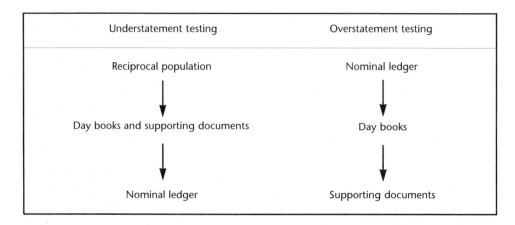

Figure 8.1 The audit trail.

sales account via the copy sales invoice and the sales day book, checking the valuation of the sale in the process. Unfortunately, there can never be any guarantee that the despatch records are, themselves, a complete population of all potential sales. The identification of an appropriate reciprocal population is always a problem; the auditor can rarely be satisfied that every potential item is included in it.

Directional testing is so called because of the nature of each type of test. When testing for understatement, the auditor tests his sample by following it through the accounting records, testing the correctness of each stage of processing, until, finally, he posts the entry to the nominal ledger. In the case of overstatement, he goes through the system backwards, starting at the entries in the nominal ledger and working towards the underlying documentary evidence. This process of following items through the system in a methodical manner is known as 'depth testing'. The records and documents which are used to trace items through the system are known as the 'audit trail' (see Figure 8.1).

8.5.3 *Vouching v. verification*

The reasoning behind the second rule, which advocates different approaches for profit and loss account and balance sheet items, is fairly obvious. Apart from anything else, it would be impossible to test the balances on the revenue and expense accounts without looking at samples of the individual transactions from throughout the year. On the other hand, with one exception, the transactions recorded in the asset and liability accounts during the year have little relevance in themselves; it is the closing balances which matter to the users of the accounts.

The testing of transactions recorded during the year is sometimes referred to as 'vouching'. The testing of balances as at the year end is often referred to as 'verification'. The audit of fixed assets provides the only exception to this rule. The Companies Act 1985 requires that all transactions involving fixed assets be summarised by means of a note to the accounts. As the note forms part of the audited accounts, it is necessary for the auditor to test the transactions involving fixed assets. In this case, the most efficient way to audit fixed assets is to agree the opening balances to the (audited) closing balance brought forward from the previous year and then to test a sample of transactions taken from throughout the year. Thus, a sample of recorded additions must be tested for validity and steps must be undertaken to ensure that disposals have not been materially understated.

This rule tends to be associated more directly with the design of detailed substantive tests. In some cases, for example, the auditor will rely on internal controls relating to balance sheet items which were designed to check the validity or completeness of transactions recorded in the account during the year.

8.5.4 *Related liabilities*

The third rule is, to some extent, an extension of the first. Several types of transaction can result in a related liability. For example, the payment of wages involves the collection of PAYE, the sale of goods may result in the collection of VAT and the purchase of goods, assets or services will result in a liability to the supplier. It is normal practice to test for the understatement of these potential liabilities while auditing the transactions to which they relate. Normally, this is done by examining the returned cheques with which they were settled. If they have not yet been settled, then they should be posted to the balance sheet.

8.5.5 *High risk transactions*

Finally, rule number four simply suggests that those items which are more likely to be misstated should be tested more thoroughly. Such items may arise because of an increased danger of fraud, e.g. salaries paid to staff working in the wages department; or because of a greater chance of deliberate or accidental misposting, e.g. entries to the repairs account which could relate to capital expenditure.

Transactions recorded during the periods just before and after the year end are particularly vulnerable to error as a result of entries being included in the wrong accounting period. Tests designed to ensure that sales, purchases, receipts and payments have been recorded in the correct period are known as 'cut-off' tests.

8.5.6 *Applying the rules*

When applying these rules, it must be borne in mind that programmes of audit tests must be designed for practical use. They must, therefore, be concise, they must break the tasks involved in achieving the objective down into manageable steps, and above all else they must be specific as to the manner in which items will be selected regarding the evidence which ought to be examined at each stage.

In designing detailed substantive tests, it will help if the tests themselves are listed in a logical order, beginning with the selection of sample items and working systematically through the audit trail. There is nothing more obvious than the student who attempts to bluff his way towards a pass mark with a statement such as 'select a sample of transactions and test their validity', without suggesting how this ought to be done.

These rules are intended to make the task of reading descriptions of audit programmes easier and the time spent revising more productive; they are certainly not intended as an alternative to either detailed study or revision. The rules which have been described should be thought of as a lamp-post – which the good citizen makes use of for illumination, but on which the drunkard relies for support!

8.6 Summary

Audit evidence is simply the information which the auditor obtains in order to arrive at his conclusion on the financial statements. The collection and evaluation of audit evidence lies at the very heart of everything the auditor does.

The auditor is obliged to ensure that he has obtained sufficient evidence to support his opinion. If he has been unable to do so, then he is required to qualify his audit report.

Audit evidence may be immediately available or may have to be created by the auditor. The auditor's deductive reasoning may also be regarded as evidence. When evaluating a potential piece of evidence, the auditor must consider the extent to which it could have been distorted by the management of the client. Evidence from an independent source is more reliable than material prepared by the client's own staff. Conclusive evidence will not always be available to the auditor. It may be possible to enhance the quality of the available evidence by corroborating different sources.

The auditor should always try to bear the shareholders' interests in mind. There is a balance between the cost of obtaining more evidence and the assurance to be obtained from it. The auditor should not collect more evidence than is necessary.

There is a logical sequence of steps for the collection of audit evidence. This process can be applied to the individual items in the profit and loss account and balance sheet by means of four simple rules of thumb.

REVIEW QUESTIONS

1. Compare and contrast the nature of the evidence used by an auditor with that which would be considered by the jury in a criminal court case.

2. What problems would be created if the shareholders' understanding of audit evidence differed from that of the auditor? How are these problems to be overcome? What further work is necessary?

3. To what extent does a lack of usable evidence pose problems for the auditor?

4. To what extent is the decision to collect more evidence a commercial one?

5. Reconcile the detailed audit objectives contained in the Auditing Guideline on audit evidence with the rules of thumb for the identification of audit objectives. Are the rules complete or do they have to be supplemented in any way?

——— **EXERCISES** ———

1. Evaluate the quality of the following pieces of audit evidence, suggesting how each could be used during an audit.

(a)   A written assurance from the client's managing director.

(b)   An analysis of standard versus actual costs, prepared by the client's staff.

(c)   A report on the value of land and buildings prepared by a firm of chartered surveyors.

(d)   An aged analysis of the balances on the client's debtors' ledger, prepared by a member of the audit staff.

2. You are the audit senior in charge of the audit of a medium-sized manufacturing company. You have asked the company secretary for the minutes of all board meetings held since the conclusion of last year's audit work. The company secretary, who has only recently been appointed, refuses to give you access to the minutes for the following reasons:

(a)   'The matters discussed at board meetings are confidential. I am not prepared to have a junior member of an audit firm, such as yourself, read them.'

(b)   'The audit report relates to the profit and loss account and balance sheet, not to the board minutes. You have no right to see anything which is not relevant to the audit.'

(c)   'It would take you hours to read through all of the detailed minutes. Your hourly charge-out rate is so high that it would cost a great deal for you to go through the minutes in our time. I do not think that the cost would be justified.'

Respond to each of the company secretary's comments.

3. You are a training manager in charge of a course for new audit staff. You have just completed a discussion on the topic of directional testing. One member of the class raises the following questions:

(a)   'If you only test debits for overstatement and credits for understatement, surely you are only half-testing the statements? What if a debit balance is understated or a credit balance overstated – you won't find the errors!'

(b)   'You say that the testing of debtors for overstatement also tests the balance on the sales account for overstatement. What if the client has deliberately overstated sales and forced the trial balance to square by omitting some of the creditors' balances? Then he has beaten your system and also made his balance sheet appear more attractive.'

(c)   'Would it matter if the auditor tested all debit balances for understatement and all credit balances for overstatement?'

4. You have been asked to audit the accounts of your friend's squash club. The income and expense account shows income from the following sources:

- Annual subscriptions.
- Enrolment fees paid by new members.
- Court fees.
- Takings from a small equipment shop.

Expenses consist of:

- Wages paid to two full-time staff who take bookings and run the shop. There are also payments to a part-time cleaner.
- A number of running costs for the rented premises, including rent, insurance and electricity.
- Stock for the shop.

The club has no material assets or liabilities.

State how you would go about the audit of the income and expenses of the club, making maximum use of directional testing.

References and further reading

1. Mautz, R.K. and Sharaf, H.A., *The Philosophy of Auditing*, American Accounting Association, 1961, p. 86.
2. APB, *Glossary of Terms*, 1995.
3. APB, SAS 400, *Audit Evidence*, 1995, paragraph 2.
4. Lee, T.A., *Company Auditing*, Van Nostrand Reinhold, 1986, pp. 158–61.
5. Flint, D., *Philosophy and Principles of Auditing*, Macmillan, 1988, p. 113.
6. APB, SAS 400, *op. cit.*, paragraph 17.
7. Mautz, R.K. and Sharaf, H.A., *op. cit.*, p. 84. This point is expanded upon in SAS 400, paragraph 18.
8. Hatherly, D.J., *The Audit Evidence Process*, Anderson Keenan, 1980, p. 26.
9. APB, SAS 400, *op. cit.*, paragraph 11.
10. APB, SAS 300, *Accounting and Internal Control Systems and Audit Risk Assessments*, 1995, paragraph 8.
11. APB, *Glossary of Terms*, 1995.
12. These rules are also described in Kneer, D.C., 'The teaching of an effective and efficient audit strategy', *Issues in Accounting Education*, 1984 and in the *Grant Thornton Audit Manual*, Longman, 1990, pp. 86–8.

CHAPTER 9

Internal control

It was suggested in Chapter 7 that internal control is one of the most important sources of audit evidence. This chapter will consider the manner in which the auditor evaluates internal control. It will be assumed throughout that the company makes use of a computerised accounting system. Despite this, the concepts described will be equally relevant to systems which do not rely upon computers. Indeed, the manual controls within computerised systems are often the most important.

By the time you have completed this chapter, you should be able to:

- Explain what is meant by internal control.
- Describe the various forms which internal controls might take.
- Explain how computers might affect the basic principles of internal control.
- Describe the inherent limitations of internal controls as a means of preventing fraud and error.
- Describe the manner in which auditors communicate their opinions concerning internal control to management.

9.1 What is internal control?

The internal control system comprises two related components: the control environment and the control procedures themselves. The control environment is determined by senior management and is essentially the embodiment of their attitude towards control within the organisation. Control procedures are the detailed checks and controls which are built into the system itself. These are related in the sense that control procedures are less likely to be rigorous (or at least formalised) if senior management places a great deal of emphasis on delegation and flexibility.

SAS 300 suggests that the internal control system has the following objectives:

1   Ensuring adherence to internal [management] policies.

2 Safeguarding of assets.
3 Preventing and detecting fraud and error.
4 Ensuring the accuracy and completeness of the accounting records.
5 Enabling the timely preparation of reliable financial information.[1]

While the auditor will usually rely on internal control as a source of audit evidence, the responsibility for the implementation of controls is a matter for management and is, therefore, at their discretion. The auditor may recommend possible improvements but is not responsible for their implementation. There is, however, a growing perception that the directors ought to implement sound systems of internal control as part of their duty. The Cadbury Committee recommends that the directors should report on the effectiveness of the company's system of internal control. It is suggested that this statement should contain an acknowledgement of the board's responsibility for internal controls and a brief description of some of the steps taken to discharge this reponsibility.[2]

The importance of the control culture was highlighted in the aftermath of the collapse of Barings Bank in 1995. A Bank of England report attributed this to a failure on the part of senior management to control the activities of a senior derivatives trader whose activities allegedly led to the bank becoming over-exposed to a risky investment.[3]

The auditor's interest in the control system will be different from that of management. The most important objectives from an audit point of view are those which reduce the likelihood of fraud and error and which ensure the accuracy and completeness of the accounting records. The directors could, however, be more concerned with the controls which are designed to maximise the profitability of the company by ensuring the implementation of management policies.

Internal control is an important source of evidence for three main reasons. First, the auditor has a duty to ensure that the financial statements have not been affected by material fraud. A properly designed system of internal controls will make such fraud much more difficult to commit. Second, a well-designed system can also check all transactions as and when they are recorded. In addition to deterring fraud, this also reduces the likelihood of error. This compares with the auditor's detailed testing of entries which must be restricted to relatively small samples of items. Finally, internal control is also a relatively inexpensive source of evidence when compared with substantive testing.

9.2 Types of internal control

The system of internal controls is not restricted to the accounting systems. A locked door could be construed as an internal control if it prevented unauthorised access to the company's assets. Internal controls have been described and classified in a number of different ways. One useful attempt to suggest the minimum requirements of a system of internal control suggested that, at the very least, a system should contain:

- Checks and balances (described below as 'internal check').
- Formal policies and procedures.
- Capable people.
- Oversight and supervision.

In designing the system, management should always be asking 'What could go wrong and what controls will prevent those errors from getting out of hand?'. In other words, controls should not be introduced for their own sake, but in response to specific problems which could arise. The cost-effectiveness of controls and their feasibility should also be taken into account.

Finally, it was proposed that the attitude of management towards internal control was the most important factor in the establishment of a sound system. If management does not display sufficient commitment to internal control then their subordinates will be unlikely to attach a high priority to it.[4]

An appendix to the (now superseded) APC Auditing Guideline on Internal Control lists the following types of internal control:

- Organisation.
- Segregation of duties.
- Physical.
- Authorisation and approval.
- Arithmetical and accounting.
- Personnel.
- Supervision.
- Management.

Each of these will be discussed in turn below.

9.2.1 *Organisation*

It is important that each member of staff within an organisation is aware of his or her duties. A system could not operate properly if supervisors were not aware of their responsibilities for the work of their subordinates. This type of control could be established by devising a detailed organisation chart which outlined the lines of reporting throughout the organisation. It would also help if every member of staff had a detailed job description which fully described the duties associated with the post and identified the person's immediate superiors.

9.2.2 *Segregation of duties*

This is one of the most important aspects of internal control and one which the auditor will usually pay a great deal of attention to. It is the main defence against fraud.

All commercial transactions involve three distinct aspects: the initial authorisation of the transaction, the custody of the related assets, and the recording of the transaction. If a member of staff is responsible for two or more of these aspects then that person will be able to defraud the company. For example, a company will have to involve at least three people, or even three separate departments, in the purchase of materials.

1 If one individual placed orders and had access to the incoming stocks then it would be possible to order goods for personal use and intercept them before they were placed in stock.

2 An individual who had access to stock and was responsible for the stock records could steal materials and conceal the theft by manipulating the records.

3 It is more difficult to envisage the problems which would be associated with the ability to authorise a transaction and update the records. Theft would be impossible if that person had no access to the assets themselves. It would, however, be possible for that individual to have other motives to distort the statements. A bad purchasing decision could be concealed by writing the stocks off as lost or stolen, thus blaming someone else for the error.

Segregation of duties can be difficult to evaluate without a detailed examination of the system. Most accounting firms have special documentation which poses questions about the duties of each member of the accounting staff. These forms are designed in such a way that any incompatible duties are highlighted.

Computerised systems may make it more difficult to identify those who have custody of assets. Many organisations make payments to suppliers and employees using instructions generated by computer programs. A person who inputs an invoice or clock card details into the system may, in the absence of other controls, also generate payments automatically, perhaps for fictitious expenses.

9.2.3 *Physical*

There is little point is designing administrative controls to prevent theft if the assets which are being protected can simply be stolen. It is important, therefore, that access to assets and the documents which control their movement, such as blank cheques and stock requisition vouchers, is restricted. Common sense should be applied in designing an appropriate level of physical security. A safe would be an unnecessary precaution for a petty cash balance of a few pounds but could be vital for valuable items such as share certificates or title deeds.

It is also important that unauthorised access to the computer system is made as difficult as possible. This could involve keeping terminals in a room which is locked when not in use, putting locks on the terminals themselves, and so on. Computer security will be discussed in greater detail in Chapter 10.

9.2.4 *Authorisation and approval*

All transactions should be authorised by staff with an appropriate level of seniority. Such a control would be ineffective if exercised by junior members of staff. It is, however, also important to ensure that senior staff are not hampered by asking them to authorise a plethora of trivial items. Formal limits should be established for each supervisor's authority. Taking fixed assets as an example, a factory manager could authorise purchases worth up to, say, £5,000. The permission of the company's board of directors could be needed for purchases worth up to, say, £20,000. More expensive items might have to be authorised by the board of the holding company.

9.2.5 *Arithmetical and accounting*

A variety of accounting and bookkeeping devices have been devised for the detection of errors in the financial statements. The trial balance ensures that double entry principles have been adhered to. The balance according to the cash book can be reconciled with the bank's records in order to ensure that all bank transactions have been recorded properly. The trial balance ensures that proper double entry principles have been applied to the recording of transactions.

9.2.6 *Personnel*

It is vital that staff are capable of applying the controls which are part of their duties. A company which did not pay sufficient attention to recruitment or which did not offer sufficient rewards to attract staff with the necessary qualifications and experience would find it difficult to operate a proper system of internal control.

9.2.7 *Supervision and management*

It has already been suggested that management must ensure that internal control is taken seriously. On a day-to-day basis, management must ensure that controls operate and that exceptions highlighted by the system are investigated. Senior management also has a part to play in this process. It would be impractical for the board to be actively employed in the daily supervision of staff. This problem could, however, be overcome by the creation of an internal audit department to conduct reviews of the system on a regular basis. The role of the internal audit department will be dealt with in more detail in Chapter 15.

9.2.8 *Internal check*

Internal check is a collective term for those internal controls which involve either segregation of duties or the checking of work done by each member of staff in the course of another's duties. Whereas segregation of duties concentrates on the prevention of fraud by eliminating the motive to distort the statements, internal check will also prevent error.

The constant checking of colleagues' work may sound sinister, but it is not intended to be so. In many cases the checking will be overt, such as the scrutiny of an expenses claim by a supervisor before it is passed for payment. In other cases, the figures prepared by one member of staff can be cross-checked against those of another. The figure for debtors can, for example, be obtained from the debtors' account in the nominal ledger or by adding up the various balances in the debtors' ledger. The two totals should always agree.

Internal check is not included in the list taken from the Auditing Guideline. It would, however, include several of the types of control described above, such as arithmetical and accounting, authorisation, and so on.

ACTIVITY

Think about the last time you bought something from a shop. Which of the above types of control did you see in operation?

There is no correct answer to this activity. The most obvious controls are likely to be the physical controls to prevent theft. There may have been electronic tags or showcases designed to ensure that high-value items could not be taken without first paying for them.

Tills are fitted with locks and produce records of the day's transactions. This makes it possible for the shop manager to implement arithmetical and accounting controls to check the day's takings against the till records.

You may have been aware of the organisational controls. Many large stores have supervisors to assist staff and to deal with any problems which might arise.

9.3 Internal control in a computerised environment

Computers have simultaneously become both cheaper and more powerful. Very few companies now rely exclusively on manual records. Computerisation has had an effect upon internal control; if programs have been written properly and data input correctly, without any interference, then it is almost impossible for a computer to make a mistake. If, however, there is an error in the program, or the processing of data is being manipulated in some way, then the machine's inability to question the logic of its instructions can lead to systematic errors which are repeated every time the program is run.

9.3.1 *Manual v. program-dependent controls*

Many of the controls within a computer-based accounting system are manual. A clerk might compare a purchase invoice with its related order to ensure that the purchase was valid before sending the invoice to a data input department for processing. This is the same manual control which would be found in a system which did not use a computer. Manual controls can be just as effective as those which are programmed into the computer. Indeed, there may be circumstances when the auditor will choose to rely on them exclusively.

Program-dependent controls are either carried out by computer programs or rely on information produced by the computer. The comparison of invoices and purchase orders could be computerised if orders were logged in the inventory files. The program which recorded purchase invoices could compare the details while they were being input against those in the order file. Any invoices which did not agree in all respects could be either rejected or processed as normal but listed on a printout of unusual or mis-matched items. Any control based on the follow-up to such a printout must also be classified as program-dependent.

The distinction between manual and program-dependent controls is an important one. If a control depends on the correct operation of a program then it may be vulnerable to interference from fraudulent programmers or even outsiders who are able to circumvent the security systems and alter program files. Manual controls cannot be interfered with in this manner. This does not invalidate program-dependent controls as a source of evidence. It does, however, mean that the auditor must ensure that the programs could not have been tampered with before relying upon them.

9.3.2 *General v. application controls*

General controls

> relate to the environment in which the computer-based systems are developed, maintained and operated, and which are therefore applicable to all the applications. The objectives of general controls are to ensure the proper development and implementation of applications, and the integrity of program and data files, and of other computer operations.[5]

Application controls

> relate to the transactions and standing data appertaining to each computer-based accounting system and are therefore specific to each such application. The objectives of application controls ... are to ensure the completeness and accuracy of the accounting records and the validity of the entries made therein resulting from both manual and programmed processing.[6]

General and application controls can be easily distinguished. If a control is specific to any given aspect of the accounting system, such as purchasing or payroll, then it is an application control. If the control is intended to protect the system as a whole, such as the requirement that users have a valid password before gaining access to files or programs, then it is a general control. The design of general controls will be described in more detail in Chapter 10. Application controls will be covered in Chapters 12 to 14 as part of the discussion of the audit of specific items in the profit and loss account and balance sheet.

The distinction between general and application controls is important. The auditor does not have to rely on every control which is in operation within the system. Some controls may be regarded as trivial; others may be considered redundant because their function is duplicated by others. The auditor will be more interested in the application controls because these are directly relevant to the completeness and accuracy of the figures in the financial statements. These will, however, have to be divided between manual and program-dependent. If the auditor wishes to rely on any of the program-dependent application controls then it will also be necessary to evaluate the general controls and ensure that they have operated. Otherwise, the auditor could be relying upon a programmed application control which had been circumvented.

In most audits, there will be some program-dependent application controls which the auditor will wish to rely upon. Once the decision has been taken to evaluate the general controls, the auditor may then decide to increase the number of application controls which are to be relied upon.

The relationship between the different types of control can be illustrated as shown in Figure 9.1.

ACTIVITY

It has been suggested that the general controls are more important than the application controls. Try to suggest why this might be so.

If the general controls are weak then the auditor will be unable to rely on the correct operation of any program-dependent application controls. For example, a payroll package could be programmed to report any claim for overtime which exceeds, say, 30 hours in any given month. This would be a program-dependent application control designed to highlight suspicious overtime claims. If the general controls were weak then a fraudulent

Figure 9.1 The control environment.

programmer could change the program so that it highlighted any claim for more than 30 hours, but not any which were for exactly 250 hours. This programmer could then submit claims for exactly 250 hours per month and would avoid detection (at least by this control).

9.4 Professional requirements in respect of internal control

Reliance on internal control has been a feature of auditing for many years. The UK professional standards and guidelines have also been in force in this area for some time. There have, however, been some interesting developments in the United States which are worth considering.

9.4.1 *Mandatory requirements*

Auditors are not really required to rely on internal control as part of their professional duties. The SASs merely lay down guidelines for obtaining evidence by this means if it is decided that it is a cost-effective source. There is, however, a statutory requirement for auditors to decide whether the company has kept 'proper accounting records' and to report any failure to do so.

The minimum requirements for the accounting system will be affected by the size and nature of the company. A small company could probably cope with a simple set of manual records. In some cases it would even be possible to prepare the financial statements from an analysed cash book and some supporting records. Larger companies would require a full double entry bookkeeping system. In some cases, it would be virtually impossible for a manual accounting system to cope and a computer-based system would be required.

The auditor need not do a great deal to comply with this requirement. It would be sufficient to prepare a list of the main records which are kept and to state whether these appear to be a satisfactory basis for the company's accounting system. Such an evaluation would not, however, yield any audit evidence.

9.4.2 *Collecting evidence from the review of the system*

SAS 300 suggests the followings steps for collecting evidence from internal control (see Figure 9.2). The first step is to decide in principle whether the controls are worth evaluating. If the system is weak then there is very little point in proceeding with the review of the system.

The next step is the identification of specific controls upon which to place reliance. The auditor will usually make use of questionnaires which list potential problems which could arise. The auditor must decide which controls, if any, would prevent these problems from arising. For example, a questionnaire relating to credit sales would ask whether the person who recorded sales

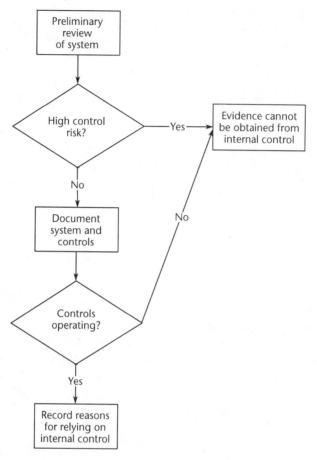

Figure 9.2 Collection of evidence from internal control.

invoices had a motive to understate this income and, if so, whether such an omission would be discovered. If the person who recorded invoices also handled receipts from customers then that employee could defraud the company. This would be accomplished by excluding an invoice from a debtor's account. When the debtor paid for the goods, the employee could steal the cheque. The theft would not be discovered because there would not be any record of the amount being due to the company. This problem could be avoided by separating the tasks of recording invoices and handling receipts. Further controls such as the prenumbering of sales invoices and regular sequence checks to ensure that they have been recorded correctly would also help.[7]

Chapters 12 to 14 will include a discussion of the various problems which could arise in each part of the system and the controls which the auditor might expect to find.

9.4.3 *Compliance testing*

The fact that the system would appear to contain controls does not, in itself, mean that the auditor has obtained any audit evidence. SAS 300 requires that the auditor carries out tests of control or compliance tests on the controls before placing reliance on them. The distinction between compliance and substantive testing is one of motive. If the auditor examines a document to ensure that an entry in one of the accounts is valid then the test is substantive. If the same test is carried out on the same document, but is done in order to ensure that an internal control has operated, then the test is a compliance test.

There are three main types of compliance test: examination of evidence, reperformance, and observation and enquiry. Examination of evidence is usually the most reliable form of compliance test. If, for example, the auditor wishes to rely upon the fact that a bank reconciliation statement is prepared at the end of every month, it would be a simple matter to examine the file of reconciliations. If a clerk is responsible for comparing an invoice with the related purchase order and goods received note before authorising payment for the goods then the auditor could obtain some assurance that this control had operated by examining a sample of invoices and making sure that they had been signed or initialled by the clerk.

Reperformance involves the auditor repeating the control on a sample of items. If, for example, the clerk who checked invoices against their supporting documents did not sign or initial them to show that the comparison had been carried out, the auditor could take a sample of invoices and conduct a similar comparison. If such a test is done on a limited sample then the auditor is only obtaining negative assurance. If the auditor attempts to replicate the control and finds that it is impossible to do so for some of the items in the sample, this would suggest that the control had not operated. The fact that the control can be reperformed for a sample is not, however, conclusive proof that it operated for all transactions.

If a control is program-dependent, reperformance may be the only viable means of testing its operation. Fortunately, the power of the computer can often be harnessed to assist in this task. For example, the payroll program might not process an employee's payment unless that person has a record in the personnel files. The auditor could write a program which would take each person on the payroll and ensure that there was a personnel record for each. The fact that this control is being reperformed electronically means that the auditor can afford to extend the testing to the entire file, thus increasing the likelihood of discovering a control failure.

Some controls do not generate any evidence which can be examined by the auditor, nor do they lend themselves to reperformance. As a last resort, the auditor can rely on observation or enquiry. The auditor may decide to test the operation of a control by observing the staff as they go about their work. This observation may be overt or covert. If the auditor is interested in the controls which operate during, say, the filling of pay packets, he may ask permission to watch the process in operation. Alternatively, the auditor will often be allocated a spare desk in the accounts department. This provides the audit team with a vantage point from which to observe the operation of the system, particularly to gauge the care with which staff carry out their duties.

The auditor may not be able to observe the operation of a control such as segregation of duties. The best way to ensure that duties are allocated to staff in accordance with the information in the audit files is to discuss the system with the staff themselves. Questions should not be asked in a leading manner, otherwise staff may give the answers which they think the auditor expects. The accuracy of the description can also be checked by asking for explanations from other members of staff and looking for corroboration.

9.4.4 *The effects of weaknesses in the system*

It is unlikely that the auditor will be completely satisfied with the system. This may be because the company has failed to include certain controls in its system or because controls which were selected during the review of the system have failed to operate.

It is not unusual for managers to refuse to change the duties of a long-serving member of staff, even if that person is in a position to commit fraud. This could be because a higher level of control would constrain that person in some way and the risk of fraud would appear to be worth taking. Alternatively, management may be afraid of offending a trusted member of staff. Sometimes slack supervision enables well-designed systems to change for the worse with the passage of time.

If the auditor discovers an apparent weakness, the first thing to be done is to re-examine the system in case any controls which would compensate for the problem have been missed. This can often happen when a company takes a slightly unusual approach to dealing with a potential problem. For example, suppose that a clerk employed in a small company was in a position to intercept payments from customers and alter the debtors' records so that this theft was concealed. This apparent weakness could not be exploited if all mail was opened by an independent person and all receipts were recorded in a register which was regularly compared with the lodgements according to bank statements.

If there are no compensating controls then the auditor will either have to abandon internal control as a source of evidence, which would be a rather extreme reaction, or increase the extent of substantive testing in order to counteract the weakness. The additional substantive testing should be carefully planned so that the auditor can be certain that a loophole in the system has not led to a material error or been fraudulently exploited. The company might not, for example, check purchase invoices against their related orders, thus making it possible for invalid purchases to be recorded. The auditor would respond to this by taking a sample of purchase invoices and examining the copy orders to ensure that the purchases were valid.

In some cases, a control weakness will be immaterial. If, for example, it was discovered that a member of staff had covered for a colleague's absence for a very short period and had been responsible for conflicting duties during this time, the auditor should evaluate the value of the transactions processed. If the total amount recorded was insignificant then the maximum overstatement would also be immaterial. This would mean that the weakness could be ignored.

9.4.5 *Professional requirements in the United States*

In 1988 the US accountancy profession published a series of new Statements on Auditing Standards (SASs), the so-called 'expectation gap' standards. One of these, SAS 55, deals with the auditor's duties with respect to internal control.[8]

The new guidance differs from the UK standards in that the US auditor is now required to obtain a sufficient understanding of the control environment, the accounting system and the control procedures within the company to plan the audit. This means that the auditor cannot simply ignore internal control and obtain evidence by means of extensive substantive testing.

The control environment is a complex collection of factors including the management philosophy and operating style of the company, its organisational structure, and so on. Control procedures are simply the internal controls within the system.

This additional requirement to evaluate internal control may not add a great deal to the auditor's duties given that internal control is a relatively cheap source of evidence and the auditor would normally wish to rely upon it anyway. It does, however, force the auditor to identify the areas of higher risk and react accordingly. This would appear to endorse the risk-based approach.

9.5 Limitations of internal control

Internal control provides high quality evidence. It must, however, be corroborated by means of some substantive testing. This is because the results of the auditor's evaluation of internal control can be misleading.

ACTIVITY

Try to suggest some of the limitations of internal control.

Most internal controls are designed to prevent fraud or error by relatively junior staff. It would usually be relatively easy for management to override the controls which they have established.

Segregation of duties can be circumvented by fraudulent collusion. If one member of staff has access to assets and the other maintains the related records it would be possible for them to work together to defraud the company and share the proceeds. The fact that two people would have to be involved would increase the likelihood of the fraud being discovered and so segregation does have some value as a means of protecting the company. In general, auditors tend to assume that collusion has not occurred unless there is reason to suspect that it is likely.

Controls can break down because of human error, poor training, or under-qualified staff. This is one reason why the auditor will take great interest in the company's recruitment and staffing policies. Care also has to be taken to investigate the effects of holidays and staff illness on the system during the year. It could be that there have been periods when duties have been rearranged to allow for absences. Serious errors could have occurred at these times.

Compliance tests can also prove misleading. The auditor can examine a document to ensure that it has been signed as correct. This signature says nothing about the care with which the person responsible checked the item. Similarly, observation could be misleading if staff modified their behaviour in the auditor's presence.

9.6 Communication of internal control weaknesses

The auditor cannot force the company to change its systems in order to eliminate control weaknesses. He can, however, inform management of the problems which have been caused by specific aspects of the system and ask for these to be rectified. The auditor will usually provide management with a list of the problems encountered during the audit. This is partly to enable manage-ment to improve the system in order to make future audits easier, partly to provide written evidence that management have been made aware of the problems with their system, and partly to provide constructive advice as a service to management. This list will usually take the form of a 'management letter' which will be discussed with the board after the audit has been com-pleted. Any major problems, such as weaknesses which could lead to a massive fraud, would, however, be reported as soon as they were discovered.

The auditor will have to take care to ensure that the letter contains appro-priate disclaimers. First, the letter cannot be construed as a list of every weakness which exists in the system. The auditor's initial review and compliance testing are both intended to highlight weaknesses which constitute major audit prob-lems. The identification of all of the system's shortcomings would require a much more thorough investigation. A statement to that effect should appear in the introduction to the letter. Second, the letter should be addressed to manage-ment. It should be made clear that it is not suitable for the needs of third parties, such as prospective investors in the company, who wish to ensure that the accounting system has been properly organised.

The letter will be of greater value if the auditor makes practical suggestions for the improvement of the system. It is also helpful to discuss the points relating to each individual aspect of the system with the relevant supervisor and to include that person's responses to the weaknesses and the auditor's suggestions. It is important to involve supervisors in this way. Otherwise, the audit could be seen as a threat because matters discovered during it were being reported straight to senior management. It is also helpful to check the accuracy of the facts in the management letter.[9]

Despite the auditor's desire to make the management letter as useful as possible, a survey of company directors revealed that the letter is not regarded as particularly useful. This is partly because the points raised are often either trivial or could not be remedied in a cost-effective manner.[10]

9.7 Summary

Internal control is the term used to describe the various procedures by which management ensure that the business is carried on in an orderly and efficient manner, ensure that their policies are adhered to, protect the company's assets, and mimimise the risk of the accounting records being incomplete or inaccurate. The auditor is interested in internal control because it provides high quality evidence that the records which must be examined as part of the audit have not been affected by material fraud or error.

The most effective means of devising a system of internal controls is to ask the question 'What could go wrong?' with regard to every aspect of the accounting system. Controls should be devised to deal with each of the problems identified, unless there is not a cost-effective means of doing so.

Computers do not affect the principles of internal control. They do, however, introduce the possibility of controls which are dependent upon programs as opposed to manual procedures. If the auditor wishes to rely upon a program-dependent control then he must first ensure that there are adequate general controls over the operation of the computerised aspects of the system.

The auditor must ensure that the company's accounting system forms an adequate basis for the preparation of a set of statements which gives a true and fair view. The auditor does not have to place reliance on the controls within the system, although there are certain steps which must be undertaken before he can do so. First, it is necessary to identify the specific controls which are to be relied upon. Second, the operation of these controls must be checked by means of compliance tests.

If the auditor's review of the system reveals weaknesses then the auditor must react either by proving that the maximum effect of the weakness could not have been material or by conducting substantive tests to ensure that the truth and fairness of the statements has not been undermined by it.

The auditor should inform management of the weaknesses encountered in the system, taking care to avoid giving the impression that the review conducted during the audit would have been capable of identifying every weakness.

REVIEW QUESTIONS

1. Compare and contrast the interests of the auditor and management in the company's system of internal controls.

2. Why is an examination of the system a vital part of the risk-based audit approach, as implied by the US requirement that the auditor should obtain an understanding of the company's control environment?

3. Why should an auditor conduct compliance tests every year, even if the company's system has always worked perfectly in the past?

4. If the company's staff are more familiar with the system than the auditor and can more easily identify compensating controls for weaknesses highlighted by the internal control evaluations, would it be more efficient for the auditor to ask the staff to complete these documents for him?

5. Why do auditors insist on sending management letters if managers do not find them useful?

EXERCISES

1. The owner of a small school of motoring has come to you for advice. She has a number of other business interests which make it impossible for her to spend more than one day of each week at the school's offices. She is concerned that the accounting records may not be properly maintained by the staff. Her two biggest concerns are that income from the sale of lessons could be understated and that the running costs of the learner cars could be overstated.

Prepare a list of possible problems and suggest controls which could prevent them from occurring. This should be laid out as follows:

What could go wrong?	Control

2. A large company which manufactures pharmaceutical products has recently opened a chain of chemists' shops across the country. This was to enable the company to sell its own brands of proprietary medicines to the public and also to diversify into the retailing industry. Other manufacturers' products are also sold through the shops.

The board of the company is concerned that gross margins are not as good as had been budgeted. All purchasing is done centrally and the cost of goods sold is roughly in line with expectations. It has been suggested that staff fraud is having an effect on recorded income, particularly as the stores have been designed to deter shoplifters.

(a) Suggest why it may be difficult to prevent staff fraud in a major retail organisation.

(b) Suggest some of the controls which could be implemented within the stores to prevent fraud.

3. A company has approximately 250 vending machines which sell childrens' toys and novelties. The machines are equipped with animated puppets which move and play tunes whenever coins amounting to the standard price are inserted into the slot. The gift is then delivered in a small plastic sphere.

The stock in the machines is replenished and their cash boxes are emptied by van drivers employed by the company. The machines are spread across a wide region and several drivers are employed. On average, each machine is emptied once every three days. All drivers are based at head office. A number of routes have been devised so that each machine is visited regularly, total mileage travelled is minimised and all drivers can return to base each evening without having had to cover an unreasonable distance.

An audit junior is unhappy with the controls which prevent fraud or error in the recording of income for this company. He has drafted the following management letter:

> To whom it may concern,
>
> We have recently completed our review of your internal controls as part of our normal auditing activities. These were generally satisfactory, although the following improvements are suggested:
>
> (a) Van drivers should travel in pairs, one to collect the cash and the other to check his calculations. Both should sign a collection book to show that they agree the amount stated.
>
> (b) On a regular basis, the counting teams should be accompanied by a senior manager, perhaps the chief accountant, to prevent staff fraud.
>
> (c) As an alternative to (b) above, spot checks could be conducted on drivers while they are emptying machines.
>
> (d) Cash should be banked immediately after each machine has been emptied. This will prevent the risks of loss, robbery or fraud which arise from having each driver bank the morning's takings at a bank on his route, with the afternoon's takings being brought back to head office when the van was being returned to the depot.

(a) List the shortcomings of the junior's letter.

(b) Suggest some cost-effective controls over income which could be implemented by the company.

References and further reading

1. APB, SAS 300, *Accounting and Internal Control Systems and Audit Risk Assessments*, 1995.

2. Committee on the Financial Aspects of Corporate Governance (Cadbury Committee), *Internal Control and Financial Reporting*, 1994.
3. *Financial Times*, ' "Failure of Controls" sank Barings', 19 July 1995, p. 1.
4. Sack, R.J., *Critical Requirements of a System of Internal Accounting Control*, Touche Ross / University of Kansas Auditing Symposium V, 1980.
5. APC Auditing Guideline, *Auditing in a Computer Environment*, 1984, paragraph 19.
6. *ibid*.
7. The completion of internal control evaluation documents is usually preceded by the creation of detailed systems notes. The manner in which systems are documented is, however, somewhat outside the scope of this text.

   Anyone who wishes to learn the standard flowcharting technique which is employed by most firms should refer to Rutteman, P.J., 'Flowcharting for auditors', *Accountants Digest*, no. 32, ICAEW, 1976. Alternatively, the recording of accounting systems is dealt with in Chapter 46 of *Grant Thornton Audit Manual*, Longman, 1986.
8. American Institute of Certified Public Accountants, *Statement on Auditing Standards*, 55, 'Consideration of the internal control structure in a financial statement audit', 1988.
9. Further information about the form and content of the management letter can be found in APB, SAS 610, *Reports to Directors or Management*, 1995.
10. Lothian, N., *Audit Quality and Value for Money Perceptions of Company Financial Management*, Heriot-Watt University, 1983, pp. 30–2.

CHAPTER 10

Computer audit

It is, in a sense, misleading to have a separate chapter on the audit implications of computers. Accounting systems were amongst the earliest commercial applications of computing. Since then, the size and cost of systems have fallen to such an extent that very few organisations rely heavily on manual accounting systems. Even the smallest companies may find it cost-effective to purchase a microcomputer for record-keeping purposes. It is, therefore, unusual to have to audit a system which has not been computerised.

This chapter will develop the previous chapter's discussion of internal control in computerised systems, concentrating upon general controls. Application controls will be considered in more detail in Chapters 12 to 14. Some of the problems and opportunities created by this technology will also be discussed. This chapter is intended to provide a brief overview of computer auditing. A comprehensive treatment of the topic would require an entire book. Guidance on further reading is provided at the end of the chapter.

By the time you have completed this chapter, you should be able to:

- Explain how the main types of computer system are organised and controlled and outline their implications for internal control and audit.
- Explain how the auditor can conduct tests using computer assisted audit techniques.
- Discuss the implications of computerisation for the auditor.

10.1 The organisation of the computerised accounting system

Computerised accounting systems can take many different forms, both in terms of hardware and the manner in which transactions are input and processed. The type of system will affect the nature of the control risks which can arise. This section makes certain generalisations about different combinations of computer hardware and processing methods. This is purely for the sake of simplicity. It is recognised that there are many different ways in which data processing can be organised.

10.1.1 *Files and records*

There are three main types of computer file. Program files contain the instructions which enable the computer to process data. Thus, a payroll program would record the various steps involved in calculating figures such as gross wages and deductions for individual employees and analyses and totals of the wages figure for both bookkeeping and management purposes.

Standing data files contain information which is of ongoing relevance to the company. Thus, the payroll system would have standing data on each individual employee's hourly rate of pay, tax codes, and so on.

Transaction data files contain details of current transactions and adjustments which will have no further significance once they have been processed. In a payroll system the number of hours worked by each employee will be entered in order to calculate the amount to be paid for that week.

Each of these files can affect the accuracy of the system's output. Errors in transaction files will, however, occur only once whereas errors in program and standing data files will be repeated during every processing cycle.

Files consist of records which contain details of individual transactions, balances or other items of interest. Thus, the payroll system would have a record for each employee. Computer records can be further broken down into fields. Thus, a payroll record would have fields for employee name, department, tax code, taxable salary for the year to date and so on.

10.1.2 *Off-line systems*

In many systems, data is processed into a form which can be read by the computer, usually by having it typed onto magnetic tape. This means that data is prepared 'off-line' for subsequent entry. In such systems, it is usually convenient for the company to create a separate data preparation department to deal with the creation of magnetic tapes. This department acts in support of the various 'user' departments who are responsible for the collection and authorisation of documents prior to their being passed to data preparation.

User departments will usually send the documents and other instructions in batches. This reduces the risk of loss or incorrect processing because the batches can be accompanied by batch header slips which state the total number of items in the batch and the total value of the transactions contained within it. These figures can then be input along with the data on the documents themselves and compared with the number and value of items actually keyed in.

The accuracy of typing may also be checked by a process called 'verification'. The transactions are typed on a machine which records them onto magnetic tape. The tape is then put onto another machine and the transactions retyped by another operator. This machine compares the tape with the second input and warns of any discrepancies. Any errors on the tape can be corrected at this stage.

On a regular basis, often monthly, users will be provided with a print-out of the records which relate to their departments. The records will be accompanied by edit or exception reports which list any transactions which could not be processed because the data was incomplete or inconsistent with details on other records. The payroll program could, for example, be written so that employees who do not have a valid record in the personnel department's files will not be paid. The exception reports could also contain details of transactions whose values exceed certain upper bounds established by management. Thus, all employees who have been paid more than £500 for a week's work or who have claimed to have worked more than 50 hours in any given week could be highlighted.

One drawback of these batch processing systems is that users often have little control over the processing of their data. The users may assume that the computerised aspects of the system are infallible and that there is no need to check the accuracy of print-outs. Conversely, the users may compensate for their dependence upon another department by insisting on high levels of application controls.

Most of the files in batch processing systems are stored upon magnetic tape. It is important that the correct reels of tape are used for each processing run and also that files on a damaged tape can be easily retrieved. Access to tapes is usually controlled by a file librarian. The librarian's role is to issue programs and data files to the operating staff so that the latest transactions and adjustments can be processed. The tapes should be kept in a room to which only the librarian has access. A register should be kept of all tapes issued and returned.

It important that program tapes are clearly labelled. The process of updating programs could lead to the existence of several different versions of any given file. Back-up copies of all programs should be kept in a separate room, preferably as far as possible from the library itself. This means that the programs will not be lost in the event of a fire or other disaster.

The protection of data files is also important. It could be catastrophic if, for example, the company lost the information in its debtors' ledger because of a computer malfunction or damage to a tape. One means of avoiding this is the adoption of the 'grandfather/father/son' or the three generation system. This involves the use of three reels of tape for every file. The approach is best understood by following a single tape through three processing cycles (see Figure 10.1).

The main advantage of this system is that it is always relatively easy to recreate a damaged current file. If the 'son' tape is lost or damaged then the 'father' tape can be brought out of storage and updated by rerunning it against the tape with the latest set of data. The 'grandfather' tape is also available as a final reserve in case both of the others are destroyed. While this is unlikely to happen, the father and son tapes will both be in the computer room at the same time during processing runs and could be vulnerable.

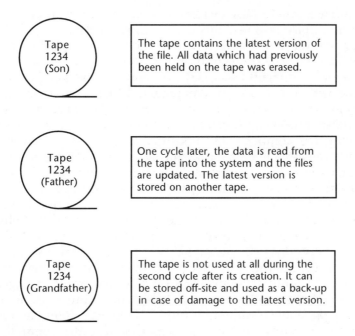

Figure 10.1 Tape processing cycles.

In a system where data tends to be entered into the computer by means of magnetic tape, unauthorised access to the system can be prevented by a combination of physical security measures and clerical controls which are designed to prevent invalid data from being processed. Physical security need not be a problem. The computer will be located in a building which has had to be specially designed to provide the necessary environment for the hardware. When this accommodation was being designed, it would have been relatively easy to ensure that access could be restricted to authorised members of staff.

10.1.3 *On-line systems*

Batch processing systems are relatively simple to design and control. They do, however, require users to accept output in the form of print-outs which may be anything up to a month old before the next computer run generates a new version. Furthermore, data which is filed on magnetic tape cannot be accessed without reading through the entire file sequentially and extracting the relevant details.

One means of overcoming these problems is to put the computer 'on-line'. In other words, data can be entered or extracted from the computer by means of a terminal. The data itself will usually be stored on magnetic disc so that specific parts of files can easily be accessed at any time. The terminals can communicate using the telephone system and need not be located in the immediate vicinity of the computer itself. This enables user departments to have their own terminals and to take responsibility for the input of data.

The nature of on-line systems changes the types of general control which must be introduced. The protection of files from unauthorised access or alteration becomes more difficult because the system could be designed in such a way that anyone with the necessary equipment, which is neither expensive nor difficult to obtain, can connect a remote terminal to the computer by means of the public telephone system. Such access has been abused by criminals intent on defrauding the company, by industrial competitors who wish to gather commercially sensitive information, and by 'hackers' who often wish only to demonstrate their ability to overcome the controls built into the system.

If possible, the company should try to restrict access. If all of the terminals are located within a relatively small area then they could be linked to the computer by dedicated communication links. If the company has branches which must be able to access files then it is possible to introduce a 'call-back' facility into the system. First, a user located at a branch would switch on his terminal, which would be connected to the computer by telephone line, and identify himself to the computer's operating system. Then the terminal would be logged off. The computer would then take that user's telephone number from its files and automatically re-establish communication. This would eliminate the possibility of an outsider imitating an authorised user because the computer would be unable to establish a link with anyone whose telephone number was not stored (see Figure 10.2).

There can be occasions when the company feels that a call-back system would be inefficient or that it would be unduly restrictive. Many organisations provide their sales and management staff with portable computers which can communicate with the company's files from anywhere in the world. Some systems, such as electronic mail networks, are intended for use by any subscriber who has paid the appropriate fee and has the necessary equipment.

Passwords are often used to limit access both to the system and also to individual files stored within it. Every user is allocated a personal code which must be entered before access is granted to the system. Having identified the user by means of the password, the software may then further restrict that person's access to those files which are related to his job description. Thus, someone working in the payroll section may be able to request information about an employee's tax code or hourly rate of pay, but would be denied access to, say, the stock files. Similarly, the range of actions which that person could undertake could also be restricted. A clerk in the payroll system may be able to read employee files but not make changes to them. The ability to add new employees or change rates of pay or other conditions could be restricted to more senior members of the department.

Passwords are not totally effective. There is always a danger that staff will select passwords which are easy to remember, such as 'password', 'FRED', their date of birth or car registration number. These are far too easy for colleagues, or even outsiders, to guess. Thus, staff should not be allowed to choose their own

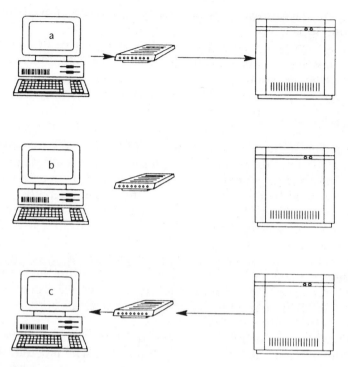

Figure 10.2 The call-back system.

passwords, but should have them issued by the manager in charge of computer security. If, however, the passwords are too difficult to remember then staff may write them down, or perhaps even tape them to their terminals!

The operating system can also be programmed to restrict the access of each terminal to designated files. Thus, regardless of passwords, anyone operating the terminal in the payroll department may be able to alter the payroll files and read from, say, the nominal ledger, but would be unable to examine anything else.

Attempts to establish unauthorised access should be recorded. The system should also restrict the number of unsuccessful attempts to connect a terminal or access a file. This avoids the possibility of someone attempting to try every possible password by programming another computer to attempt to log on to the system.

Technology is constantly providing new means of restricting access to systems. Companies can encrypt all data files so that it is impossible for someone to alter or even read anything unless they have the necessary hardware and codes to translate instructions into the format understood by the system or to decode its responses. Biometric techniques are also being developed so that a computer system can identify users by their fingerprints or by the pressure patterns created when they sign their names on a special pad. Inevitably, there will have to be further advances in such technology as ways of overcoming these methods are developed.

It is important that data is protected from loss by regularly 'dumping' it from the discs to magnetic tape. This means that the loss of data due to a hardware malfunction can be overcome.

10.1.4 *Database systems*

It is not always efficient to have a separate set of files for every user department. The accounts department's records on customers could have a great deal in common with those of the sales department. This leads to wasteful redundancy in the storage of data. It could also make it difficult for a department to make legitimate use of data recorded by another. These problems can be overcome by the use of the database structure for files. This permits the use of a query program to extract information quickly and without the need for complicated programming. Thus, the sales manager could produce a report which listed every customer who had purchased a certain product within the previous three months, but excluding those whose current balances exceeded their credit limits. This could then be used to concentrate marketing efforts on customers who were also good credit risks.

In general, database systems tend to be on-line and many of the controls described in the previous sub-section are still relevant. The fact that the system is designed to make access to all of the data as easy as possible can, however, lead to control problems. There may also be difficulties in designing controls because of the complexity of the operating system.

A further control weakness is created by the appointment of a manager to oversee the operation and structure of the database. This 'database admin-istrator' is responsible for the overall control and supervision of the database. This individual is, therefore, in a unique position to commit fraud.

10.1.5 *Microcomputers*

Microcomputers can make it extremely difficult to control access to data. The machines are usually located in offices, often without any special security precautions. It is, therefore, relatively easy to copy the floppy discs which are used for storage purposes or even to make changes to records when the room is unoccupied.

The control problems associated with microcomputers are often compounded by management attitudes. The hardware is easy to obtain and is relatively inexpensive. A new system could, for example, be purchased from the office equipment budgets of individual departments. They can also be purchased from a range of outlets including retail stores. Managers could, therefore, be tempted to acquire a system without first considering the need for adequate levels of control or even basic protection of data. The department could, for example, become dependent upon the system for the recording of data. A moment's carelessness with a disc could destroy the only copy of a vital file.

It is important that every organisation should establish a policy for the purchase of microcomputers. Otherwise there is a danger that different departments will choose machines which are incompatible with the others. This could make it difficult for data to be shared within the company and could also complicate the provision of technical support.

Broadly, microcomputers are on-line systems. Many of the controls for such systems, such as password protection and data encryption, still apply. Physical protection of the data can often be achieved by means of locks which prevent access to the data stored on hard discs. Microcomputers may be self-contained and, therefore, safe from interference from outside. They can, however, be linked together in networks for communication purposes.

10.1.6 *Networks*

Two myths which have persisted for many years are that computers will create a 'paperless office' and that large computers will be replaced entirely by PCs. Both of these myths are related to the fact that it is becoming increasingly common for organisations to make use of networks of smaller computers, linked either to a mainframe or to each other through a server. The size and configuration of networks can vary from a simple connection between a small number of PCs in a single office to a massive series of interconnected networks, possibly operating internationally. All networks share the characteristics of enabling users to communicate and to share access to certain files and also to facilities such as printers. This can reduce costs and enhance flexibility but it can also lead to security problems.

A large-scale system may enable individual users to use their PCs to connect to, say, the minicomputer serving their location. The minicomputer could allow further access to a corporate database held on a central mainframe. There could also be gateways which enabled the users to connect to suppliers or customers to exchange data concerning orders. It may be possible to run data collected from any of these sources on the local PC or minicomputer or on the mainframe. This type of system creates the possibility of users having unrestricted access to the whole network once they have accessed any given part of it. Alternatively, they may have to enter passwords or user identities at each stage of connection. The latter approach increases security, but at the cost of much greater effort on the part of users – who may decide to use the same password for each of their accounts anyway.

On a smaller scale, the network may be localised and could comprise a number of PCs linked by cables to a server which is itself a powerful PC. Such systems are easily capable of processing data for a reasonably large organisation. Such a system does, however, depend on the security of the server. It might be necessary to restrict physical access by keeping it locked away from all users apart from the network administrator. The server should also be equipped with a tape drive so that the files can be backed up regularly.

While networking is a specialised area, many of the controls are similar to those which would be appropriate for any on-line system.

10.1.7 *Software development and maintenance*

The development and maintenance of software are crucial to the efficiency of the company. Payroll programs, for example, would have to be amended if there was a significant change in the rules for the calculation of income tax or if a new method of calculating bonuses was agreed. It is important that all alterations to programs are properly controlled to prevent the possibility of incorrect or even fraudulent changes.

Many organisations employ their own full-time analysts and programmers who develop and update programs. The analysts will be responsible for the design of the program specification which describes the various inputs, the processes which are to be carried out by the program and the output. The programmer uses these specifications to write the program coding for the computer.

It is important that the analysts and programmers do not have unrestricted access to the computer files. Anyone with programming skills could alter the programs which control the movement of assets. It would also be relatively easy to override the controls within programs which are designed to prevent such abuse. A programmer could increase his salary tenfold. This excessive payment would probably be highlighted in the edit report listing of salaries which exceed a certain amount. The programmer could, however, prevent this by rewriting the coding which identifies large payments so that it automatically excludes items with his personnel number from the listing.

The systems development staff should submit their proposed changes to their supervisor for inspection. These should then be input by the data processing staff in the case of an off-line system. In on-line systems, the terminal used by the programming staff should be unable to access live program files. The ability to effect changes to programs should be restricted to their supervisors. Quite apart from preventing fraud, these precautions ensure that changes are properly documented so that the company can make further changes, even if the current systems staff are promoted or leave.

All new and updated programs should be tested before the company becomes dependent upon them. In an ideal world, the company would operate the new program in parallel with the existing system for one or two months. Errors in the program would be highlighted if the new system's figures differed from those produced by the original. Unfortunately, this type of check is rarely possible in practice because of the cost and inconvenience of running both systems. Many of the computer assisted audit techniques described in the next section can be used by the company to check the logic of new programs. Indeed, many of these techniques were first developed for this purpose.

10.2 Computer assisted audit techniques

The auditor must choose between two different approaches to the audit of a computerised system. In some cases there is sufficient detailed information in the form of print-out to enable the auditor to approach the audit using traditional manual tests. Effectively, the only difference is that the accounting records are neatly printed instead of being written out manually. This approach is known as auditing 'round the machine'. Auditing round the machine can yield satisfactory audit evidence. It may, however, take longer to complete the audit using this approach. If this is the case, the auditor could be replaced by a firm which took advantage of the computer's processing power.

The auditor may, however, decide to take advantage of the fact that much of the information is available in a form which can be tested electronically. Alternatively, the auditor could be forced to abandon manual tests because there is no visible audit trail. In either case, the auditor must use either software or specially prepared audit data to test the inner workings of the company's system. This is known as auditing 'through the machine'. The methods by which this is done are known as 'computer assisted audit techniques' (CAATs).

CAATs enable the auditor to save time by examining data stored on computer media rather than on print-outs or other documents and, in some cases, to conduct tests which cannot be done manually because there is no visible evidence or audit trail. CAATs can be used for both compliance and substantive testing.

There are two main types of CAAT: audit software and test data. These are supplemented by several further techniques, some of which were originally designed as tools for use in the development and testing of new programs.

10.2.1 *Audit software*

A number of large accounting firms have their own special software which can be adapted for use on their clients' systems. These usually offer a wide range of facilities which can be used for sampling, analytical review and comparisons. Some of these are available on a commercial basis under licence.

The auditor can use computer programs for compliance testing, particularly in the reperformance of controls. The payroll program could, for example, ensure that payments were made only to bona fide employees by checking their clock card details against the information in their personnel files. The auditor could test the operation of this control by running a special program to compare all of the employees on a weekly transaction file with their personnel records. This comparison would then highlight every possible compliance error.

Reperformance is not usually a very conclusive form of compliance test. Audit software can, however, carry out such a large number of tests that the auditor can be reasonably certain that the results of the test are not misleading. Once a program has been installed, the auditor might decide to test every item in the file.

It would also be possible to conduct compliance tests which would be completely impossible to do using manual testing. It would be possible, for example, to repeat the preparation of an aged analysis of stock or debtors to ensure that management controls which rely upon such analyses are effective.

Audit software has many uses in substantive testing. The auditor will often use statistical sampling schemes which involve an enormous amount of tedious arithmetical calculation. These can be automated using audit software and the sample items printed out for subsequent testing. The auditor can also automate analytical review by using a program to generate a more detailed analysis of a balance than is provided by the company's system. Items can be selected for detailed testing by defining a variety of criteria for selection, such as debtors' balances which exceed their credit limits or which are more than one month overdue or employees whose hourly rate calculated by dividing their gross pay by the number of hours worked exceeds, say, £15.

10.2.2 *Test data*

The auditor can ensure that program-dependent controls are operating by running fictitious data through the company's system. The test items will contain several types of error or inconsistency which are designed to trigger certain responses from the program.

Test data can be run 'live' by inserting it into a normal processing run or can be run 'dead' in a special run designed for audit purposes. In general, live runs are more meaningful because there is less risk of the company using a different version of the programs or running the procedure under artificial conditions.

The auditor must predict the effects of the fictitious data and be ready to correct them when the test has been concluded. There could be complications if, for example, a cheque was printed out for a bogus employee who had been invented for audit purposes or non-existent stock lines appeared in the inventory records. The correction of such errors could be complicated by the fact that certain items will have to remain in the system for some time in order to test ageing programs. The auditor could wish to leave a dummy debtor's account in the system for several weeks in order to see whether the balance is highlighted in a report on overdue debts.

10.2.3 *Parallel simulation*

Parallel simulation is, in a sense, the opposite of test data. The auditor writes a program which is intended to simulate the operation of the company's own software. This is used to process the company's data and the results are compared with those produced by the client. Any discrepancies are then investigated.

It is unnecessary to replicate the entire suite of programs used by the company. The auditor could simply wish to repeat the calculation of bonus payments to employees or the preparation of sales invoices from despatch note details.

10.2.4 *Embedded audit facilities*

Embedded audit facilities are a form of audit software. They are, however, inserted into the company's normal operating programs and are designed to test the operation of controls and even conduct substantive tests or select items for detailed testing during live processing. The results of this testing are written to a special file which can be read only by the auditor.

This type of facility would have to be implemented with the active cooperation of management. It could be argued that it is an extension of internal control and is, therefore, somewhat inconsistent with the role of the external auditor. Various types of embedded facilities can be used to overcome the loss of audit trail which can arise even when the auditor is willing to interrogate the system with audit software. There is, for example, a technique called 'tagging' which can be used to select transactions for testing. This program traces each step of the recording of the transaction in a separate file for subsequent review by the auditor.

10.2.5 *Systems software data analysis*

The computer's operating system usually maintains a record of operations which have been conducted on the computer. This operating log enables the computer manager to monitor usage of the system and also to warn him or her of any unusual actions, such as the alteration of a program file.

The fact that such a record exists and is examined is an important control in its own right and the auditor should conduct compliance tests to ensure that the supervisor is examining it on a regular basis and taking appropriate action in respect of any unauthorised activities. The auditor could also prepare an analysis of the log, which is often on magnetic tape, to produce a listing of events such as unsuccessful attempts to obtain access to files and attempted changes to programs.

10.2.6 *Application program examination*

The auditor might wish to examine the logic of parts of programs, such as the calculation of staff bonuses or deductions. This could be done by obtaining a listing of the relevant section of the program and checking that it has been written properly.

The examination of a program can be assisted by the use of a flowcharting package which produces a diagram from program code. This will be easier to follow than the original code. Alternatively, 'tracing' software can be used to identify the program instructions executed during the processing of a single transaction. This can assist in the review of the program's logic.

The examination of the actual program itself will require programming skills and could be extremely time-consuming. The auditor could conduct a less complicated review of the program by running a package which compares the copy of the program file which is used during operations with the original version which is stored as a back-up. This comparison would highlight any differences between the copies. The reasons for these, and the extent to which they were authorised, should be ascertained.

10.2.7 *Mapping*

Mapping software is similar in concept to the tracing software described above. A mapping program is used to identify 'hidden' routines in programs. These are routines which only come into operation when certain conditions are met. A fraudulent employee could, for example, have changed the payroll program to identify his clock card number and multiply his net salary by ten. Alternatively, someone with access to program files could have inserted a 'logic bomb' or 'virus' program which can erase large amounts of data. These are sometimes used to blackmail companies into paying for the necessary codes to deactivate the routines.

10.3 Is computerisation an opportunity or a threat?

The auditor can use computers in a number of ways. CAATs are the most obvious example of this, although developments in portable microcomputers are providing audit staff with a variety of powerful tools. The increasing use of computers by companies can, however, create problems for the auditor.

ACTIVITY

Computers have obviously changed the approach taken by auditors. Try to think of some of the opportunities and problems which computers might have created.
This issue will be discussed in the remainder of section 10.3.

10.3.1 *Microcomputers as audit tools*

Portable microcomputers can be as powerful as the desktop machines which are in everyday use. Many of the traditional packages such as spreadsheets and wordprocessing software can be used during audit fieldwork, although recent advances in programming and storage have created much more imaginative possibilities.

One consequence of the increasing use of networks is that systems are often designed so that data can be extracted by managers so that they can build models and conduct enquiries on their PCs using standard spreadsheet and database packages. These facilities can also be used by auditors to collect data, possibly without even having to visit the premises where it is stored.

Spreadsheet packages, which were amongst the earliest microcomputer applications, can be used in a number of ways. The auditor can use their statistical functions to increase the effectiveness of analytical review. Alternatively, although it is a rather trivial use of the technology, they can be used to record the results of audit testing. Apart from making the resulting audit files easier to review, the discs are cheaper than the equivalent paper files and are much easier to store.

Wordprocessing packages can also be used during audit fieldwork. The audit team can use these for correspondence, particularly in producing personalised letters to, say, debtors when requesting confirmation of balances. It is also relatively easy to maintain files of permanent information, which is of ongoing relevance to the audit, on disc. This can then be updated as and when required.

Expert systems provide an exciting means of assisting relatively junior staff to arrive at relatively complex decisions which accord with the firm's standards. An expert system is a computer program which has been developed to replicate the thought processes of a specialist in some field. An accounting firm could, for example, develop an expert system which decided upon the materiality of some item for disclosure purposes. This program could then be distributed throughout the firm. Its use would be twofold. First, the staff engaged in the audit fieldwork would be able to use this software for guidance if they are faced with a difficult materiality problem. Second, senior members of the firm could compare their own opinions in this area with those generated by the expert system. This should lead to a greater degree of consistency in such decisions.

CD-ROMs have several audit applications. These devices can store enormous quantities of data which can then be accessed by a computer equipped with a drive. An accounting firm can, for example, store the entire text of its audit manual, the SASs, FRSs and the Statements of Standard Accounting Practice on one CD. This can then be duplicated at extremely low cost and distributed in sufficient quantities to every office so that every audit team could have access to this information without having to carry large quantities of reference material in more conventional forms. Special software can locate the relevant sections appropriate to any problems which the audit team encounters.

10.3.2 *Problems for the auditor*

One of the most pressing problems created for the auditor by the computer is the need for specialist staff. The evaluation of general controls and the selection and implementation of CAATs require the services of a fully qualified computer professional. This is becoming increasingly necessary because of advances such as database technology which further complicate the systems used by companies. Accounting firms have responded to this challenge by creating computer audit departments staffed by auditors who have had systems training and computer specialists who have been trained as auditors.

New applications are being developed on an almost constant basis. Companies are becoming increasingly dependent upon communication and payment systems such as the Banks Automated Clearing System (BACS) and are beginning to realise the benefits of such innovations as electronic funds transfer at point of sale (EFTPOS). These could expose the company to increased control risks because of the involvement of third parties.

Electronic communications might have enormous implications for the nature of audit evidence. Invoices could, for example, be transmitted to the company by suppliers' computer systems. This would improve the efficiency with which such transactions were processed but would also reduce the quality of the evidence available for the auditor's inspection. Perhaps this problem could be overcome by using audit software which selected items for testing from the company's records. If there was no documentary evidence to support a sample item then the software could confirm the details automatically with the supplier's computer records.

In the long term, it has been suggested that the annual report might eventually be dispensed with. Companies could simply provide shareholders with access to the accounting records themselves. These could be interrogated and users could compile their own statements in whatever format best met their needs. This would change the role of the auditor to one of ensuring that the underlying accounting records did not contain material errors. The fact that these records could, in principle, be accessed by readers at almost any time could lead to much heavier use of embedded audit facilities.

10.4 Summary

Computers do not change the auditor's duties, but they can have an effect on the manner in which they are discharged. The auditor must examine the general controls within the system before placing any reliance upon the program-dependent application controls which are of more direct relevance to the truth and fairness of the financial statements. The nature of these general controls is affected by the type of computer system in operation.

The auditor may wish to make use of CAATs which can help in the collection of evidence from both compliance and substantive testing. Audit software and test data are used most frequently in practice, although there are other types.

Microcomputers can be useful tools for the auditor, providing a number of facilities from simple storage of working papers to the provision of advice from expert systems. These machines can be sufficiently portable for audit staff to take them to client companies' offices.

Computer systems are becoming increasingly sophisticated. Auditors will require sufficient expertise to handle the demands which these systems will impose. It may be, in the relatively distant future, that computers will even affect the manner in which accounting information is distributed. This could change the fundamental objective of the audit.

━━━━━━━━━━━━━━━ **REVIEW QUESTIONS** ━━━━━━━━━━━━━━━

1. To what extent should companies consult their auditors before acquiring or updating their computer systems? Consider the implications of such consultation for audit risk and independence.

2. The use of CAATs requires the active cooperation of the company's staff. This may mean that the company's management can learn a great deal about the general approach to the types of test conducted by the auditor, materiality levels, and so on. Describe the problems which this could create for the auditor.

3. If the auditor can reduce the time taken to complete the audit then the level of the audit fee will be reduced accordingly. Is it wise for accountants to invest in audit software packages and portable microcomputers?

4. The ICAEW's discussion paper *IT and the Future of the Audit* points out that the auditor can use CAATs to conduct very detailed substantive tests at relatively low cost. The amount of evidence collected in this manner could reduce the need for any investigation of internal control.

    The discussion paper argues that an audit based on substantive testing alone would be unacceptable to client companies because they would wish the auditor to advise them on the quality of the internal controls in their system. Discuss the merits of this argument, bearing in mind the objectives of an audit.

5. It is possible that traditional financial statements will be replaced by the interrogation of company accounting systems by shareholders using their own personal computer systems. Discuss the possible effects of this innovation on the role of the auditor.

━━━━━━━━━━━━━━━ **EXERCISES** ━━━━━━━━━━━━━━━

1. When the payroll system of DPE Ltd was first installed it was decided that the possibility of overpayments should be avoided by programming the system to produce a print-out of every employee whose wages exceeded £100 in any given week and everyone who claimed to have worked for more than forty-three hours.

Since then, the system has worked well although the parameters built into the exception report have not been updated. Inflation has pushed the minimum weekly wage up to well over £100 and most employees are encouraged to work sufficient overtime to claim at least forty-five hours. As a result, almost every worker is listed on both exception reports every week.

(a) How effective are the exception reports in these circumstances?
(b) Assuming that £400 and forty-eight hours were considered more realistic for the reporting thresholds, describe the controls which should surround the alteration of the program by the company's systems staff.
(c) Assuming that the new thresholds have been implemented and that the auditor wishes to rely upon the exception report as an internal control, suggest two ways in which the auditor could test its operation.

2. Mr Dickens is a partner in Quill, Penn and Co., a firm of accountants. The firm has recently been appointed as auditors of IT Ltd, a company which maintains its accounting records on a mainframe computer. This is Mr Dickens' first experience of auditing in a computer environment. None of his staff have a great deal of knowledge in this area either, although the manager in charge of the audit did take a one-year class entitled 'Introduction to Computers' whilst at university and also attended a training course in computer audit shortly after qualifying as an accountant.

Rather than appear old-fashioned, Mr Dickens has spent £4,000 on an audit software package. He then despatched his manager to IT Ltd with the tape, manual, and an instruction to 'go and check out their system!'. Shortly afterwards, he received a telephone call from IT's systems director. The following points were made:

(a) The company maintains its files on a database. The audit package purchased by Dickens is intended for use in a more traditional system where records are filed sequentially. The CAAT cannot be run unless the company spends a great deal of time converting its records to a different format.
(b) There was no need to waste money on a new piece of software. The query program in the company's database software can do everything that the audit manager wishes. One of the company's programmers can write the necessary instructions.
(c) The computer system is operating at almost full capacity. The company simply cannot spare a great deal of computer time for the auditor.

Answer the following questions:

(a) Discuss the wisdom of Quill, Penn and Co.'s decision to accept nomination for this audit. Should they have done so?
(b) How should the approach to the company's computer system have been planned?
(c) What problems could be created if the company converts its files before the CAAT is run?
(d) Should the company's programmer be permitted to produce the reports required by the auditor?
(e) If the use of a CAAT is an indispensable component of the audit, what action should the auditor take if access to the company's system is denied?

Further reading

This chapter was intended to provide a broad overview of some of the issues associated with computer auditing and to introduce the CAATs which will be applied in later chapters. Rather than provide specific references during the chapter itself, the following books and articles are recommended for further information.

Readers who are unfamiliar with the different types of computer hardware and software may find it helpful to consult a text which describes data processing within the context of management or information systems. See, for example, K.N. Bhaskar and R.J.W. Housden, *Accounting Information Systems and Data Processing*, Heinemann, 1985, and H.C. Lucas, *Information Systems Concepts for Management*, McGraw-Hill, 1990.

The following general texts on computer auditing are extremely helpful: A.D. Chambers and J.M. Court, *Computer Auditing*, Pitman, 1991; I. Douglas, *Computer Audit and Control Handbook*, IIA/Butterworth-Heinemann, 1995; B. Jenkins, *Audit Approach to Computers*, ICAEW, 1990, and D.A. Watne and P.B.B. Turney, *Auditing EDP Systems*, Prentice Hall, 1990.

Chambers and Court and Douglas both provide a concise coverage of computer auditing. Either would, therefore, be the most suitable book for someone who simply wished to develop some of the topics dealt with in this chapter. The other two books are much more detailed. Jenkins examines computer auditing from the perspective of practising computer auditors. The text is, however, clear and well written and does not require specialised knowledge of computer auditing. Watne and Turney provide a similar coverage to Jenkins, Perry and Cooke, although their text has been aimed more directly at the student readership. These books should, of course, be supplemented with the APC Auditing Guideline, *Auditing in a Computer Environment*, 1984.

Detailed coverage of the design of controls in computerised systems can be found in *Computer Control Guidelines*, CICA, 1986. Despite its practical bias, this text would be extremely useful to anyone who wished to explore the control issues raised by computers.

The manner in which microcomputers can be adapted for use by auditors is dealt with by D. Clark, 'The use of microcomputers by the auditor', in D. Kent, M. Sherer and S. Turley, *Current Issues in Auditing*, Harper and Row, 1985. There is also a very helpful discussion, including a case study and a description of the merits of several generalised audit packages for microcomputers in S.D. Jacobson and C. Wolfe, 'Auditing with your microcomputer', *Journal of Accountancy*, February 1990, pp. 70–80. A more detailed coverage can be obtained in *Application of Computer Assisted Audit Techniques Using Microcomputers*, published by the Canadian Institute of Chartered Accountants in 1994.

A research study into the development and uses of expert systems in accounting is contained in A. Edwards and N.A.D. Connell, *Expert Systems in Accounting*, Prentice Hall / ICAEW, 1989. Systems developed specifically for audit applications are described on pages 54–61.

A discussion paper published by the ICAEW entitled *IT and the Future of the Audit*, 1989, provides a stimulating introduction to the effects of increasingly complex and sophisticated computer systems on the audit.

Finally, the arguments underlying the replacement of traditional published accounts by providing interested parties with access to the company's computerised accounting records are discussed in more detail in K. Pratt, 'The end of the Annual Report? – an events data base alternative', *The Accountant's Magazine*, October 1987, pp. 45–9.

CHAPTER 11

Audit sampling

This chapter will consider the manner in which the auditor selects and evaluates samples of items for compliance and substantive testing purposes. This will concentrate on the integration of audit sampling into the audit risk model developed in earlier chapters. Despite the availability of sophisticated statistical techniques, this is an area where the auditor must apply a great deal of professional judgement.

Audit sampling is

> the application of a compliance or substantive procedure to less than 100 per cent of the items within an account balance or class of transactions to enable the auditor to obtain and evaluate evidence of some characteristic of the balance or class and to form or assist in forming a conclusion concerning that characteristic.[1]

In general, auditors must restrict compliance and substantive tests to samples of items. It would cost too much and take too long for tests to be conducted on every item in the financial statements. Furthermore, the auditor is not required to guarantee the truth and fairness of the financial statements, merely to apply 'reasonable skill and care' in forming an opinion on them. The only exceptions are those figures for which an acceptable means of testing the entire population exists, such as proof in total, or those cases where each item within a population is considered material in its own right, such as individual directors' emoluments.

By the time you have completed this chapter you should be able to:

- Describe the various parameters which arise in the context of sampling and explain how they are related.
- Explain how the quality of sample results might be improved by stratifying the population.
- Explain how judgement sampling differs from statistical sampling and describe the advantages and disadvantages of each.
- Describe some of the main methods of statistical sampling.

11.1 Sample parameters

The auditor must establish three parameters before a sample can be taken (see Figure 11.1). These factors are interrelated. Once the auditor has determined two of them then the third follows automatically. The auditor will usually determine the most appropriate levels of tolerable error and sampling risk and the sample size is derived from these.

11.1.1 *Tolerable error*

The tolerable error is the maximum amount of error which the auditor is prepared to accept in a population under examination and still accept that the audit procedure has achieved its desired objective. In substantive testing, the auditor will usually determine a monetary limit for the acceptable level of error. Thus, the auditor could wish to establish that the purchases figure has not been overstated by more than, say, £50,000.

If sampling risk remains constant then the sample size will fall as the tolerable error is increased. The tolerable error cannot, however, be a material amount. The auditor cannot claim that the financial statements give a true and fair view unless he is certain that the errors contained within them are not significant.

Turley and Cooper studied the auditing methodologies of twenty-one large accounting firms by means of interview and examination of the firms' documentation and manuals.[2] Table 11.1 shows the relationship they discovered between materiality for reporting and the tolerable error.

Grant Thornton, an international firm of accountants, distinguish between materiality for sampling and reporting purposes. The tolerable error for sampling is described as 'Touchstone'. This is based on a percentage of the higher of turnover and total assets. This percentage is taken from a table of rates which reduce as turnover or assets increase. The materiality level for reporting purposes is based upon another set of parameters which will usually give a figure which exceeds Touchstone.[3]

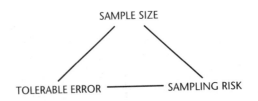

Figure 11.1 Sample parameters.

Table 11.1 Relationship between materiality for reporting and the tolerable error

Number of firms	Relationship between materiality for reporting and the tolerable error
9	Distinguish between materiality for testing and reporting purposes. While these decisions must be linked, the latter can only really be determined during the closing stages of the audit. In some cases, this distinction is put into effect in a slightly mechanical manner by estimating reporting materiality at the planning stage and reducing this by a percentage for the sake of prudence.
6	Make no explicit distinction between tolerable error and reporting materiality.
3	Suggest that materiality decisions should be taken for individual areas within the financial statements. None of these firms laid down any mechanical decision rules for doing so. (Such an approach could pose problems for firms using directional testing because the assurance obtained from corollary testing might be inadequate.)
3	Did not mention the relationship between testing and materiality for reporting.

Source: Turley and Cooper, 1991

11.1.2 *Quantifying tolerable error*

There are no agreed guidelines for the calculation of the most appropriate materiality level in testing. This could lead to disparities in the extent of testing carried out by different accounting firms. It would, however, be difficult to lay down any prescriptive guidance on this matter. A study by Leslie identified the following seven basic approaches from a review of the literature in this area and also from discussion with auditors in practice:

1. Five per cent to 10 per cent of income before tax.
2. A variable percentage of gross profit, with the percentage rate decreasing as gross profit increases.
3. Percentage of assets.
4. One per cent of equity.
5. One-half per cent of turnover.
6. The average of items (1) to (5).
7. A variable percentage of turnover. This approach is similar to Grant Thornton's.[4]

It would appear reasonable to suggest that, in general, the users of financial statements are likely to expect materiality decisions to be based upon net income. It is, however, possible that a simple percentage of profit would produce inconsistencies. If, for example, a large company had a poor year and generated a very small profit figure then the resulting materiality figure could be ridiculously low.

The consistency problem could be overcome by establishing a 'normal' income figure for the company and applying the percentage to that. This could, however, create further difficulties. It would be difficult to estimate the relevant figure for a company which had had a succession of poor years, or one whose profits had been growing over time but which had suffered a sudden dip in income.

The rates based upon assets, gross profit, turnover and equity are, in different ways, attempts to produce less volatile surrogates for a normal profit figure. If, for example, a company aims for a return on equity of 20 per cent, basis (4) above is equivalent to the 5 per cent of income referred to in (1). Equity is also likely to be a relatively stable figure over time. Again, this approach is fraught with problems. Two similarly sized companies may have different target returns because they are in different industries. This would render the adoption of a standard percentage of equity meaningless if it is intended to produce similar tolerable errors to those generated by the percentage of net income approach. Similar criticisms could be made of the other surrogate measures.[5]

It has been suggested that the auditor should communicate the level of tolerable error used during the audit to the users of the financial statements. At present, these figures are not published. It has been suggested that market forces could then regulate the relationship between the benefits of higher precision in reporting and the cost of its achievement. Furthermore, accounting firms would be able to compare their approaches and could, therefore, work towards a greater degree of consistency.[6]

Despite its apparent merits, this proposal would be difficult to implement. The auditor could be put at a disadvantage if the directors of a company had too great an insight into the materiality thresholds which were in force. It is common for matters to arise which are serious enough for the auditor to request a change to the financial statements, but are not quite important enough to warrant a qualification. The directors would be less inclined to yield to the auditor's arguments if they knew that he would not qualify over an issue. This information could also be used to support an accusation of negligence against the auditor. It could be argued that almost any figure chosen for the tolerable error was too high.

ACTIVITY

It would appear that firms tend to use quantitative measures to determine materiality for testing purposes. What problems might this create and how might these be overcome?

Materiality is defined in terms of the extent to which knowledge of the matter might affect the behaviour of users of the financial statements.[7]

This can mean that materiality has a qualitative dimension. Any tests which were structured entirely in terms of the monetary value of the amounts involved could lead to 'material' items being missed. A good example of this would be the audit of directors' salaries which may amount to only a very small proportion of profit or turnover but which tend to be of immense interest to the shareholders.

The only really effective way to overcome this problem is to take great care to identify areas where sampling may lead to an inadequate level of audit coverage and to test these in more detail – possibly even to the extent of abandoning sampling altogether and testing 100 per cent of the relevant populations.

11.1.3 *Tolerable error and compliance testing*

The auditor conducts compliance tests in order to establish whether specific controls identified during the review of internal controls have operated or not. The design of a sampling scheme still requires the definition of the level of tolerabie error. This raises the question of how the tolerable error should be defined. There are two main alternatives.

It could be argued that compliance deviations are equally significant regardless of their monetary value. This would suggest that tolerable error should be defined as a percentage of the total number of transactions. If the auditor was testing a control involving the comparison of purchase invoices with their supporting documents, he could attempt to ensure that this would appear to have been done in at least 95 per cent of all cases.

Alternatively, it could be argued that compliance deviations are more serious if they relate to large transactions. This would suggest that compliance testing ought to be biased towards high value items. Such an approach would lead to tolerable error being defined in monetary terms. The auditor could, for example, attempt to ensure that the maximum value of purchase invoices which had not been checked before being recorded was less than, say, £30,000.

Leslie suggests that the latter approach is superior.[8] He points out that the purpose of audit testing is to identify monetary errors in the accounting records. Compliance errors do not, in themselves, imply that there is anything wrong with the figures. They do, however, mean that the ability of a control to detect fraud or error is impaired. By concentrating on the higher value items, the auditor can ensure that the exposure created by any failure of the control has not led to irregularities in the recording of the more material transactions.

11.1.4 *Sampling risk*

Reliance on samples exposes the auditor to a certain amount of risk. This could be because the sample itself had been badly designed and was unrepresentative of the population from which it was drawn or it could be the result of chance. It would, therefore, be possible to conclude that the accounts give a true and fair view when they do not. Such an error could lead to the auditor being accused of negligence.

It would also be possible for the auditor to be misled into expressing an unnecessary qualification. This latter type of error could irritate the directors and lead to the auditor's replacement. Alternatively, the auditor may feel obliged to extend the sample size in order to confirm the initial findings. It could be difficult to recover the cost of this extra work from the company. The consequences of this type of error may be undesirable, but are unlikely to be as damaging as the incorrect expression of an unqualified report.

Sampling schemes can be designed so that the auditor can quantify, and therefore manage, both types of sampling risk. Unfortunately, this requires large samples. In practice, auditors concentrate on managing the risk of missing a material error and accept the possibility of the sample being over-sensitive.

It is important to differentiate between sampling and non-sampling risk. Assuming that the method of selecting sample items is unbiased, sampling risk is related to the number of items selected. It is the risk that the conclusions based on the sample would differ from those which would have been reached if the entire population had been examined. The auditor can always reduce sampling risk by increasing the size of the sample. Sampling risk can be eliminated altogether by testing every item in the population.

Non-sampling risk arises because of the possibility that the audit tests themselves will not be properly designed or conducted. If, for example, the auditor wished to test creditors' balances for completeness and did so by selecting a sample of the balances recorded in the creditors' ledger for detailed testing, then the test would be misspecified because it ignored the possibility of balances being omitted from the ledger. Similarly, if the audit of a complicated stock calculation was delegated to an inexperienced junior it is unlikely that the work will be done properly. Non-sampling risk can only be reduced by implementing stringent quality control procedures, such as those described in Chapter 3 of this text.

The relationship between sampling risk and sample size is not linear. It would be possible for the auditor to obtain 95 per cent assurance by testing a relatively small proportion of the population. A small increase in assurance could require a substantial increase in the number of items tested. This is best illustrated by the fact that a reduction from 5 per cent risk to no risk at all may require the auditor to increase the sample from, perhaps, 2 per cent of the population, depending on the nature of the items within it and the sampling approach adopted, to 100 per cent.

11.1.5 *Sampling risk and the risk-based audit*

Chapter 7 described the risk-based approach to auditing. This approach requires the quantification of the risks that material errors will be missed by each of the sources of audit evidence. This is not difficult to achieve in substantive testing because this figure is usually a residual after the other types of risk have been evaluated. It is, however, necessary to place a value on the other risks before achieving this objective.

In theory, there is no reason why the audit partner or manager could not simply make use of subjective judgement to arrive at an appropriate risk factor for each element of the audit. This would make the maximum possible use of the knowledge and experience gained during previous audits and collected during the planning stage of the current year. There would, however, be inconsistencies between individual audits. The factors chosen could prove difficult to defend if the audit opinion was ever challenged.

An alternative is to develop some heuristic decision rules to standardise the evaluation of risk throughout the firm. Thus, a list of indicators of inherent risk could be developed, and some weighting attached to each. The company could then be evaluated in the light of these weightings and a score calculated. Ranges of scores could then be listed which would be associated with specific levels of inherent risk. Thus, a score between 0 and 3 could be associated with an inherent risk factor of 50 per cent. A score between 3 and 6 could be assigned an inherent risk of 70 per cent and a higher rating with a 100 per cent audit risk.

Similar guidance could be created for control risk and analytical review risk. Internal controls could be evaluated in terms of both the potential effectiveness of the controls identified during the review of the system and also by the extent of compliance discovered during detailed testing. Thus, the auditor might decide to place a maximum reliance of, say, 80 per cent on a system of controls which appeared capable of preventing any material fraud or error and provided that these controls appeared to have operated in at least 95 per cent of all cases. Lower levels of reliance could be placed on control if there are higher levels of compliance deviations or if there are minor control weaknesses.

The level of reliance placed on analytical review would depend upon both the sophistication of the techniques applied and also the results obtained. The successful application of a statistical regression package could, for example, justify a reliance of, say, 40 per cent. A lower level of reliance could be placed on less rigorous techniques.

The restriction of possible levels of reliance to predetermined amounts which are applied in accordance with a standard set of criteria could lead to inappropriate decisions being taken. Different companies are subject to different types of risk. It is highly unlikely that a firm of accountants could devise a set of risk factors which was totally effective for all circumstances. This need not be a major problem provided that staff are properly trained in the use of the rules and are encouraged to make exceptions where necessary.

In practice, auditors do not think in terms of percentage rates of risk or assurance. It is simpler to attach 'R' factors to the various sources of evidence. These factors are calculated using simple algebra and are added together rather than being multiplied. If, for example, the auditor decides to define a total R

Table 11.2 R factors and the level of assurance

R factor	Level of assurance (%)
0.5	39
1.0	63
1.5	78
2.0	86
2.5	92
3.0	95

factor of 3 as being equivalent to 95 per cent certainty, the related subsidiary R factors would be as shown in Table 11.2.

If the auditor decided that an R of, say, 0.5 could be taken from the review of inherent risk, an R of 1.0 from internal control, an R of 0.5 from internal control and an R of 1.0 from detailed testing this would give a total R of 3. The risks associated with these factors are 61 per cent, 37 per cent, 61 per cent, and 37 per cent, giving a total risk of $0.61 \times 0.37 \times 0.61 \times 0.37 = 5$ per cent.

In theory, any number could be defined as being equivalent to any desired level of total assurance. If, however, the auditor is working to 95 per cent assurance then the number 3 has a certain amount of significance when some types of statistical sampling are employed. This will be demonstrated in section 11.5.1.

11.2 Stratification

Many of the populations which must be examined during an audit consist of mixtures of items which are differently sized, which have been recorded differently, or which display different risk characteristics. A company could, for example, use a single account to record all purchases. The transactions in this account could vary in value from a few pounds to many thousands. The larger items could have been recorded differently, perhaps because of different author-isation procedures for purchases worth more than a certain amount. The account could also contain import purchases. There is an increased possibility of error if invoices have to be translated from a foreign currency into sterling.

ACTIVITY

Why would it be dangerous to rely on the results of a sample taken from the population with the characteristics described in the previous paragraph? How might these be overcome without abandoning sampling altogether?

Table 11.3 Stratification of debtors' ledger

Size of balance (£)	Number of items	Value £m	%
100,000 +	2	0.3	18
10,000 – 99,999	15	0.9	52
1,000 – 9,999	112	0.4	24
0 – 999	200	0.1	6
		1.7	100

These differences could render a sample unrepresentative of the population as a whole. It would be possible for a sample of purchases to contain too few large, small or imported items. If one of these types of item was under-represented then the auditor could miss a material error. The solution is to stratify the population, that is separate it into various sub-sections and draw a sample from each stratum.

Sometimes stratification can be by size of item. A debtors' ledger could, for example, be analysed as shown in Table 11.3. In this case, the auditor might wish to concentrate on the two largest strata. The examination of the seventeen balances worth £10,000 or more would enable the auditor to test a total of 70 per cent of debtors by value. This would, however, ignore the smaller balances which are still worth 30 per cent of the total value of debtors. The auditor should then decide whether the value of these smaller balances is material and, if it is, should select an appropriate number for testing.

The testing of every item in a population or stratum is not a sampling technique. It may, however, be worthwhile in cases of high risk items which are relatively few in number.

The auditor will often have other criteria for stratification. In examining debtors' balances, the auditor might, for example, decide that overdue balances are more likely to be incorrect and may extend the sample to include some of these.

Items which have been included in a sample because they are of a high value or high risk are often referred to as 'key' items. The possible existence of such items should be considered at the planning stage of the audit, during the review of inherent risks, and also during analytical review. The auditor would ensure that these items have not led to a material misstatement by testing a representative sample of them or even by examining them all. This avoids the danger of key items being omitted from the sample because of chance.

11.3 Judgement versus statistical sampling

ACTIVITY

Which of the following statements would be the more satisfactory conclusion on an audit area? Why?

1   I have tested sixty purchase transactions. One error was discovered: a £500 item which had been incorrectly recorded as £750. In my opinion, purchases are not materially overstated.

2   I have tested thirty-six purchase transactions. On the basis of the sample results, I am 95 per cent certain that purchases have not been overstated by more than £120,000.

The second statement is preferable because it quantifies the relationship between sample size, tolerable error and sample risk. This suggests that the auditor would find it easier to defend the decision to accept that purchases had not been materially overstated. It also suggests that the sample size could be justified in a formal way. The first statement raises too many doubts. In particular, the reference to the error could be interpreted in a variety of ways: at one extreme it could be assumed that this is the only error in the population; alternatively it is possible that one item in sixty is overstated by 50 per cent – suggesting a major potential overstatement.

While the second approach is preferable, it relies heavily on the use of a rigorous statistical basis for the selection and evaluation of sample results.

There are two basic approaches which can be taken to sample selection and the evaluation of sample results. Under judgement sampling, the auditor measures the relationship between the various parameters described in 11.1 above in an intuitive manner. Sample items may be selected in a haphazard manner in an attempt to select a random cross-section. Alternatively, the auditor may deliberately bias the sample towards the key items, supplementing this by testing some items from the remainder of the population. This is effectively a stratified approach to sample selection. The number of items tested is based on subjective judgement.

Statistical sampling differs in that the sample parameters are quantified. The auditor can decide, for example, that the tolerable error in a population is £40,000 and that the reviews of inherent risk, internal control and analytical review suggest that an 84 per cent level of assurance is required from substantive testing. Once these factors have been inserted into a statistical sampling scheme, the sample size becomes fixed. The selection of specific items for detailed testing will also be done in accordance with the sampling scheme.

The advocates of judgement sampling would argue that it enables audit staff to apply their professional judgement to the selection of items. By concentrating on the items of highest risk, the audit team can reduce the overall probability that the records contain material errors. Another advantage is that judgement sampling does not require time to be spent on the design of elaborate sampling schemes or the identification of items in accordance with complicated selection procedures. This is in direct contrast to statistical sampling.

Judgement sampling does, however, have several drawbacks. It is impossible to justify the sample size if anyone claims that the extent of audit testing has been inadequate. The auditor may remedy this by selecting a very large sample. The cost of this additional testing could, however, outweigh the time saving associated with the simplicity of the approach and there is still no guarantee that the sample size will be accepted as adequate. A related problem is that it is impossible to evaluate the effects of any errors contained in the sample in an objective manner. This creates yet another opportunity for criticism of the auditor.

Judgement-based samples may also prove to be unrepresentative. It would be difficult for staff selecting straight from the population to ensure that each stratum had been sampled to an appropriate extent. Bias can also creep in because some items may appear less 'random' than others to the audit staff. Thus, the first few and last few items in the population may never be selected. Individual members of staff could be tempted to bias the sample towards those items which are easiest to test or may even select too few items. It would be difficult for the audit partner or manager to identify such behaviour during their reviews of the audit working papers.

Statistical sampling can overcome these problems, although this may be at the expense of creating others. The required sample size can be calculated by referring to the levels of tolerable error and sampling risk. This means that the auditor can tailor the sample size and justify the decision to test, say, 47 rather than 46 or 48 items in these terms. This has the advantage of minimising sample sizes and, therefore, reducing the overall cost of the audit. The time spent designing the sample and selecting items will rarely exceed the time saved by the smaller sample size. Grant Thornton suggest that statistical samples tend to be 40 per cent smaller than the corresponding non-statistical ones.[9] The statistical basis for the sample size and selection procedures also enable the auditor to extrapolate the results from the sample in order to project the likely level of error in the population itself.

Statistical sampling is just as subjective as judgement sampling. It could be argued that the auditor accepted too high a tolerable error or too much sampling risk. Such an accusation is relatively easy to make because these are matters for professional judgement which cannot be arrived at objectively. There is also an obvious temptation for audit managers or partners to choose relatively high materiality and risk levels in order to reduce the sample size. Another problem with statistical sampling is that the selection rules for identifying items for testing tend to be relatively mechanical. While some approaches tend to bias the sample towards high value items, it is impossible to introduce bias in favour of high risk items. This can, however, be overcome by stratification.

Despite its inherent subjectivity, statistical sampling does force the various decisions which have to be made to be arrived at during the planning stage of the audit. This means that the various sampling parameters will be determined by senior members of the audit staff, perhaps the partner and manager, and documented in the audit working papers. This means that much of the intuitive element of sample selection has been taken away from junior, relatively inexperienced, members of the audit team. It also means that the reasoning behind the choice of parameters will be recorded and can be referred to in case of complaint. On balance, the advantages of statistical sampling would appear to outweigh the disadvantages. It has been suggested that it would be easier for an auditor to defend an opinion which had been based upon a statistical approach.[10]

Despite the alleged advantages of statistical sampling, the survey conducted by Turley and Cooper suggests that firms have rather mixed views. A number of audit manuals make no clear statement about whether statistical or judgement sampling should be used. Many describe variations of both approaches and leave the final choice to the partners in charge of individual audits.[11] On a similar vein, the APC tried for many years to provide some guidance on sampling but did not produce a definitive Guideline. The APB has published a SAS on the subject.[12] This lays down some very broad guidance on the principles involved, but deliberately avoids such issues as the relative merits of statistical and judgement sampling and the quantification and measurement of the factors involved.

11.4 Evaluation of errors

A plan should be drawn up for every sample. This should describe the objectives of the audit procedures which are to be conducted and should also define the conditions which will constitute an error. These conditions are related to the objective of the audit test and could include incorrect amounts, the recording of items in the wrong accounting periods, or even incorrect classifications such as the treatment of capital expenditure as revenue.

11.4.1 *Qualitative evaluation of errors*

If the auditor is using a statistical sampling scheme it might be tempting to evaluate the errors discovered in a mechanical manner, applying the formulae associated with the particular method in use and concluding that the population as a whole is either acceptable or not depending upon the results. While such extrapolation of the results of errors is necessary, the auditor must also consider their underlying causes as well. Quite apart from their effect upon the specific objectives of the compliance or substantive tests which are being carried out, the discovery of certain types of error could also require the auditor to revise the estimates of inherent risk.

There are several qualitative aspects to the evaluation of errors. If, for example, an error appears to have been caused intentionally or deliberately concealed then the possibility of fraud should be considered. The auditor would have to investigate such suspicions. The auditor's assessment of the directors' motives would have to be altered if the error had been caused by management. Such a discovery could indicate deliberate manipulation of the records. If several of the errors discovered had occurred during the same period, the auditor would have to investigate the possibility of a breakdown in internal controls at that time, perhaps because of staff holidays or illness.

11.4.2 *Quantitative evaluation of errors*

The quantitative evaluation of errors will vary in accordance with the nature of the test and the sampling method in operation. In general, the auditor is trying to project the extent of the errors discovered during testing to estimate the overall level of errors in the population as a whole. This sub-section will concentrate on the evaluation of judgement samples. The quantitative evaluation of errors during statistical sampling will be dealt with in section 11.5.

If the auditor is conducting a compliance test then the proportion of compliance errors in the population as a whole will usually be assumed to be similar to that in the sample.

In substantive testing, the level of errors in the sample could be projected to establish the possible error in the population as a whole in a variety of ways. The auditor could calculate the average error per sample item and extrapolate from this by multiplying the number of items in the population by this amount (the 'difference' method). Alternatively, the total error could be divided by the value of the sample items. The value of the population as a whole could then be multiplied by this ratio (the 'ratio' method). Take the following example.

Suppose thirty items were selected from a population of 600 transactions. The sample items were worth a total of £500 and the population £12,000. These were tested and three overstatements worth a total of £15 were discovered. It could be assumed that the average error in each item of the population was £15/30 = £0.50. This would imply that the population as a whole could have been overstated by a total of 600 × £0.50 = £300. This approach assumes that errors do not vary in proportion to the size of items in the population.

Alternatively, the errors discovered during detailed testing amounted to £15/500 = 3 per cent of the value of the sample. This would imply that the population had been overstated by a total of £12,000 × 3 per cent = £360. This method is more suitable when it is suspected that larger items are likely to contain larger errors.

This approach to the evaluation of sample results is intuitively attractive. Unfortunately, it is unlikely to prove accurate because of the relatively small number of errors which tend to be discovered in samples. In addition, it is unusual for samples to represent a significant proportion of the population itself. If the auditor has deliberately biased the sample by the inclusion of key items, this could exaggerate the projected level of error. Some statistical techniques have been designed to cope with this problem.

11.4.3 *Isolation of errors*

Auditors often ignore certain errors in the sample because they appear to have been due to some isolated cause. It is argued that these isolated errors do not indicate any underlying errors in the remainder of the population and should, therefore, be omitted when projecting the sample results to the population as a whole. A survey of audit staff in the United States suggested that this logic is often applied during audits, with one respondent claiming that a rubber stamp marked 'Isolated Error – Do Not Project' would be used frequently during the review of audit files.[13]

The same paper went on to point out that this attitude was based on a misunderstanding of the assumptions inherent in the evaluation of sample results. It might be true that certain errors are unique and could not have occurred more than once in the population. It is even possible for the auditor to prove that the error has not been repeated by conducting an exhaustive test of the items which are similar to the one which was incorrect. This does not alter the fact that the purpose of a sample is to identify the proportion of items in the population which are in error. The fact that the items may have other qualitative attributes is, to a large extent, irrelevant. Furthermore, one could argue that every sample item is unique in one sense or another.

The only errors which should be ignored are those which are outside the population being sampled or those which are irrelevant to the purpose of the audit procedure. The transactions in the purchases account, for example, could consist largely of domestic purchases with a small number of high-value imports. If the auditor decided to stratify the transactions and test all of the imports and only a sample of the domestic items, it would be inappropriate to include any errors in the import items in the projection of errors in the domestic population. As another example, suppose that the auditor was examining the balances in the debtors' ledger and discovered that a sale had been posted to the wrong debtor's account; this error should not be included in the evaluation. The purpose of the test was to establish whether the total debtors' figure had been overstated. This misposting would not have led to an error in the total debtors' figure and is not, therefore, relevant to the audit procedure.[14]

11.4.4 *Unacceptable levels of error*

The auditor's evaluation of errors and their projection to the population as a whole may reveal that the tolerable error has been exceeded. There are three possible courses of action in these circumstances:

1 Request that the financial statements be corrected.
2 Qualify the audit report, or
3 Establish that the sample results were unrepresentative of the population as a whole.

It is unlikely that the first two options will be considered acceptable. The directors are unlikely to make an adjustment to the financial statements on the strength of a relatively small sample. Similarly, the auditor may have misgivings about taking the fairly drastic step of qualifying the audit opinion on the basis of a sample. Sampling schemes are usually designed in such a way as to ensure that the risk of accepting an incorrect figure is kept within acceptable limits. It was pointed out in 11.1.4 that controlling both this risk and the risk of the incorrect rejection of a correct figure requires much larger samples and is usually considered inefficient.

The third option may involve the extension of the sample to control for the possibility that there has been an unintentional bias towards incorrect items in the population. Alternatively, the company could be asked to conduct a detailed investigation of the transactions or balances in question in order to assure the auditor that there is not a major problem. If the directors refuse to accommodate the auditor then, regardless of the risk of the sample being invalid, the auditor will be forced to publish a qualified report.

11.5 Methods of statistical sampling

It is important that statistical sampling methods are theoretically sound and yet remain simple enough for audit staff to apply in practice, even if they are not mathematically minded. This is usually achieved by issuing staff with detailed sample evaluation forms which give step-by-step instructions on the projection of the errors discovered in the sample to the population as a whole. Broadly speaking, there are three approaches which can be taken to statistical sampling: variables sampling, attribute sampling, and Bayesian methods.

Variables sampling is similar to the hypothesis testing applied in many fields including finance and biological sciences. In auditing, it would involve the selection of a representative sample from an accounting population and testing the hypothesis that the amount has not been materially misstated. The auditor could, for example, conclude that he is 95 per cent certain that the correct balance on an account lies within the range £50,000 to £70,000. If the recorded balance lies within this range then the figure would be accepted.

The variables sampling approach is rarely the most efficient of those available to the auditor. It does not cope well with the relatively low error rates and the skewed populations which tend to be encountered. It is usually necessary to draw a relatively large sample in order to overcome these problems. As a general guide, the sample would have to be large enough to include 50 errors before this method could be considered reliable.

Attribute sampling is the most common of the approaches taken by the auditor. It is concerned with identifying the rate of occurrence of an event or a characteristic within a population. This makes it ideal for compliance testing where, for each item tested, the auditor will establish that either the control has worked or it has not. The fact that attribute sampling would appear to be restricted to situations where there are only 'yes' or 'no' answers would appear to restrict its usefulness when conducting substantive tests. This problem can, however, be easily overcome. Attribute sampling schemes tend to be based on the Poisson distribution. The mathematics behind this distribution make it ideally suited to those populations in which there is a relatively low incidence of error.

The Bayesian methods involve the combination of statistical and non-statistical evidence. The auditor uses a combination of experience of the company, knowledge gained during the initial stages of the audit and so on to estimate the distribution of errors in the population. A sample is then taken and the sample results are combined with the auditor's subjective prior distribution using Bayes' theorem. This results in a 'true' error rate for the population as a whole.[15] The approach is mathematically sound, but is limited in practice by the problems associated with developing the prior distribution.

The remainder of this chapter will concentrate on the various methods of attribute sampling which are used in practice.

11.5.1 *The statistical background to attribute sampling*

The purpose of this section is to provide a very brief outline of the statistical background to this sampling approach.[16] The Poisson distribution is used to calculate a series of RELIABILITY FACTORS (R factors). This results in a table which the auditor can use to estimate the true distribution provided the following conditions are met:

1   The population must be large.
2   The error rate in the population must be relatively low.

This table can be obtained from several texts on statistical techniques in auditing.[17] Some of the values contained in it are listed in Table 11.4. The R factors in this table are related to the tolerable error and sample size as follows:

$$R = \text{sample size} \times \text{tolerable error} \tag{11.1}$$

This relationship can be used in a number of ways. Suppose, for example, an auditor has conducted thirty compliance tests and has discovered no deviations; he could rearrange formula (11.1) as follows:

Table 11.4

Number of	Confidence levels		
sample errors	80%	90%	95%
0	1.61	2.31	3.00
1	3.00	3.89	4.75
2	4.28	5.33	6.30
3	5.52	6.69	7.76
4	6.73	8.00	9.16

$$\text{Tolerable error} = \frac{R}{\text{sample size}} \qquad \qquad (11.2)$$

By taking the various R factors from the row of the table which corresponds to 0 errors, he could then conclude the following:

- Either: 'I am 80 per cent confident that there are fewer than 5.4 per cent of compliance deviations in the population' (1.61 / 30 = 0.054).

- Or: 'I am 90 per cent confident that there are fewer than 7.7 per cent of compliance deviations in the population' (2.31 / 30 = 0.077).

- Or: 'I am 95 per cent confident that there are fewer than 10 per cent of compliance deviations in the population' (3.00 / 30 = 0.10).

Notice the relationship between the confidence level and the tolerable error. The auditor is forced to accept a less attractive tolerable error as the confidence level increases.

If the auditor had decided to accept a 95 per cent confidence level and had discovered one error while testing the sample of thirty items then the tolerable error would be increased to 4.75 / 30 = 15.8 per cent. If the auditor had already decided not to rely upon the control if the level of compliance errors exceeded, say, 12 per cent, it might be worth extending the sample. If, for the sake of argument, a further forty items were tested and one further error discovered then the auditor would have a total sample of seventy items which contained two errors. In these circumstances, the tolerable error would be 6.3 / 70 = 9 per cent. The auditor must decide whether this level of risk is acceptable.

This is a 'one tailed test'. In other words, the auditor is 95 per cent certain that the level of compliance errors in the population does not exceed this level. There is no means of calculating the risk that the level of error is lower. Thus, the initial finding from the sample of thirty items could have been misleading and the additional tests carried out unnecessary.

Table 11.5

Number of errors in sample	Tolerable error (%)	Extent of reliance on control
0	7	High
1	11	Medium
2	14	Medium
3	17	Medium
4	20	Medium

11.5.2 *Acceptance sampling*

Acceptance sampling is the application of the concepts introduced in the previous section to the decision to accept or reject a population. It is most commonly used in compliance testing. The auditor sets the tolerable error, selects a sample and decides whether or not the extent to which the control appears to have operated permits any reliance to be taken.

If, for example, the auditor is working to 95 per cent certainty, he may decide to place maximum reliance on an internal control if it has operated in at least 90 per cent of all cases and medium reliance if it has operated in at least 80 per cent. If forty-five sample items were to be selected, a table could be constructed using the table of R factors and formula (11.2) as shown in Table 11.5. Thus, the auditor will only place high reliance on this control if no errors are discovered. The auditor will place medium reliance if no more than four errors are encountered. If a larger number is found then no reliance can be taken unless the sample size is increased and the initial results are found to be misleading.

11.5.3 *Monetary unit sampling*

Acceptance sampling is of limited value if the auditor wishes to express a conclusion in monetary terms. There is little comfort in knowing that a relatively low proportion of the items in the population is incorrect unless it can be established that the monetary value of these errors is also immaterial. This problem can be remedied by the adoption of another form of attribute sampling known as Monetary Unit Sampling (MUS). This can be used in substantive testing and also in compliance testing when the auditor wishes to measure compliance deviations in monetary terms.

It has already been pointed out that attribute sampling can only be used in circumstances in which each item sampled is either correct or not. This would appear to make it invalid for the examination of populations which consist of items of different sizes and whose values could be partially misstated. This problem is, however, neatly overcome by defining each £1 unit in the population as a separate sampling unit. Thus, an invoice worth £500 contains 500 separate units each of which stands an equal chance of being selected. This invoice contains twice as many units as one which is worth £250 and is, therefore, twice as likely to be selected.

The tolerable error will usually be expressed in monetary terms. This figure will be converted into a fraction which can be inserted into formula (11.1) as follows:

$$\text{Tolerable error rate} = \frac{\text{tolerable monetary error}}{\text{population value}} \quad \textbf{(11.3)}$$

The sample size is then calculated by rearranging formula (11.1) to give:

$$\text{Sample size} = \frac{R}{\text{tolerable error}} \quad \textbf{(11.4)}$$

Formula (11.3) is then substituted for the tolerable error in the denominator of (11.4) to give the final formula:

$$\text{Sample size} = \frac{R \times \text{population value}}{\text{tolerable monetary error}} \quad \textbf{(11.5)}$$

The most effective means of selecting items for detailed testing is to establish a sampling interval and select £1 units in accordance with this fixed interval. The sampling interval is simply:

$$\text{Sampling interval} = \frac{\text{population value}}{\text{sample size}} \quad \textbf{(11.6)}$$

Once the auditor has calculated the sampling interval, it is a simple matter to start from a random starting point which must be between zero and the sampling interval and then work through the population, identifying every £1 unit which falls on the sampling interval thereafter. The random start is necessary in order to ensure that every £1 stands an equal chance of selection.

Let us take an example. An auditor wishes to be 95 per cent certain that the purchases figure of £1,000,000 has not been overstated by more than £60,000. This would imply that a sample of $(3 \times 1,000,000 / 60,000) = 50$ items must be selected. This, in turn, means that the sampling interval must be $(1,000,000 / 50) = £20,000$.

A random start between 0 and 20,000 has to be generated. Suppose that the random number function of a pocket calculator or a set of random number tables yielded 5,000 as the starting point. This means that the auditor must identify the 5,000th £1, the 25,000th, the 45,000th, and so on until all fifty items have been obtained.

The entries in the purchases account are as shown in Table 11.6. Thus, looking at the cumulative total, batch 2 contains every £1 from 2,001 to 6,000. This batch must, therefore, contain the first sample item. Batch 5 contains the 25,000th unit and so on.

In practice, the main accounting records tend to summarise the various

Table 11.6 Entries in the purchases account

Batch	Value (£)	Cumulative total (£)	Selected?
1	2,000	2,000	
2	4,000	6,000	yes
3	6,000	12,000	
4	11,000	23,000	
5	7,000	30,000	yes
6	8,000	38,000	
7	9,000	47,000	yes
etc.			

transactions by means of day books, batching and so on. This is apparent in the example where purchase invoices were batched before being recorded in the nominal ledger. It is, however, important for the auditor to identify individual invoices for detailed testing. This is achieved by sub-sampling.

The process of MUS sampling generates random numbers which can be used to identify specific items for detailed testing. This number is obtained by subtracting the lower bound of the cumulative range within which the sample item lies from the number of the £1 unit being sought. Thus, the 5,000th £1 is also the 3,000th £1 unit within Batch 2. This requires a further arithmetical exercise as shown in Table 11.7. Thus, invoice number 3461 contains the 3000th £1 unit in Batch 2, which corresponds to the 5,000th in the population as a whole. This invoice will now be tested for validity.

It can be seen that sample selection under MUS can be a long, tedious process. It could be argued that the cost of selecting individual items using this approach would outweigh the advantages of this approach. Two points must, however, be borne in mind. First, it is possible to check the arithmetic in the various records while selecting sample items. This means that very little additional time has to be spent on this task because the totals calculated by the company would have to be checked anyway. Second, very few companies keep their accounting records manually. There are many audit software packages which can extract MUS samples, thus automating the process.

Table 11.7 Batch 2 in the purchases account

Invoice number	Value (£)	Cumulative total (£)	Selected?
3456	900	900	
3457	400	1,300	
3458	300	1,600	
3459	800	2,400	
3460	500	2,900	
3461	700	3,600	yes
etc.			

If the auditor examined all fifty items and found no errors, then it would be legitimate to conclude that there is 95 per cent certainty that the purchases figure had not been overstated by £60,000.

If one error has been discovered, the R factor will increase to 4.75. This amount can then be fed into formula (11.5), along with the other sample parameters, and the formula rearranged to give the tolerable error implied by this discovery. This gives:

$$\text{Tolerable monetary error } = \frac{R \times \text{population value}}{\text{sample size}} \qquad \textbf{(11.7)}$$

$$\text{Tolerable monetary error } = \frac{4.75 \times 1,000,000}{50} = £95,000$$

The auditor must then decide whether the conclusion that there is 95 per cent certainty that the purchases figure has not been overstated by more than £95,000 is acceptable. If this potential error is too high then it may be necessary to extend the sample or request that the company conduct an investigation.

A similar approach would have been taken if two or more errors had been discovered. If, however, the number of errors discovered had been large then the assumptions inherent in the Poisson distribution would not be valid and an alternative approach to sampling would have to be adopted.

The evaluation described above is extremely conservative. It assumes that all of the item examined had been invalid. In practice, most errors result in the partial misstatement of an item. In such cases, it is possible to calculate a more accurate implied tolerable error by means of a process known as 'tainting'.

11.5.4 *Numerical sampling*

The MUS approach has the advantage of relating the likelihood of an item's selection to its value. This makes it ideal for testing populations to which a monetary value has been attached, most notably when conducting overstatement tests. Unfortunately, many populations have not been valued in this manner. If, for example, the auditor wished to sample from a population of despatch notes, these documents would state the quantities of goods sent to customers but would not have been priced.

If the auditor wishes to select a sample for understatement testing from a population which has not been valued, then it is possible to determine a sample size using similar logic to that applied to MUS sampling. This can then be divided into the number of items in the population in order to arrive at a numerical sampling interval and the sample items selected in the same systematic manner as under MUS. Thus, the auditor could examine every 200th despatch note starting from a random point. As with MUS, the errors encountered during a numerical sample should be evaluated, again making use of statistical tables.

11.6 Summary

Auditors rarely examine every item in a population. It is usually possible to obtain an adequate level of assurance from the examination of a sample of items. When designing and evaluating a sample, the auditor must ensure that a satisfactory relationship is maintained between the three interrelated factors of sample size, tolerable error and sampling risk. Under judgement sampling, these relationships must be measured in an intuitive manner. They can, however, be quantified if statistical sampling techniques are used.

There is no agreed method of calculating the most appropriate levels of tolerable error or sampling risk. Sample sizes increase as these factors are reduced and so the auditor must conduct a cost-benefit analysis in order to arrive at an appropriate balance.

The populations from which samples are drawn often consist of different types of item or balance. This can lead to the possibility that a random sample will contain too few items of a particular type and could prove misleading as a result. This problem can be overcome by separating populations into different strata and selecting a separate sample from each.

All errors discovered in the sample must be evaluated in order to determine the likely level of error in the population as a whole. The qualitative nature of the errors discovered are just as important as their quantitative effect on the sample results. There are very few circumstances in which it is acceptable to ignore an error on the grounds that it occurred in an item which was unusual or unrepresentative of the population as a whole.

If the sample results suggest that the level of error in the population as a whole is unacceptably high, the auditor will usually either extend the sample or will request that the company conducts an investigation into the population. If the sample results are confirmed then the directors will either have to correct the statements or have the audit report qualified.

There are several methods of statistical sampling. The most common approach is attribute sampling. This enables the auditor to estimate the level of error in the population as a whole with reasonable accuracy. A high incidence of errors in the population as a whole would tend to invalidate the assumptions upon which this approach is based. Monetary Unit Sampling is the most effective method of selecting from a population where the value of the items can be easily determined. It is unusual for the reciprocal populations used in tests of understatement to be valued in this way and so the auditor will often resort to a numerical sample in these circumstances.

———————————— **REVIEW QUESTIONS** ————————————

1. The importance of audit sampling is underlined by the fact that this was one of the first topics covered by an SAS. Despite this, the standard does little more than define terms and lay down broad guidance at a very high level

(e.g. that the effects of errors should be evaluated). Describe the difficulties which would have to be overcome by the APB if it were to produce a more detailed standard which would assist practising auditors in the design and evaluation of samples.

2. It would appear that the quantification of materiality levels and the residual risk which is to be dealt with by substantive testing are the most difficult aspects of designing a statistical sample. Given the developments of expert systems, discuss the benefits which could be obtained from automating these decisions. If such a system is feasible, should it be left to individual firms, or should the accountancy profession become involved in its development?

3. Leslie suggested that the company's audit committee should be involved in the setting of the tolerable error. Discuss the merits of this proposal.

4. Discuss the assertion that the failure to use statistical sampling techniques during an audit is indicative of negligence.

EXERCISES

1. You are an audit manager employed by the accounting firm of Misconceive and Bluff. You are discussing statistical sampling with the senior partner of the firm. He makes the following comments:

(a) 'Look at this conclusion on the audit of purchases. "I am 95 per cent certain that the purchases figure has not been overstated by more than £50,000." That was written by one of our most junior assistants. It proves that our audit approach is objective.'

(b) 'The tolerable error which you have suggested for the audit of XY Ltd is far too low. The time taken to select and test all those sample items would cost more than the client is prepared to pay. Rearrange the figures so that the sample size is brought down to a more sensible level.'

(c) 'What is all this nonsense about the "qualitative" nature of errors? Our approach is scientific, just look at those statistical tables! There is no need to worry about all of this subjective evaluation.'

You are required to respond to the partner's comments.

2. You are about to commence the audit of the wages figure produced by a computerised payroll system. Within the payroll files, each disbursement is flagged with a single digit which states the nature of the payment. The following code is in use:

    1 = Hourly paid staff (UK)
    2 = Salaried staff (UK)
    3 = Directors' salaries
    4 = Staff on long-term overseas secondment
    5 = Adjustments and unallocated payments

A computer print-out analyses the total cost:

$$£$$

```
1 = 800,000
2 = 450,000
3 =  98,000
4 = 170,000
5 =  50,000
```

The tolerable error is £60,000. You are required to suggest how the above population should be sampled.

3. You are auditing the transactions in the repairs account of MN Ltd. These were worth a total of £300,000. A MUS sample was extracted using a sampling interval of £50,000. One of the items in the sample was totally invalid; the recorded expense had not occurred.

Evaluate the effect of this error, assuming that you have been trying to obtain an R of 3 at the 95 per cent certainty level (you should refer to Table 11.4).

Assuming that this led to an error which was unacceptable, recalculate the figure on the basis that the audit partner had agreed to accept a sampling risk of 90 per cent.

References and further reading

1. IFAC Auditing Guideline 19, *Audit Sampling*, 1985, paragraph 3.
2. Turley, S. and Cooper, M., *Auditing in the United Kingdom*, ICAEW/Prentice Hall, 1991, pp. 72–4.
3. Grant Thornton, *Grant Thornton Audit Manual*, Longman, 1990, Chapter 7.
4. Leslie, D.A., *Materiality: The concept and its application to auditing*, CICA, 1985, Chapter 4.
5. Chapter 5 of Leslie, *op. cit.*, discusses the drawbacks of the various methods in greater depth.
6. This proposal is put forward in Chapter 6 of Leslie, *op. cit.*
7. APB, SAS 220, *Materiality and the Audit*, 1995.
8. See Chapter 8 of Leslie, *op. cit.*
9. Grant Thornton, *op. cit.*, p. 255.
10. See Randall, B. and Frishkoff, P., *An Examination of the Status of Probability Sampling in the Courts*, Touche Ross / University of Kansas Auditing Symposium III, 1976.
11. Turley, S. and Cooper, M., *op. cit.*, pp. 108 and 109.
12. APB, *Audit Sampling*, 1995.
13. A detailed description of the survey and the related normative model generated to demonstrate the fallacy of error isolation can be found in Burgstahler, D. and Jiambalvo, J., 'Sample error characteristics and projection of error to audit populations', *The Accounting Review*, April 1986, pp. 233–48. The same authors summarised their arguments in 'Isolation of errors in audit sampling', *The CPA Journal*, November 1986, pp. 66–70.
14. The qualitative aspect of this error could have some implications for the auditor. If there are a significant number of mispostings in the debtors' ledger, it could be argued that the company has failed to maintain proper accounting records as required by the Companies Act 1985.
15. The Bayesian approach to audit sampling is described in greater depth in Bailey,

A.D., *Statistical Auditing: Review, concepts, and problems*, Harcourt Brace Jovanovich, 1981, Chapter 11.

16. A more detailed description can be found in chapter 11 of Smith, T.M.F., *Statistical Sampling for Accountants*, Haymarket, 1976.

17. See, for example, Leslie, D.A., Teitlebaum, A.D., and Anderson, R.J., *Dollar Unit Sampling: A practical guide for auditors*, Pitman, 1980.

CHAPTER 12

The sales cycle

This chapter and the two which follow are intended to illustrate the application of the various concepts introduced throughout Chapters 7 to 11. It is intended to describe the manner in which the risk-based approach is applied to the various figures which appear in a company's profit and loss account and balance sheet.

This chapter will concentrate on the figures within the sales cycle. This commences when a customer places an order, continuing through the despatch of goods and the preparation and recording of an invoice until the customer's payment is received and recorded. The chapter will, therefore, concentrate upon the audit of the figures for sales and debtors.

In practice, turnover and debtors will be regarded as two separate audit areas. A great deal of the audit work on sales can be done during the year, whereas debtors cannot be tested until the year end. The audit of debtors may require an experienced member of the audit team, whereas the audit of sales can usually be entrusted to a relatively inexperienced junior. These areas are, however, closely connected. The concept of directional testing, introduced in Chapter 8, suggests that the auditor will test debtors for overstatement and income for under-statement. The work done on sales provides the auditor with assurance that the debtors figure is complete and the work done on debtors provides assurance that no invalid sales have been recorded. It is, therefore, important that the relation-ship between these two figures is borne in mind during the review of the working papers.

By the time you have completed this chapter you should be able to apply the risk-based approach to audit to:

- Credit sales
- Cash sales
- Trade debtors.

12.1 The general approach

This chapter and the two which follow will describe the audit of most of the major figures which are to be found in the financial statements. The audit of each figure will be described in roughly the same manner. The treatment will commence with a simple description of the accounting systems which are likely to be found in practice. The more common inherent risks associated with the figure will be discussed.

The section will describe the internal controls which are usually associated with the item, along with the compliance tests which can be used to ensure that they have operated. The section will then conclude with a description of the analytical review techniques and the detailed substantive tests which the auditor will usually apply.

The approaches described in these chapters are indicative of the approach which will be taken in practice. They would not, however, be followed mechanically in every audit. Every company's system will differ to some extent. The factors which affect management's motives will also vary. Thus, it could be necessary to conduct additional tests. Conversely, some of the tests described will prove to be redundant if the systems contain a high level of controls and the risk of misstatement is considered to be low.

12.2 Credit sales

The systems outlined below are typical of those used by many companies. There are, however, many different titles for the various records and documents described. It would also be possible to organise the records differently.

Figure 12.1 shows the documents which are likely to be found in the credit sales system.

12.2.1 *A typical accounting system*

Customers may place orders in writing, by telephone, or in person during a visit from one of the company's salesmen. The efforts of a number of departments will have to be coordinated in order to complete the sale and so it is usually worth recording every order on a standard order form. The order form will show the customer's name and address, details of the items ordered and the date. This form should be prenumbered so that the loss of any forms will be noticed. One copy of the order form will be attached to the customer's written order, if any, and filed in the sales department.

A second copy of the order form will go to the credit control department. This department will ensure that the customer is considered creditworthy. This may be done by reviewing the customer's payment history. Usually, customers are allowed pre-set credit limits. This is the maximum amount of credit that they are allowed to have outstanding at any time. If the company has not dealt with

Customer order

Detailed description of the type and
quantity of goods ordered.
Details of delivery instructions.
Statement of the customer's
understanding of the terms and
conditions of sale.

Despatch note

Multi-part, prenumbered document
prepared as:

1. Instruction/authorisation
   to release stock.
2. Notification to accounts
   department of the despatch
   so that an invoice can be raised.
3. Notification of delivery
   to customer.

Sales invoice

Multi-part, prenumbered document
prepared as:

1. Request for payment
   from customer.
2. Record of value of sale,
   both net of VAT and gross.

Credit note

If goods are returned, the credit
note is prepared as:

1. An acknowledgement to the
   customer of the return.
2. Notification to the accounts
   department to deduct the value
   of the return from the customer's
   balance.

Figure 12.1 The credit sales system.

the customer before then the credit control department may request a credit reference from one of the customer's existing suppliers or will purchase a credit rating from one of the organisations which compile records of poor payers.

If the customer's credit rating is acceptable then a third copy of the order form will be passed either to the production or to the stores department, depending on whether the goods are in stock. This copy will constitute an instruction to manufacture the goods or take them out of stock.

The goods will be taken to the despatch area where a despatch note will be prepared. This will state the name and address of the customer, the reference number of the order, the quantity and type of items despatched and the date. This document will also be prenumbered. Two copies will be sent with the goods, one to inform the customer of the source of the delivery and the other to be signed by the customer and returned as a receipt for the goods. A third copy should go to the sales office to advise them that the order has been filled and a fourth copy to the accounts department to advise them that the sale has occurred.

On receipt of the copy despatch note, the accounts department will prepare an invoice based upon the information on the despatch note. The quantities on the invoice will be priced in accordance with the company's official price list. This amount will be adjusted for any discount to which the customer is entitled and the relevant amount of Value Added Tax (VAT) will be added. The customer will receive a copy of the invoice and another will be kept by the accounts department where it will be used to update the accounting records.

The company may find that it is more convenient to work with manual records of goods ordered and despatched. Alternatively, the initial recording of the order could be on a computer file and, instead of paper documents, the program could request a credit rating before passing instructions to production or stores. Credit checking could be done automatically for existing customers by ensuring that their balances were not overdue and did not exceed their credit limits. The program could also check any computerised stock records so that the order could be routed to the appropriate department. A printer in the despatch area could then produce the despatch note once it had been confirmed that the goods were ready.

If the entire system has been computerised then the invoice would be prepared from the file of despatch records and would be priced, totalled and recorded without any further manual intervention. In less sophisticated systems, the invoice may have to be typed and the details keyed into the computer at this stage.

The information on the invoice is summarised in the sales day book. The total sales figure for the month is extracted from this book and debited to the debtors' account and credited to the sales and VAT accounts in the general ledger. The general ledger is the principal accounting record and is used to prepare the accounting statements. The total owed by debtors can be broken down into individual balances by referring to the debtors' ledger, which contains an account for each customer. Each entry in the sales day book will be entered into the individual debtors' accounts. In computerised systems, the sales day book will be replaced with a file of invoices processed during the period. This will, however, serve exactly the same function and be dealt with in the same manner as its manual equivalent. Once the invoice has been sent to the customer, the accounting system will simply keep track of the customer's balance, perhaps listing the balance on an exception report if the payment becomes overdue and possibly even printing out reminders. At the end of every month the system will also produce a detailed statement for each customer stating the amounts invoiced and received during the month. These statements are sent to the customers, enabling them to compare their records with those of the company and query any discrepancies which arise.

The customer's payment will usually come in the form of a cheque received by mail or in a credit transfer straight into the company's bank account. A list of receipts will be compiled and this will be used to update the cash book, the general ledger and the individual debtors' accounts.

There may be occasions when the customer's account will have to be adjusted. In most cases, this will be because the goods sent were defective. If the company agrees that the items sent were faulty then it will issue a credit note. One copy will be sent to the customer and another will be used to record the return of the goods in the general ledger and in the customer's account in the debtors' ledger.

It is also possible that the debtor will default on the debt. If the amount due becomes uncollectable then the balance should be written off.

12.2.2 *Inherent risk in the audit of credit sales*

The sales figure has an obvious relationship with profit. The directors may feel compelled to inflate turnover, often by recording sales made at the beginning of the following accounting period as if they had been made during the current year. Alternatively, income could be deferred by delaying the recording of sales to a later period in order to smooth profits from one year to the next.

The auditor may feel constrained by the lack of third party evidence to support the assertion that there has been no material omission of sales income. Virtually all of the documents and records which are available for inspection will have originated from within the company.

The company's staff could be tempted to suppress the recording of sales. If a sale is not entered in the ledgers then it will be relatively easy to intercept the debtor's payment. Even crossed cheques can be converted into cash by opening false bank accounts.

12.2.3 *Internal controls over credit sales*

Perhaps the most important control is to ensure that the staff who are involved in the preparation or recording of invoices do not also have access to receipts from debtors. This would create both the motive and the opportunity to understate sales. The actual extent of segregation of duties should be tested by observation and enquiry.

It is also important that records are kept of all despatches of goods. The company's security staff could be instructed to check all outgoing vehicles and ensure that their drivers have the necessary documents for any goods on board. It would be difficult to design a compliance test for this control. It would be possible to obtain some assurance by asking several people to explain the operation of the system without asking specific, closed questions about the paperwork and security arrangements. If their descriptions tended to agree, then the controls are probably operating in a satisfactory manner.

Further confirmation that all despatches are recorded can be obtained by matching despatch notes to orders. If a large number of orders appear to remain unfilled some time after their being placed then it is possible that goods have been sent to customers without the delivery having been recorded. The auditor should ask for evidence that such a review is conducted on a regular basis, preferably by someone who has no access to receipts.

The files of despatch notes should be checked regularly to ensure that they are not being lost or suppressed. The auditor should either request evidence that sequence checks are being conducted or reperform this control. Sequence checks could be conducted by the accounting software. The auditor may, therefore, have to use a CAAT to conduct a compliance test.

If sales invoices are prepared manually then the details should be checked by someone independent of the preparer. If the details are supposed to be checked manually, this could be compliance tested by a combination of reperformance and enquiry.

Finally, someone should check the posting of invoices to the sales day book and, thereafter, to the general ledger. This might be accomplished by means of a sequence check on recorded invoice numbers.

Any credit notes should be properly authorised before they are recorded. The auditor should review a sample of these to ensure that this is being done.

12.2.4 *Analytical review and credit sales*

Any unusual fluctuations in the sales figure from one year to the next should be investigated. The auditor should also review the monthly management accounts to identify months in which the recorded sales figures appear suspiciously low. The auditor should calculate the gross profit percentage. Any understatement of sales would depress this ratio unless the company was also failing to record purchases.

If the company keeps detailed statistics of units sold, the auditor should be able to relate these to selling prices and ensure that this provides a reasonable approximation of the recorded turnover figure. The validity of this test will be enhanced if the unit sales are calculated outside the accounts department.

12.2.5 *Substantive testing of credit sales*

The first, and most difficult, step is to identify a population which contains every potential sale. Preferably, this should consist of items which have been created at the earliest possible stage in the sales cycle and there should be a low risk of omissions. A file of invoices would, therefore, be unacceptable on both counts because the invoice is prepared late in the cycle and because there is a possibility that an invoice might not be prepared in respect of every sale. A file of written orders placed by customers is produced early but could be incomplete because of the possibility of telephone orders and also because there is no way to ensure that none of the orders have been removed from the file.

A sample could be drawn from a number of possible populations. The auditor could trace a sample of goods purchased to their subsequent sale. This would be an ideal starting point in, say, a vehicle dealership where every purchase can be identified by a chassis or registration number. If the auditor is satisfied that the sales staff prepare a prenumbered order form every time an order is placed then a sample of orders can be taken. In the absence of detailed stock records or prenumbered order forms, the auditor might start with a file of prenumbered despatch notes.

If statistical sampling is being used, the auditor may have to resort to the numerical approach. Orders and despatch notes are unlikely to have been valued and so monetary unit sampling will not be possible.

Having selected a sample of potential sales, the auditor must then follow each item through to the sales account in the nominal ledger. The documents examined at each stage will have been prepared by the company's staff and so the auditor will wish to corroborate them against each other in order to enhance the overall quality of the evidence obtained.

The auditor should obtain the following for each item selected:

- The customer's order.
- The despatch note.
- The copy invoice.

The most important of these is the invoice because this is posted to the general ledger. The details on it should be checked against the other documents. The auditor should also check the pricing, discount and arithmetic. Prices should be compared with the company's official prices list, preferably a copy obtained for audit purposes from the sales director. Discounts should be checked against the customer's file or the official discount list.

Once the auditor has done as much as possible to check that the invoice is correct, its value should be traced to the sales day book or a print-out summarising sales. The total of this record should be checked to ensure that the selected invoice is included and then posted to the sales account in the general ledger. The auditor should ensure that the liability in respect of VAT on each sale has. been properly recorded by checking the calculation of the tax on the copy invoice and posting it to the sales day book and, subsequently, to the VAT account in the general ledger.

The despatch records for the final few days of the year should be reviewed for any major deliveries. This is to ensure that sales have not been deliberately understated by a deliberate delay in the recording of sales. Any major despatches should be traced to their related invoices and posted to the sales account, making sure that they have been recorded in the correct period. This is known as a 'cut-off' test.

If recorded returns of goods are material then the auditor should select a sample, preferably using monetary unit sampling. These should be tested for validity by examining any correspondence to support the return and checking that the return has been authorised by an appropriate person.

ACTIVITY

Read through the selection of schedules from the sales section of an audit file shown in Figure 12.2. Try to relate these back to the material in section 12.2.

12.3 Cash sales

The audit of cash sales can differ from the audit of credit sales in a number of ways. The auditor may find it relatively difficult to collect sufficient evidence, partly because of the nature of the system and partly because of the higher inherent risk.

12.3.1 *A typical accounting system*

Cash sales usually arise in the context of retail organisations. There tends to be very little documentary evidence to support the recording of the transaction. Supermarket customers do not, for example, complete order forms. In most cases, sales staff record sales using tills. These machines print out two copies of every entry made by the staff, one of which is given to the customer as a receipt and the other is wound on to a spool within the till for subsequent checking.

At the start of every day, till operators are given a float of coins and low denomination notes for change. Every time a sale is made, the amount of cash taken is recorded by the till. During the day, the shop manager or a checkout supervisor will collect, and sign for, customers' cheques and large accumulations of cash. This reduces the risk of robbery and ensures that tills do not become over-full. At the end of the day, till operators will lodge the cash remaining in their tills and their till rolls with the shop manager. It should be possible to reconcile the day's takings as follows:

	float at start of day
+	takings according to till
=	cash collected during day and submitted after closing

The manager will check these reconciliations. Any excessive differences will be investigated. The day's takings will then be summarised and recorded in the cash book for subsequent posting to the general ledger and the takings themselves banked.

12.3.2 *Inherent risk in the audit of cash sales*

The fact that the company's income is in the form of cash makes it a relatively tempting target for fraud. There will also be large numbers of staff involved in the collection of cash from customers, thus reducing the opportunity for tight control over individual till operators.

The recording of cash income is also difficult to test because of the poor quality of the documentary evidence. If a till operator sold an item costing £5 but keyed only £4 on the till then the £1 difference could be misappropriated without the loss being discovered.

Client	Ritter PLC		Schedule	50/1
Year end	31/12/95		Prepared by	JAD 12/2/96
Area	Sales		Reviewed by	MGR 16/2/96
			Reviewed by	PIR 27/2/96

Client	Ritter PLC		Schedule	50/2
Year end	31/12/95		Prepared by	JAD 12/2/96
Area	Sales		Reviewed by	MGR 16/2/96
			Reviewed by	PIR 27/2/96

Sales – Lead schedule

The figure for sales comprises:

	1995 £000	1994 £000	Change
10200 Credit Sales	9,826	8,324	+18%
10201 Export Sales	1,354	1,543	−12%
10202 Returns Inward	(427)	(276)	+55%
per draft p & l	10,753	9,591	

- Domestic sales have risen by an amount in excess of the general rate of inflation for the year.

- Export sales have fallen dramatically because of the strengthening of the £ sterling against the DM and US $.

- Returns inward have increased because of problems encountered with quality control.

Conclusion

On the basis of the work described on schedules 50/2 – 50/37, I am 95% certain that the figure for sales has not been understated by more than £60,000.

Work done

Inherent risks were evaluated by MGR at the planning stage of the audit (see sch. 6/1-4). Reliance of 20% was placed on the review of inherent risk.

The systems notes were updated by means of a walk-through test and the standard ICQ completed (50/3). The system is basically sound and reliance of 50% has been placed on internal control. Compliance tests are described on sch. 50/4-5.

Most sales are of a standard material which is sold by weight. The statistics compiled by the shipping office were used to estimate the turnover figure for the year (see sch. 50/8). Reliance of 30% was placed on analytical review.

It was necessary to test 47 domestic sales and 7 exports in order to obtain 82% reliance from detailed substantive testing. (see sch. 50/9-20)

80% x 50% x 70% x 82% = 5%

Client	Ritter PLC		Schedule	50/3
Year end	31/12/95		Prepared by	JAD 14/7/95
ICQ for SALES			Reviewed by	MGR 18/8/95
			Reviewed by	PIR 27/2/95

Client	Ritter PLC		Schedule	50/4
Year end	31/12/95		Prepared by	JAD 12/2/96
Area	Sales		Reviewed by	MGR 16/2/96
			Reviewed by	PIR 27/2/96

		yes/no/n.a.	Ref
(1)	Are staff responsible for the creation or recording of sales invoices independent of those who handle receipts from debtors?	NO	SYS 8
(2)	Are despatch records prepared for all sales goods and services?	YES	–"–
(3)	Does an independent official review the despatch records on a regular basis to ensure that an invoice has been raised for each?	YES	–"–
(4)	is there a file of unfilled customer orders?	YES	–"–
	Is this reviewed regularly by an independent official?	YES	–"–
(5)	Are sales invoices properly controlled and accounted for? (e.g. by means of sequence checks on pre-printed serial numbers)	YES	–"–
(6)	Are sales invoices checked prior to despatch for: – Quantities – Pricing – Arithmetic	YES	–"–
	By someone independent of those who handle receipts?	NO	
(7)	Is the sales day book checked to ensure that all sales are recorded?	YES	–"–
(8)	Are the additions in the sales day book checked to ensure that the correct totals are posted to the nominal ledger?	YES	–"–

Evaluation of ICQ and compliance tests

(1) G Hamilton is responsible for the preparation of invoices and handles incoming cheques. This is not, however, a real problem because all mail is opened by two senior managers. A cheque register is maintained. Details on the cheque register are posted to the bank statement at the end of every month. Thus, G Hamilton would be unable to conceal the theft of a cheque by the suppression or alteration of an invoice.

The operation of the register and the regular posting were checked by the inspection of the register and scrutiny of the chief accountant's initials to show that the comparison was being made.

(2) The creation of despatch records was checked by enquiry of the staff responsible for despatch and the security staff who inspect delivery notes before permitting vehicles to leave the factory. The inspection of documents was observed on several occasions during the audit.

(6) There is no documentary evidence of the checking of invoices. This control was checked by reperformance. All of the invoices selected for detailed testing were cast, compared with their related orders and delivery notes and were checked against price lists. No compliance errors were discovered.

(7 & 8) The system is computerised. There is no sales day book as such and there is no detailed print out of transactions. The program is supposed to conduct a sequence check on all invoice numbers (invoices are prepared manually and input in batches) and produces a total which is automatically posted to the sales account. Our standard audit package was used to conduct an independent sequence check and to test the total of the invoices.

Figure 12.2 Schedules from the sales section of an audit file.

Client	Ritter PLC		Schedule	50/8
Year end	31/12/95		Prepared by	JAD 12/2/96
Area	Sales		Reviewed by	MGR 16/2/96
			Reviewed by	PIR 27/2/96

Analytical review

Tonnage shipped during the year according to despatch records:

January	12,465
February	13,571
-	-
-	-
-	-
December	11,098
	155,844

Selling price per tonne = £72.00

155,844 x 72.00 = £11,220,768

Gross sales (before returns inward) £11,180,985*

Difference = £39,783 (not material)

* All sales (including those to export customers) are invoiced in sterling

Client	Ritter PLC		Schedule	50/10
Year end	31/12/95		Prepared by	JAD 12/2/96
Area	Sales		Reviewed by	MGR 16/2/96
			Reviewed by	PIR 27/2/96

Sales - Detailed tests

(1) Selected 47 despatch notes from domestic sales and 6 from exports by numerical sampling.

(2) Obtained the related invoices for each despatch note selected.

(3) Checked the quantities and descriptions of the goods on the invoice against those on the despatch notes. Checked pricing and arithmetic.

(4) Checked calculation of VAT on each invoice.

(5) Posted net value and VAT from each selected invoice to relevant batch. Batch totals checked.

(6) Posted batch totals to credit sides of sales and VAT.

(7) Checked cut-off by reviewing year end despatch records for major despatches. (The last despatch note no. was recorded during the stock count.) No major despatches occurred during the final ten days of the year.

Results

One minor error discovered. This was evaluated (see sch. 50/xx). The extrapolated error was not material.

Figure 12.2 continued

Client	Ritter PLC		Schedule	50/9
Year end	31/12/95		Prepared by	JAD 12/2/96
Audit programme			Reviewed by	MGR 16/2/96
SALES			Reviewed by	PIR 27/2/96

		Work done by	Ref.
(1)	Select, from the most appropriate records, a sample of <u>potential</u> sales.	JAD	50/10-20
(2)	Trace the related copy sales invoice for every item selected at (1).	JAD	50/10-20
(3)	Test the sales invoice as follows: Quantity - trace order and despatch note Pricing - see official price list Discount - see official list or customer file Arithmetic	JAD	50/10-20
(4)	Post the sales invoice to the sales day book (or equivalent)	JAD	50/10-20
(5)	Cast the sales day book	JAD	50/10-20
(6)	Post the sales day book total to the sales account	JAD	50/10-20
(7)	Check the VAT on each sale selected at (1) and post the amount to the credit of the VAT account	JAD	50/10-20
(8)	Compare major despatches recorded during the last few years with their related copy invoices. Ensure that these sales have been recorded in the correct accounting period.	JAD	50/10-20

Client	Ritter PLC		Schedule	50/11
Year end	31/12/95		Prepared by	JAD 12/2/96
Area	Sales		Reviewed by	MGR 16/2/96
			Reviewed by	

Detailed tests

ITEM NO.	DESPATCH NOTE NO.	DATE	INVOICE NO.	AMOUNT	CHECKED DETAILS	CHECKED PRICING	CHECKED ARITHMETIC	CHECKED VAT	POSTED TO BATCH	POSTED BATCH CH
1	34598	24/1	708324		√	√	√	√	√	√
2	35586	8/2	717900		√	√	√	√	√	√
3	36573	19/2	728498		√	√	A	√	√	√
4	37536	2/3	B		N/A	N/A	N/A	N/A	N/A	N/A
5	38549	16/3	747835		√	√	√	√	√	√
ETC										

Client	Ritter PLC		Schedule	50/15
Year end	31/12/95		Prepared by	JAD 12/2/96
Area	Sales		Reviewed by	MGR 16/2/96
			Reviewed by	

A These goods were sold at cost price to a potential customer who wanted to compare the quality of the company's product with that of a competitor. The memo from the sales director agreeing to this price was inspected.

B This despatch was of poor quality goods being returned to their supplier. The correspondence with the supplier was reviewed to ensure that the treatment of the despatch was valid.

12.3.3 *Internal control over cash sales*

The company's management will be well aware of the possibility of staff fraud and should have reacted by implementing an effective system of controls. The possibility of incorrect entries via the till's keyboard can be remedied by asking customers to check their receipts before leaving the till. Tills are often fitted with a second display which is clearly visible to the customer. Many stores are also equipping their tills with barcode readers which identify the customer's purchases by reading a symbol printed on the packets by their manufacturers. A rather draconian, but nevertheless common, control is the requirement that staff lock their personal belongings in a room to which they have no access during the working day. Till operators may then be asked to turn out their pockets at any time and any cash found in their possession is assumed to have been stolen. The auditor can only check the operation of these controls by enquiry and observation.

The daily reconciliation of takings also acts as a control. The auditor should review a sample of these to ensure that they are being done regularly and that any abnormal discrepancies discovered were actually dealt with. The company could also keep records of the amounts taken by each operator. Anyone whose takings were consistently lower than average should be observed more closely.

12.3.4 *Analytical review of cash sales*

The auditor should examine trends in annual and monthly sales, comparing them with competitors and any relevant indices. The gross profit percentage should be examined and any sudden changes investigated, although a decrease could be due to changes in pricing policy or because of an increase in 'shrinkage' or shoplifting.

12.3.5 *Substantive testing of cash sales*

The auditor will be forced to rely upon the till rolls as a starting point. A sample of till rolls should be selected, perhaps by selecting dates from throughout the year on a random basis and then making a further random selection of individual till operators on each chosen date. The figure for the day's takings should then be traced to the sales account through the daily summary prepared by the shop manager.

The auditor should review the shop manager's summary of differences. The results of any investigations should be studied and the possibility of significant losses because of fraud considered.

12.4 Trade debtors

The auditor will wish to ensure that debtors have not been materially overstated, either by the recording of balances which do not exist or by a failure to write off bad debts.

12.4.1 *Inherent risk in the audit of debtors*

The users of the financial statements will usually be interested in the company's solvency, as measured by the relationship between current assets and liabilities. Thus, even a relatively minor overstatement of debtors could be deemed material because of its effect on the liquidity ratios.

The fact that most of the company's cash receipts come from debtors makes this a potentially lucrative target for fraud. The auditor must also ensure that an adequate provision has been made for bad debts. This can be difficult because the provision is based upon forecast information which may be difficult to check.

12.4.2 *Internal control over debtors*

It is important to ensure that the staff who are involved in the recording of debtors do not have a motive to overstate the balances. Staff who maintain the debtors' ledger should not also have access to customers' payments. A member of staff who was responsible for both activities could steal cheques and manipulate the debtors' balances to conceal the theft.

The fact that debtors are provided with monthly statements would appear to prevent the possibility of fraud in this area. It is, however, possible to conceal the theft of a debtor's payment by means of the quaintly titled process of 'teeming and lading'. This works as shown in Table 12.1. This process would continue until the clerk is caught or returns the £100 to the company.

It is very difficult to detect teeming and lading once it is in operation. It must be prevented by proper segregation of duties. The staff who maintain the debtors' ledger should have no access to debtors' cheques. This could, of course, be difficult because the debtors' ledger staff must be aware of the amounts received from debtors in order to update their accounts.

All incoming mail should be opened by two members of staff, at least one of whom should hold a reasonably senior position. A list of all cheques received should be compiled and copies of this can be circulated to the cashier and

Table 12.1 Teeming and lading

Time	Action undertaken
Month 1	Customer A pays £100 at the end of the month. This payment is intercepted by a dishonest clerk. Customer A's statement would not include the cheque, but this would be of little concern because the payment could have been delayed in the post.
Month 2	Company B pays £100 at the end of the month. This payment is deliberately misposted to A's account. A's statement will now show the correct balance. B will not be concerned about the omitted payment because it was sent at the end of the month.
Month 3	C pays £100. This is misposted to B's account.

debtors' ledger staff. The list can be used to maintain the cash book and the debtors' ledger. The bank lodgements recorded in the bank statements can also be checked against this list in order to ensure that cheques are not being intercepted in other ways. The auditor could check the operation of this control by reviewing the register to make sure that it is in regular use and also that there is evidence that its contents are compared with the bank statements every month.

If the accounting records are maintained on a computer then the software will almost certainly update both the debtors' account in the general ledger and also the debtors' ledger at the same time. In manual systems, the general ledger and the debtors' ledger will often be prepared by different departments. This means that there are usually two independent records of the total owed by debtors. These totals should be compared every month, any differences implying an error in either one or both of the records. This control can be compliance tested by comparing the totals generated by each of the records as at the end of every month during the year.

The debtors' ledger staff should not be permitted to deal with customers' queries about their statements. Most companies find it worth employing a credit controller to monitor overdue balances and press slow-paying customers. This person will have access to the debtors' records but will have no responsibility for updating them. The credit controller will not, therefore, have a vested interest in the concealment of fraudulent errors in the debtors' ledger and can be trusted to deal with possible misstatements in an honest manner.

Staff will be less likely to resort to teeming and lading if their duties are changed on a reasonably frequent basis. This would interrupt the process of misposting and would reveal the fraud. This could, however, be counter-productive. Constant shuffling of duties could affect staff morale. The fact that staff will be unfamiliar with their new jobs could lead to mistakes. On a smaller scale, a similar effect can be obtained by requiring staff to take their full annual holiday entitlement.

Fraud is not the only possible problem. The auditor will wish to ensure that the valuation of debtors is not affected by the inclusion of balances which are uncollectable. Many of the controls which will be relied upon in this area will be relatively expensive to implement. Fortunately for the auditor, management may find these controls cost-effective for reasons other than ensuring that the debtors figure in the balance sheet is correct.

The auditor would start by checking the company's procedures for authorising trade credit facilities. It is of little concern to the auditor that such precautions can reduce the incidence of bad debts. The financial statements will still show a true and fair view provided that the bad debts are written off and shown as an expense in the profit and loss account. The fact that the debtors are regarded as creditworthy is, however, one step towards ensuring that the balances shown in the debtors' ledger at the year end are collectable.

The auditor should ensure that the credit checking system is operating properly by selecting a sample of debtors and ensuring that their balances do not exceed their predetermined credit limits or that, in the case of new customers, an acceptable credit reference has been obtained. A CAAT might be a useful means of comparing balances with their limits or of identifying a sample of new customers.

The auditor should also examine the operation of the credit control procedures. The company may chase slow payers in order to manage their working capital more effectively. This process would also be of interest to the auditor because overdue balances would be more likely to default after the year end. If the company is identifying such customers on a regular basis and taking action to ascertain their intentions then it is unlikely that any worthless balances will be left in the financial statements.

The auditor could check that this process is working effectively by examining the credit controller's correspondence files in order to see whether overdue balances are being followed up. This could be supplemented by reviewing an aged analysis of debtors and asking for explanations of any large amounts which are long overdue. Finally, a CAAT could be used to identify those balances which are overdue and the credit controller asked to explain why they are still considered recoverable.

12.4.3 *Analytical review of debtors*

The rate at which debtors are settling their balances provides the auditor with an insight into the risk of bad debt and also of the possibility of significant overstatement due to fraud. If the average time taken to settle a balance appears to be increasing then the auditor may suspect that uncollectable balances have not been written off.

The rate at which debts are settled can be measured by the debtors' turnover ratio:

$$\frac{\text{trade debtors}}{\text{credit sales}} \times 365$$

If, for example, this has crept up from forty-five days to sixty then the auditor would become suspicious of the possibility of unadjusted bad debts.

Alternatively, the auditor could examine an aged analysis of debts or a list of long overdue balances. Rather than rely upon the company's figures, it would be better for the auditor to prepare an independent analysis using audit software.

A decrease in the rate of turnover does not necessarily imply that the risk of bad debts has increased. The company could have decided to allow more attractive credit terms to increase sales. Some large companies are notoriously slow payers. Their suppliers are often afraid of losing their custom and are unwilling to demand prompt payment.

The provision for bad debts can also be tested by examining the company's past experience of default. Actual bad debts written off should be calculated as a percentage of credit sales. The provision for bad debts in relation to recorded debtors should be roughly in line with this proportion.

12.4.4 *Substantive testing of debtors*

Debtors are tested largely by means of direct confirmation. A sample of balances is selected at a certain point in time, preferably the year end, and the debtors are contacted and asked to confirm the amounts owed. The selection of balances is usually from the debtors' ledger, having first made sure that the total of the balances on this agrees with the balance on the debtors' account in the general ledger. Monetary unit sampling provides the most appropriate sample because it automatically stratifies the population according to size. The auditor could, however, wish to stratify the debtors in other ways first, perhaps dealing with overseas debtors or amounts due from members of the same group of companies separately.

Once the debtors have been identified, the auditor will then write to each one, stating the amount owed according to the company's records and asking for either positive or negative confirmation of this balance. Positive requests ask the debtor to reply to the auditor either stating that the balance on the letter is the same as that shown in the debtor's records or that a different amount is shown. In negative requests, the auditor writes stating the amount and also that it will be assumed that the debtor agrees with the balance shown unless a response is received to the contrary. The assumption inherent in negative requests is somewhat difficult to defend because of the poor response rates received in respect of positive requests. In general, an auditor would be pleasantly surprised if more than 30–35 per cent of debtors replied to such a request.[1]

The auditor should use positive requests unless the review of inherent and control risks and the analytical review suggest that there is very little risk of material error. In this case, it might be worth risking the use of negative requests.

Many of the debtors who reply to the auditor's letter will claim that the company's balance is overstated. This is usually because of timing differences between the supplier's and customer's records. The debtor will record payments before the cheques have actually been received by the company. The company will record sales whenever the goods are despatched whereas the debtor will wait until the goods have been received and invoiced. The auditor must test the validity of these timing differences as shown in Table 12.2.

The auditor would have to ensure that the £3,500 difference between the company's records and those of the debtor is valid. The date on which the cheque for £1,500 was received and banked would be obtained from the list prepared by the manager who opens the mail and by referring to the bank statements. This date should fall after the confirmation date. Any excessive delay in the recording of the receipt could indicate teeming and lading and should be investigated. The auditor should also make sure that the goods worth

Table 12.2 Debtor's balance

Debtor – ABC Ltd	£
Balance according to debtor's reply	7,000
Add back payment made by debtor but not received by the company	1,500
Add goods despatched by company but not received by debtor	2,000
Balance according to company's records	10,500

£2,000 were despatched before the confirmation date by examining the despatch records.

Debtors are not obliged to reply to confirmation requests. If they ignore the first request then it might be worth sending a reminder. If they refuse to reply to this then the balance can often be confirmed by telephoning the customer and asking for verbal confirmation. This is more time-consuming, but does at least provide some assurance.

If the debtor cannot or will not confirm the company's balance then the auditor will have to use alternative procedures to test for validity. These involve analysing the balance into its constituent invoices. For each invoice, the auditor will conduct the following tests:

1 Examine the customer's order to ensure that the goods were requested before the confirmation date.
2 Examine the despatch note to ensure that the goods were sent to the customer before the confirmation date. Preferably, the auditor should examine the copy which is signed by the debtor's staff and returned to the company as a receipt.
3 Check the pricing, discount rate and arithmetic on the invoice.
4 Ensure that the customer paid for the goods after the confirmation date.

The debtor's subsequent payment is an acknowledgement of the balance owed to the company. It is, however, necessary to ensure that this balance had been owed before the confirmation date otherwise the company could have over-stated debtors by bringing sales forward from the following accounting period.

These alternative procedures are much more time-consuming and provide relatively poor audit evidence. A written confirmation from a third party is much more conclusive than a procedure based largely on documentation prepared by the company's staff.

The auditor should ensure that the debtors' balances have not been overstated by cut-off problems at the confirmation date. This can be checked by examining a sample of invoices debited to the records just before the confirmation date and checking the dates on the despatch records to ensure that the sales have been recorded in the correct period. A sample of receipts should be selected from the cheque listing for the period immediately before the confirmation date and posted to the records, making sure that they have been recorded in the correct period.

The confirmation date might not coincide with the year end. If the directors of the company wish to report as quickly after the year end as possible, the auditor might use the normal procedures to confirm a sample of debtors' balances as at an interim date. The fact that the auditor has established that the debtors' figure was not materially overstated at, say, 30 November does not in itself prove that the balance was correct at 31 December. The auditor must ensure that the debits recorded during the intervening period have not been overstated and the credits understated using the same tests as those described in the preceding paragraph for checking cut-off.

The auditor must also ensure that the debtors' figure does not contain any material irrecoverable balances. This is best done by means of the analytical review techniques described in the previous section. These can, however, be supplemented by a review of post-balance sheet events. The management accounts for the first few weeks of the following year and the credit controller's files for the same period should be examined. If there is a significant incidence of bad debts written off during this period then the auditor should ensure that any balances which were outstanding at the year end have been included in the provision for doubtful debts.[2]

Bad debts written off during the year should be sampled and tested to ensure that the amounts written off were actually irrecoverable. The credit controller's files and the related correspondence should be inspected to check that an attempt was made to collect the balance.

12.5 Summary

Sales should be tested for understatement. The basic approach is to ensure that there are controls which would prevent income from remaining unrecorded and then to sample from a reciprocal population of potential sales. The evidence to support the sales figure is of relatively low quality because most of the documents and records are prepared within the company.

Debtors are tested for overstatement. A sample of debtors is selected from the debtors' ledger and tested by requesting direct confirmation. The replies to the confirmation provide high quality evidence, although the response rates tend to be relatively low. The valuation of debtors should be tested by reviewing the debtors' ledger for potential bad debts.

─────────────────── **REVIEW QUESTIONS** ───────────────────

1. Understatement tests are usually difficult to design because of the problems of identifying an appropriate reciprocal population. This is demonstrated in

the audit of sales. Should auditors abandon the concept of directional testing because of this?

2. How can accounting firms overcome the dangers associated with inter-related aspects of the audit being completed in isolation?

3. Is it dishonest for an auditor to suggest improvements to a client's credit control system if he is doing so to reduce the level of audit risk and not out of a desire to reduce the cost of bad debt for the company?

EXERCISES

1. You are auditing the rental income of a car hire company. Suggest the types of inherent and control risk which would be encountered in this type of audit and describe the analytical review and substantive procedures which you would undertake.

2. You are the auditor of a mail order company which sells clothes on an approval basis through a large number of customers spread across the country. Customers are given 30 days to pay for goods after they have been despatched. They are also allowed to return the goods within this period. All balances are recorded on-line on the company's computerised accounting system. Describe the particular inherent risks associated with the audit of debtors for this company and suggest how the balances should be tested.

3. You are the audit manager in charge of the audit of THI Ltd. One of the audit juniors was responsible for the audit of debtors and has filed the following comments on the audit approach taken.

(a) 'A great deal of time was saved by asking the company's staff to type out the confirmation requests and post them straight to the debtors. This appears to have had a dramatic effect on the response rate, over 80 per cent and hardly a disagreement!'

(b) 'The company's chief accountant did not want me to pester two of the largest customers because their balances were in dispute. Rather than risk provoking these debtors, they were removed from the sample and replaced with two other balances of a similar size.'

(c) 'Six of the responses to the confirmation request suggested that the company's balances had been overstated. A brief review of the company's records showed that these problems were almost certainly due to timing errors and so no further action was taken.'

List the shortcomings of the junior's work on debtors.

4. A company's major customers are in a specialised line of business which complicates the recording of invoices for purchases. The auditor attempted to confirm several of their balances by means of a positive request and received a 15 per cent response rate.

The audit senior contacted the debtors by telephone and discovered that it would be impossible for them to confirm the balance as at their supplier's year end. This suggests that the replies received to the confirmation requests have been made recklessly. The audit partner's response to the query raised by the audit senior regarding the evidence obtained to support this part of the debtors sample was 'My files contain their written confirmations. I do not need to worry whether they signed them recklessly or not.'

State whether you agree with the audit partner's attitude. If an unqualified report was issued and the debtors figure was later found to be incorrect, could the partner be accused of negligence?

References and further reading

1. Some suggestions for improving the response rates to positive requests are contained in Rouse, R.W. and Lathan, M.H., 'Improving the confirmation process', *The CPA Journal*, December 1986, pp. 58–61. The American Institute of Certified Public Accountants has published a US SAS (number 67) on the confirmation process.
2. This is defined as an 'adjusting event' in SSAP 17.

CHAPTER 13

The purchases cycle

The purchases cycle comprises the procedures which deal with the ordering and receipt of goods and services and the settlement of the resulting liabilities. This chapter will discuss the audit of purchases and trade creditors in the context of the risk-based audit approach. It will conclude the treatment of profit and loss account items by describing the audit of wages.

By the time you have completed this chapter you should be able to apply the risk-based approach to audit to:

- Purchases
- Trade creditors
- Wages and salaries.

13.1 A typical purchases system

Individual departments will notify the buying department of the need for stocks to be replenished. Most purchases will be of raw materials and components for production, although there will also be requests for other items such as stationery and computer consumables. The buying department will be responsible for finding the most appropriate supplier.

The buying department will prepare a purchase order. One copy of the order will go the the supplier, another to the accounts department and a third will be retained in the buying department. In computerised systems, the buying department may receive requests from the inventory control program which monitors stock levels. The buying department might then authorise the preparation of an order. The fact that an order had been placed would then be input into the system.

All deliveries should be directed to the stores department. The staff there will inspect the goods to ensure that the details on the supplier's delivery note are correct and that the goods appear to be undamaged. They will also prepare a goods received note which records the items received, the name of the supplier and the date. Copies of the goods received note will go to the buying department and accounts and another will be filed in stores. Details from the goods received note will also be keyed into the inventory files. The goods are then available for collection by the department which placed the order.

The accounts department will maintain a file of unfilled orders. Whenever a goods received note comes from stores, the accounts staff will attach it to its related order and file the two documents together. When the supplier's invoice arrives these documents can be used to make sure that the goods were ordered and received in good condition before the invoice is passed for payment.

Invoices which have been passed for payment are recorded in a purchase day book or in a computerised file of purchase invoices. The totals from these records will be posted to the purchases and creditors' accounts in the general ledger. The individual invoices are posted to their respective creditors' accounts in the creditors' ledger.

At the end of every month, the amount which is due to each creditor is calculated. Computerised systems can either print out cheques, complete with the amounts and payee details, or produce magnetic tapes which can be used by a bank to transfer funds straight into the suppliers' current accounts. This program would also record the payments in the general and creditors' ledgers.

Each supplier will send a monthly statement to enable the account balances to be checked and also to discourage late payment. The statement will, for example, highlight any overdue items.

Purchase order

Prenumbered, multi-part document, prepared by the buying department:

1. To send to the supplier.
2. To inform the production or sales staff that the stock has been ordered.
3. To enable the accounts department to check that all requests for payment are supported by a properly authorised order.

Goods received note

Prenumbered, multi-part document prepared by the staff taking delivery of stock:

1. As a receipt for the supplier.
2. To enable the inventory records to be updated.
3. To enable the accounts department to check that requests for payment are, in fact, for goods which have been received.

Purchase invoice

Prepared by the supplier as a request for payment.
The details can be checked for validity against those on the copies of the order and goods received note held by the accounts department.

Suppliers' statement

Submitted by the supplier to enable cross-checking of balances against that of the customer.
The balances are likely to disagree because of deliveries of goods and payments prior to the end of the month appearing in one record but not the other.

Figure 13.1 The purchases cycle.

The various documents in the purchases cycle can be summarised as shown in Figure 13.1.

13.2 Purchases

Purchases should be tested for overstatement. In other words, the auditor should select a sample of transactions from the purchases account in the ledger and ensure that the items selected are valid.

13.2.1 *Inherent risk in the audit of purchases*

Staff might have a motive to record fictitious purchases in order to collect the resulting payment. Computerised systems which automatically generate payments are particularly vulnerable to such attempts. The management of the company could wish to smooth profits by recording purchases on the wrong dates. There could be a temptation in good years to bring transactions forward from the first few weeks of the following financial year in order to reduce the current year's tax charge and provide a relatively easy profit target for the next period.

13.2.2 *Internal control over purchases*

The purchases cycle contains three main elements which must be segregated. The authorisation of purchases, the custody of the related goods and access to the payments must all be kept separate otherwise there will be scope for the fraudulent overstatement of purchases. In general, this segregation is not difficult to achieve, especially in larger organisations. The buying department would not have access to stock or be involved in authorising payments. The staff receiving stock in the stores department will not raise orders and any errors on their goods received notes will be detected when they are compared with the suppliers' invoices. The staff passing the invoice for payment and entering it into the computer may be unable to overstate the amount of the purchase provided there are adequate controls over the signing of cheques. This segregation of duties should be checked by enquiry and observation.

This system will only prevent fraud if someone checks that all invoices are supported by both an order and a goods received note. All three documents are usually matched and, indeed, filed together as evidence that the invoice is valid. This control could, therefore, be tested by inspecting a sample of invoices to ensure that they had been signed or initialled by the person responsible for the comparison. The fact that all three documents are usually stapled together means that the auditor can easily test the control by reperformance.

The software used to record invoices might repeat the comparison described above by checking the details on the invoice against those relating to the order and the receipt of the goods within the inventory files. This second comparison could result in the rejection of unmatched invoices or their appearance on an exception report. The auditor could test the operation of this control by means of a CAAT.

The possibility of invalid purchases being recorded could be further reduced by restricting the creation of new creditors' accounts to senior staff who are independent of the recording of invoices and the handling of payments. The auditor could test the operation of this by attempting to process an invoice whose sender did not have a valid accounts code or by attempting to open a new account without the necessary authorisation.

Cheques should be signed by two signatories, each of whom should inspect the invoices which support the payment. The signatories should stamp the invoices 'paid' to prevent them from being presented more than once. The auditor should examine a sample of cheques to see whether they have been properly signed. The signatories' examination of invoices will be difficult to test, although some assurance can be gained from observation and enquiry. The cancellation can be checked during the examination of invoices.

Management can exercise control of purchases by using budgets and standard costing techniques to identify apparent excessive spending. The auditor should review the monthly management reports to ensure that any large variances have been investigated.

13.2.3 *Analytical review of purchases*

The figures for purchases and other expenses can be reviewed by comparison with previous years and budgets. It is also helpful to relate these expenses to the level of activity as measured by turnover or some non-financial measures such as labour hours.

It might be possible to estimate the total cost of the purchase of certain basic commodities such as coal or ore by obtaining weighbridge records and multiplying the total weight received by the average unit price.

13.2.4 *Substantive testing of purchases*

Monetary unit samples should be extracted from the purchases account and from the other accounts which are used to record bought-in goods and services. It may be necessary to stratify the population if there are any high risk transactions such as imports. The entries to the purchases account will consist of totals from the purchase day book or invoice file. These records will have to be sub-sampled in order to provide a sample of individual invoices.

The auditor should inspect the supplier's invoice for each sample item. Invoices are third party, documentary evidence and are, therefore, fairly conclusive evidence that the transaction occurred. The auditor should, however, ensure that the purchase was valid by checking the details against the related order and goods received note. This is, in fact, the same test as has already been conducted in the reperformance of one of the company's controls. There is no reason why compliance testing and substantive testing cannot be conducted simultaneously using the same sample of transactions. The auditor should ensure that each selected invoice has been paid by tracing it to a print-out of bank credit transfers or by examining the returned cheque. This is not part of the audit of the purchases figure but is done as part of the testing for the completeness of creditors' balances at the year end. If the invoice has not been paid by the end of the year then the auditor should ensure that it has been included in the creditors' figure in the balance sheet.

The purchase day book or its equivalent transaction file should be reviewed for any large amounts recorded during the last few days of the financial year. The related goods received notes should be examined to ensure that the purchases have been recorded during the correct accounting period.

13.3 Trade creditors

The figure for creditors should be tested for understatement. In other words, the auditor should obtain a sample of potential creditors, establish the amounts owed to them, if any, and ensure that they have been properly dealt with in the balance sheet. There are many similarities between the basic approaches taken to the audits of debtors and creditors.

13.3.1 *Inherent risk in the audit of creditors*

Staff could wish to understate the total due to creditors in order to conceal fraud. Management could also wish to understate current liabilities in order to manipulate the company's apparent solvency. The fact that creditors are being tested for completeness creates the difficulty of obtaining an acceptable reciprocal population.

13.3.2 *Internal control and creditors*

The staff who authorise payments should not be responsible for the maintenance of the creditors' ledger. These staff should also be denied access to the signed cheques to suppliers. It is easy to misappropriate a payment to a creditor unless duties are segregated in this way.

It would be possible to conceal the theft of a cheque to a supplier by a variation of teeming and lading. A cheque payable to supplier A could be stolen. At the end of the following month a cheque to supplier B could be intercepted and used to settle A's balance. This process would have to be repeated until the original amount stolen was returned. This type of fraud would be made more difficult if suppliers' queries about their balances were directed to someone independent of the staff who maintained the records and passed invoices for payment. The auditor will have to test the segregation of duties by enquiry and observation.

The company can control the recording of creditors more easily if the order forms and goods received notes are prenumbered and regular sequence tests are conducted to make sure that they are all accounted for. The matching of these documents to the incoming invoices also makes it easier for the company to estimate the amount due to suppliers with greater accuracy. The auditor can test the operation of the sequence checking by reperformance. The matching of orders, goods received notes and invoices is tested as part of the audit of purchases.

There should be some means of ensuring that all invoices are recorded in the records. The totals of the entries in the purchase day book could be checked to ensure that all invoices have been included or there could be batch controls if the system is computerised. In manual systems, where the creditors' account in the general ledger is updated independently of the creditors' ledger, the fact that there are two records which should produce the same figure is a useful control. The auditor should test the operation of these controls by looking for initials to indicate the checking of totals or for reports which indicate that the two totals for creditors agree.

Any long-outstanding orders or goods received notes should be followed up. There is a possibility that a liability has been incurred in respect of these items but has remained unrecorded because of the loss of the invoice. If there are no reports to indicate that such reviews have been conducted, the auditor could reperform the control by examining the files of unmatched orders and goods received notes in the accounts department.

The accounts staff should reconcile the suppliers' statements with their balances in the creditors' ledger at the end of every month. There are likely to be timing differences between these records and these should be investigated in more detail if there appears to be an excessive delay between the recording of a transaction by the supplier and its appearance in the company records. The reconciliations should be filed and should be inspected by the auditor to ensure that they have been produced.

13.3.3 *Analytical review of creditors*

The creditors' turnover should be calculated using the following formula:

$$\frac{\text{creditors}}{\text{purchases}} \times 365$$

This gives the average number of days taken to settle a creditor's balance. If the period appears unusually short then it is possible that the creditors' figure has been understated. This could be because purchases made during the last few days of the year have not been recorded or because payments made at the beginning of the following accounting period have been brought forward.

13.3.4 *Substantive testing of creditors*

It is necessary to select a sample of suppliers with whom the company has had a trading relationship. The suppliers whose invoices were examined during the audit of purchases is a useful starting point. If purchases were selected by means of monetary unit sampling then the larger suppliers will have stood a greater chance of being selected. This list could be supplemented by any large suppliers whose identities are known but who have been omitted from the initial sample.

The balances owing to these suppliers can be obtained from their statements as at the end of the year. Statements might not be available for every supplier, perhaps because there are no outstanding invoices as at the confirmation date. The auditor could, therefore, be forced to request written confirmation from some of the potential creditors in the sample. It is often simpler to write to every supplier in the sample. Direct confirmation provides a slightly higher level of assurance and also avoids having to wait for suppliers' routine statements.

Replies should be reconciled with the company's records. Timing differences can arise because the company will record payments before the supplier and the supplier will record invoices before they have been received by the company. The validity of these timing differences should be tested.

If suppliers do not respond to a written request for confirmation and there are no current statements available at the confirmation date then the auditor could request verbal confirmation by telephone. If the supplier still refuses to cooperate then it will be necessary to confirm the balance by alternative procedures.

The alternative to direct confirmation is a time-consuming search for unrecorded liabilities to the supplier. The purchase day book or its equivalent transaction file should be reviewed for invoices from the supplier during the several weeks leading up to the confirmation date. If these are recorded on magnetic tape then they could be identified using audit software. Each invoice should be traced to the supplier's account in the creditors' ledger. If this suggests that the invoice is no longer outstanding then the returned cheque should be inspected. The cash book for the period after the year end should also be reviewed for payments to the supplier. If any such payments have been made then the auditor should obtain the invoices to which they relate. If the goods in question were purchased before the year end then they should appear in the creditors figure in the balance sheet.

Cut-off should be tested by reviewing the goods received records during the period after the year end and ensuring that any major receipts of goods have been recorded in the correct accounting period. The date of any large payments made immediately before the year end should be confirmed by examining the returned cheque and ensuring that it appears to have been recorded in the correct period.

It is possible to conduct an interim confirmation of creditors in much the same manner as was described for debtors. The payments recorded during the period between the confirmation date and the year end should be tested for validity by examining the cheques. The invoices recorded during the intervening period should be tested for completeness by selecting a sample of goods received notes completed between the two dates and tracing the related entries in the creditors' ledger.

The balances according to the creditors' ledger are always slightly out of date because they do not record purchases until the related invoices are received. This does not usually matter although it could lead to an understatement of liabilities at the year end. The company will usually accrue such purchases by estimating the value of the unmatched goods received notes at the year end. The auditor can ensure that this accrual has not been understated by tracing a sample of the items in the unmatched file to the accrual calculation and checking that the values placed on them appear reasonable. The invoices received after the year end should also be reviewed and traced to the accrual if they relate to goods delivered during the current year.

13.4 Wages and salaries

Labour costs are likely to be a major component of total expenses. The wages system has to ensure that staff are paid the correct amount each week or month and that the appropriate amounts are deducted for income tax, national insurance, union subscriptions and so on.

13.4.1 *A typical wages system*

Weekly paid staff are usually paid on the basis of the number of hours worked or units produced. Hourly paid staff will either have a clock card stamped with their times of arrival or departure each day or will have to give their payroll numbers to a timekeeper when they enter and exit the factory. The number of hours worked each week will be entered into a payroll system. This obtains the employee's hourly rate from another file and multiplies this by the number of hours worked to give the gross wage for the week. The employee's deductions are then calculated, taking the necessary information about tax codes, union membership, pension arrangements, etc., from the appropriate file maintained by the personnel department.

If employees are paid in cash, the payroll system will print out pay packets and will produce a coin analysis for the company's bank. This will enable the company to obtain the necessary notes and coins of each denomination to pay each employee's net wage. The system will also provide details of the total gross pay and the totals for each type of deduction so that the correct amount can be entered in the related accounts in the general ledger.

The wages staff will then fill the pay packets with the amounts printed by the payroll system. Staff can then collect their pay packets in person from the wages office or they can be issued to foremen who will distribute them to the employees in their section.

In piecework systems, where employees are paid for output rather than time, the system will operate in exactly the same way except that staff will have to keep records of their productivity. These will have to be signed by a supervisor to ensure that only work which meets the official quality standards is paid for.

Wages need not be paid in cash. Some companies have persuaded their staff to accept payments by credit transfer into their bank accounts. This avoids the cost of filling pay packets.

Salaried staff tend to be paid a fixed amount each month. This means that the system is similar to that for wages, except that there is less need to maintain detailed records of attendance or output. The payroll department need only be informed of any days on which salaried staff were absent so that the appropriate adjustment can be made to their gross salary for the month.

ACTIVITY

Before reading on, try to draft your own outline list of risk factors, internal controls, analytical review techniques and substantive tests. These issues will be discussed in the remainder of section 13.4.

13.4.2 *Inherent risk in the audit of wages and salaries*

The fact that this system generates substantial payments, often in cash, makes it a tempting target for fraud. The auditor will have to ensure that the recorded figure for wages has not been materially overstated.

The shareholders are very interested in the amounts paid to directors. Furthermore, the auditor has statutory responsibilities to examine the disclosure made in respect of directors' emoluments. This means that directors' emoluments are always material, regardless of their monetary value.

13.4.3 *Internal control and wages and salaries*

Segregation of duties should ensure that the wages staff do not have an incentive to overstate the amount paid for wages. It is particularly important that the staff who can determine the amounts to be paid should not have access to the related cash or wages cheques.

Standing data containing employees' pay grades and other personal details should be maintained by a personnel department which is independent of the payroll section. This reduces the risk of someone creating a bogus employee and collecting the related wages. In computerised systems, this could involve the use of special passwords for the personnel staff. The operating system should be programmed so that the ability to amend or alter personnel records is restricted to the terminals in the personnel department. The payroll staff may be able to read these files, but should not be able to change them.

The auditor could use CAATs to run compliance tests on this part of the system. Test data, consisting of clock cards for fictitious employees who do not have valid personnel files, could be entered. These should be either rejected by the system or listed on an exception report. The control could also be tested by running a program which compares the employees listed on the payroll with those on the personnel files. Any discrepancies should be listed and investigated. Finally, the auditor should attempt to update the personnel files using a terminal located in the payroll department. The system should refuse to process the change.

Time and production records maintained by individual employees should be authorised by their supervisors. This will reduce the risk of wages being overstated by staff clocking each other in and out. The effectiveness of this authorisation can be enhanced by making supervisory staff responsible for the productivity of their department. Standard costing can be used to calculate labour efficiency variances. These can be used to identify departments where staff hours appear excessive for the quantities produced.

The payroll staff themselves should be controlled by an overall review of the amounts on the weekly payroll by a senior member of staff. This could be supplemented by programming the system to list employees who claim to have worked more than the normal number of hours or whose gross wages exceed a realistic upper limit. The auditor should examine the payroll for evidence of the supervisor's scrutiny and should also obtain evidence that the exception reports were being reviewed and investigated.

13.4.4 *Analytical review of wages*

If staff are required to fill in time sheets which are used to charge customers for the amount of time spent on individual jobs, the auditor might be able to reconcile the number of hours charged to the number of hours paid. This could be a reasonably effective test, provided that there were not significant numbers of unallocated or unchargeable hours on the time sheets. The number of hours claimed and the total cost of wages might be monitored by means of a standard costing system. The auditor should review these reports for any excessive variances.

The average wage per employee should be calculated and compared with that of previous years. Any increase in excess of the annual pay award which cannot easily be explained by an increase in overtime should be investigated.

13.4.5 *Substantive testing of wages*

A monetary unit sample should be taken from the wages account in the general ledger. This will provide a sample of payroll totals for a number of weeks or months. These payrolls should be subsampled to generate a sample of payments to individual employees.

The payment to each employee should be tested for validity by doing the following:

1 Ensuring that the employee actually worked for the company at that time, perhaps by referring to the personnel records.
2 Checking that the hours or output referred to on the payroll were valid

by obtaining the employee's clock card or production report for the relevant week.

3 Checking the rates of pay given against the official rates in force at that time.

4 Checking the calculation of the employee's wages.

The auditor will also have to ensure that there are no unrecorded liabilities in respect of wages. The payment of the net wage should be checked, perhaps by referring to a returned cheque paid to the employee or by examining the book signed by staff to acknowledge receipt of their pay packets. The calculation of each of the deductions from the employee's gross wage will have to be checked and posted to the appropriate accounts in the general ledger.

13.4.6 *Directors' emoluments*

The auditor must undertake additional substantive testing of the amounts paid to directors. It must be ensured that full disclosure has been made of all salaries and benefits in kind. Assurance could be obtained in a number of ways including the following.

1 Requesting each director to sign a letter stating the amounts of salary and benefits according to the draft accounts. This should acknowledge that the director is aware of the disclosure requirements regarding these items and that all relevant information has been published.

2 Reconciling the information in the financial statements to the tax forms which the company must submit to the Inland Revenue in respect of directors and higher paid employees.

3 Reviewing directors' contracts of employment and board minutes for details of remuneration packages.[1]

13.5 Summary

Purchases are tested for overstatement. A sample of items is selected from the accounting records and tested by inspecting the invoice and other related documentation.

Creditors are tested for understatement. The auditor will select a sample of potential creditors and ensure that their balance has been correctly stated in the balance sheet.

Wages are tested for overstatement by sampling from the payroll and testing the selected payments for validity. The only major problem associated with the audit of wages is the need to ensure that directors' emoluments have been accounted for properly.

─────────────── **REVIEW QUESTIONS** ───────────────

1. Interim confirmations of debtors and creditors cost more because of the need to audit transactions recorded during the period from the confirmation date to the year end. They also provide poorer quality evidence because of the additional reliance on documents which have been prepared by the company's staff. Should this approach to testing be discouraged on the grounds that it is against the shareholders' best interests?

2. Should the auditor have a statutory right to demand responses to confirmation requests?

3. Discuss the advantages and possible dangers of conducting compliance and substantive tests simultaneously using the same sample of items.

─────────────────── **EXERCISES** ───────────────────

1. You are auditing the creditors' figure for ZYX Ltd. You have prepared the following reconciliation of a supplier's statement to the company's records as shown in Table 13.1.
  Describe the tests which you would conduct upon the reconciling items.

2. You are the audit partner in charge of the audit of SDE Ltd, a small company employing eighty staff. A junior has just completed the audit of wages and has written the following memo regarding the company's wages system.

> There are several glaring weaknesses in the company's system of internal controls. The company should be asked to rectify each of these as soon as possible:
> (a) The payroll and personnel records are maintained by two staff. These employees could invent bogus workers and overstate wages. I suggest that the company finds a separate room for the personnel records and makes one member of staff responsible for these. The other staff member should prepare the payroll.
> (b) The hourly paid workers operate a two-shift system. They clock themselves

Table 13.1 Reconciliation of supplier's statement to company records

	£
Balance according to supplier	9,000
Less: Invoices not yet recorded by company	(2,000)
Interest charged on overdue balance not recorded by client	(200)
Cheques recorded by client, not yet on statement	(3,000)
Balance according to company	3,800

in and out of the factory at the beginning and end of each shift. This process is supervised by a gatekeeper. The process of supervising up to thirty-five staff entering and leaving at any given time is too great a responsibility for one person. The company should employ two additional gatekeepers to increase the level of control over this activity. This should be further enhanced by requiring the presence of a senior manager, perhaps the production director, at the beginning of every shift to prevent staff clocking their friends in.

(c) Every week, the factory foremen are asked to review the number of hours claimed by the staff in their sections. There are between five and eight workers in each section. These hours are then processed by the payroll department and are also incorporated into the calculations of the labour efficiency variances. This review should not be entrusted to such junior supervisors. The hours should be reviewed by the chief accountant.'

Discuss the merits of the junior's criticisms of the system and of the proposed remedies for its shortcomings.

References and further reading

1. The audit of directors' emoluments is dealt with more fully in an APC Audit Brief entitled *The Companies Act 1980 and the Auditor.*

CHAPTER 14

Audit of the balance sheet

This chapter will complete the discussion of the audit of the balance sheet. Two areas (debtors and creditors) have already been covered.

By the time you have completed this chapter you should be able to apply the risk-based approach to audit to:

- Fixed assets
- Stock
- Investments
- Bank
- Taxation
- Long-term liabilities
- Capital.

14.1 Fixed assets

In general, balance sheet items are tested by examining the closing balances on their accounts as at the year end. This tends not to be done for fixed assets because the Companies Act 1985 requires the company to disclose details of acquisitions and disposals in the audited financial statements. The easiest way to test fixed assets is, therefore, to compare the opening balance with the previous year's financial statements, test the additions during the year for overstatement and the disposals for understatement.

14.4.1 *Inherent risk in the audit of tangible fixed assets*

There is a great deal of flexibility inherent in accounting for fixed assets. This can be seen in the calculation of the depreciation charge and in the capitalisation of intangible fixed assets. Management could abuse this freedom to manipulate the profit figure. The problems created by such estimates are discussed in an SAS. Essentially, this stresses the need for auditors to take reasonable steps to ensure that the estimates have not led to any material misstatement. In the context of fixed assets this could include drawing on knowledge of the business to determine whether, say, management estimates of asset lives are credible.[1]

14.1.2 *Internal controls over tangible fixed assets*

The accounting system relating to fixed assets is extremely simple. The general ledger will have two accounts in respect of each type of fixed asset, one to record cost and the other to record depreciation. The balances on these accounts can be analysed quite easily by means of a plant register which contains a record in respect of the individual assets. This register includes the cost of each asset, its date of acquisition, the depreciation charged to date and its location.

The plant register is usually maintained on a computer and the depreciation charge and the totals of cost and accumulated depreciation can be calculated on a monthly basis. The totals can be compared with the balances on the cost and depreciation accounts in order to ensure that the plant register agrees back to the accounting records.

The acquisition and disposal of fixed assets will have to be properly authorised. There could be different levels of authority depending upon the amounts involved. Small purchases could be authorised by the production manager, perhaps working within an annual budget. Larger amounts would require the sanction of the company's board. In some cases, really large purchases might have to be authorised by the directors of the holding company.

There should be a formal system for requesting capital expenditure. This could involve the use of special forms which are designed to ensure that the staff who are authorising the expenditure have sufficient information to arrive at an intelligent decision. There should be a similar system for the authorisation of disposals. It is important that the staff who maintain the plant register are unable to authorise acquisitions or disposals. The auditor should ensure that these controls are operating by selecting samples of acquisitions and disposals and making sure that the appropriate forms have been completed and authorised.

The details on the plant register should be checked regularly by means of physical inspection. Someone independent of the staff who have custody of the assets or who maintain the plant register should check that all of the items which should be within a selected area or department are present. The auditor should examine the reports produced as a result of these checks to ensure that they are being conducted with reasonable frequency.

14.1.3 *Analytical review of tangible fixed assets*

The auditor should compare the amounts of acquisitions and disposals against the company's budgets for the year. It is possible to get some insight into the usage of fixed assets by means of the fixed asset turnover ratio:

$$\frac{\text{sales}}{\text{fixed assets}}$$

Trends in this ratio give an indication of the relationship between the book value of fixed assets and the level of activity. If this ratio is decreasing then there is a danger that the fixed assets figure has been overstated.

Analytical review is also a useful means of ensuring that the depreciation charge is adequate but not excessive. If the company is constantly recording substantial losses on the disposal of its fixed assets then it is not charging enough depreciation. If it is making gains then the depreciation charge is excessive.

If the company uses the reducing balance method to calculate depreciation then the auditor can use proof in total to ensure that the depreciation charge is in line with the stated accounting policy.

14.1.4 *Substantive testing of tangible fixed assets*

The company should provide the auditor with a schedule stating the opening balance on the fixed asset accounts, the adjustments for acquisitions and disposals and the movements due to depreciation. The opening balance on this schedule should agree to the closing balance according to the previous year's audited financial statements.

A monetary unit sample of acquisitions should be extracted from the debits to the fixed asset accounts. These should be tested for validity as follows:

1   The authorisation of the purchase should be checked by examining the relevant form or board minute.
2   The cost of the acquisition should be checked. In some cases this will be done by examining an invoice or contract. There could, however, be other costs such as the wages paid to staff for the installation and testing of the asset.
3   The accounting treatment should be considered. The decision to capitalise the expenditure should be evaluated. The company could be trying to carry the costs of major repairs forward to future years.

The auditor should ensure that there are no unrecorded liabilities in respect of the selected acquisitions by examining the related paid cheque.

The disposals should be tested for understatement. This is done by taking a sample of the items which could have been disposed of, namely the assets recorded in the plant register at the beginning of the year and those which were acquired during the year, and investigating their present status and condition. The auditor has already extracted a sample of acquisitions and so a second sample must be taken from the plant register print-out as at the end of the previous year.

For each item in the combined sample, the auditor should enquire whether the asset has been disposed of. If it has, then the auditor should check any supporting documentation or correspondence to see whether the proceeds of disposal have been recorded correctly. The adequacy of the amount recovered should be investigated in case there has been fraudulent collusion between the employee who negotiated the selling price and the buyer. Finally, the auditor should ensure that the disposal has been properly accounted for.

If the item has not been disposed of, then the auditor should ensure that it still exists and, as far as possible, check that it is the property of the company. The title documents of any property in the sample should be examined. If the documents are in the custody of a third party then the auditor should request written confirmation that they are being held on the company's behalf. The existence of other assets should be tested by physical inspection. The auditor may not have sufficient legal or technical knowledge to examine the documents properly or to identify the equipment belonging to the company. It may be necessary to obtain independent advice.[2]

The depreciation charge for the year has to be tested to ensure that it is adequate but not excessive. There are two aspects to this. The simplest is to ensure that the amount charged is arithmetically correct in terms of the company's stated accounting policy. The auditor could check the amounts charged on each of the assets in the combined sample used to check for the understatement of disposals. It could, however, be simpler to use a piece of audit software to repeat the calculation. It is also necessary to consider the validity of the assumptions underlying the accounting policy. If the company has assumed, for example, that most of its machinery has an estimated useful life of ten years, then the auditor should obtain an explanation for the selection of this rather than a greater or lesser period.

If it is some time since the company has had its property revalued or if the market prices of property have changed substantially since the last revaluation, then the auditor should discuss the need for an appraisal with management. Revaluation is, however, an inexact science. One of the most controversial cases in recent times involved the hotel group Queens Moat Houses. The company's 1991 financial statements carried the properties at a value, supplied by an independent firm of chartered surveyors, of £2bn. The same firm valued the properties at £1.35bn one year later. While this slump in value was a matter of some concern, it was even more worrying that a second firm used exactly the same information and valuation basis to arrive at a value of only £861m. The company's 1992 statements carried the hotels at a value of £732m after a write-off of over £1.3bn.[3]

14.1.5 *The audit of intangible fixed assets*

There are many different types of intangible fixed assets, including goodwill, patents and trade marks. The audit of these figures requires a great deal of professional judgement on the part of the auditor, particularly because this is an area where there is a great deal of disagreement over the merits of different accounting policies.

There are two basic aspects to the audit of these assets. First, the auditor must examine the manner in which the company has calculated the figures. If they have been purchased and are to be recorded at cost, then the auditor should examine any documentary evidence which exists to support the calculation. If some other basis is being used then the auditor must make sure that the figure has been arrived at in accordance with the company's stated accounting policy.

The second, and most difficult, aspect of the audit of intangibles lies in the accounting treatment of intangibles. This has led to a great deal of controversy in the past. When SSAP 22 introduced the requirement that purchased goodwill should be eliminated from the balance sheet, a number of companies responded by capitalising the estimated values of their brand names.

14.2 Stock

The figure for stock must be audited for misstatement. The concept of directional testing suggests that the debit entry, which results in the appearance of a current asset in the balance sheet, must be tested for overstatement and the credit entry to the trading account must be tested for understatement.

The estimated value of stocks according to the accounting records must be corrected by means of a physical stock count. The physical quantities must then be valued in order to generate the closing stock figure.

14.2.1 *Inherent risk in the audit of stock*

The process of physically counting stock can be difficult to organise properly. Any errors which occur in this process will lead to an incorrect valuation. The auditor may not have sufficient specialised knowledge to observe the count properly. The stock could be spread across many different locations, thus making it difficult to visit every one.

The valuation of stock creates further opportunities for manipulation or error. There is a great deal of subjectivity associated with determining the net realisable value of stocks, the apportionment of overheads, and the realisation of profits on long-term contracts. The subjectivity and uncertainties associated with the counting and valuation of stock make it an ideal vehicle for the distortion of the profit figure. If the auditor is suspicious of the directors' motives then he should take extra care over the audit of stock.

14.2.2 *The audit of the stock count*

The importance of the auditor's attendance at the stock count is underlined by the fact that an Auditing Guideline has been published on this topic.[4] It is the responsibility of company management to organise the stocktaking and to ensure that the counting is carried out correctly. The auditor's role is to observe the procedures and carry out test counts as part of the collection of audit evidence. The auditor should take great care to ensure that the count is properly planned and that any problems which arise during the count are brought to management's attention immediately. It is unlikely that the company will be prepared to repeat the exercise for audit purposes.

Management should prepare written instructions for the employees who will carry out the count. These should cover such areas as follows:

1   The stock should be tidied before the stock count. Lines are often painted on the floors of factories or warehouses so that specific areas can be identified during stock counts. Foremen or other supervisors should ensure that stock does not straddle these lines.
2   There should be a designated controller who will take responsibility for the issue and collection of pre-numbered stock sheets. This controller will maintain a list of areas within the factory and stores and will allocate count teams so that no area is either missed or counted twice.
3   Employees should work in pairs. This reduces the risk of arithmetical errors.
4   Areas which have been counted should be identified by coloured cards or chalk marks on the floor to reduce the risk of double counting.

It is not the auditor's responsibility to check these instructions, although they should be reviewed as part of the planning process. If there are any omissions then the auditor should bring these to management's attention.

The date and locations of the stock count should be discussed with management. Ideally, the stock count should be conducted at the year end. Sometimes companies bring their stock counts forward to avoid disrupting operations at a busy time or to ensure that the count is conducted over a weekend. This requires the stock count figures to be updated for receipts and despatches of stock during the period between the count and the year end. Stock is sometimes calculated by means of stock records which are checked by means of continuous stock counting procedures. This involves a cycle of stock counts during the year, each one concentrating on a different area.

The auditor will have to ensure that an adequate number of staff are available to attend the counts. If there are several locations then the auditor might decide to send staff to a representative sample of counts. During the count, the audit team should observe the manner in which stock is being counted to ensure that the instructions issued by management are being complied with. The auditor should also conduct test counts. The stock records should be tested for overstatement by selecting items from the sheets and recounting them to make sure that they are there. The records should also be tested for completeness by selecting items of stock and making sure that they have been properly counted and recorded on the sheets. Any obsolete or damaged stock should be identified as such on the stock sheets to ensure that it is recorded at the correct price.

Some of the stock on the company's premises could belong to third parties. Stock could be held on consignment and will not become the company's property until some time after its delivery. The company could also hold stock which it is going to process and return to its owners. The auditor should, at least, enquire about the ownership of stocks during the stock count. The company's stocktaking instructions should require that all stock belonging to third parties be properly identified so that it is excluded from the count.

14.2.3 *The valuation of stock*

The auditor should check that all of the stock sheets have been accounted for after the count. It is possible to prevent insertions or alterations by counting the sheets immediately after the count and either cancelling any blank lines or photocopying the original sheets.

The valuation of the items selected during the auditor's test counting should be checked. In the case of raw materials, the valuation may be obtained from invoices or standard costing schedules. The cost of work in progress and finished goods will include the direct labour and overhead costs incurred in their creation as well as the material cost. The apportionment of overheads should be done in accordance with the requirements of SSAP 9. In particular, all manufacturing overheads should be apportioned and the allocation of costs should be done on the basis of normal levels of output. If the company values stock at standard cost then the auditor should review the variance accounts to ensure that standard costs are reasonably close to actual.

Any inter-departmental or inter-company profits on stock should be cancelled. Once the valuation of the individual items and the totals of the stock sheets have been checked, the auditor should use analytical review to ensure that the valuation is reasonable. The physical stock figure should be compared with the book stock. If there is a significant difference, then the company should identify the reasons for it. There could have been significant losses because of theft or deterioration. Alternatively, there could have been errors in the counting and valuation of the stock.

The auditor should calculate the gross profit percentage and the stock turnover ratio:

$$\frac{\text{stock}}{\text{cost of goods sold}} \times 365$$

Any trends in this ratio are worth noting. If the average number of days taken to sell an item of stock is increasing, it could be that the stock figure has been overstated because damaged or obsolete stock has been valued at cost and not written down to net book value.

Aged analyses of raw materials, work in progress and finished goods should be inspected. Again, the auditor should look for any indication of obsolete stocks which should have been written down to their net realisable values. In some cases, the auditor will be able to ascertain the net realisable value of stocks by referring to the selling prices obtained after the year end. This review is, however, likely to be of limited value because there are unlikely to be many sales of obsolete, slow-moving stocks during the relatively short period between the year end and the completion of the audit.

If the stock count has been conducted at an interim date, the auditor should test receipts and issues for both under- and overstatement. Issues can be tested for overstatement by sampling from the issues in the stock records and examining the supporting documents, such as materials requisitions or despatch notes. Issues are tested for understatement by sampling from the files of requisitions and despatch notes and posting the selected transactions to the stock records. Receipts would be tested for overstatement by sampling from the inflows recorded in the stock records and examining the related goods received notes. They would also be tested for understatement by sampling from the goods received notes and posting the inflows to the stock records.

14.2.4 *Long-term contracts*

The accounting treatment of long-term contracts is dealt with in SSAP 9.[5] This requires that the proportion of a long-term contract which has been completed during the year should be recorded as turnover. The costs incurred in bringing the contract to this stage should be shown as part of the cost of goods sold for the period. The expenses will be in respect of labour and materials, many of which can be easily attributed to specific projects. These can be tested using the methods described in Chapter 13.

The stage of completion of the projects will have to be evaluated by referring to the reports produced by the architects or surveyors who have been appointed to visit the site and certify the value of the work completed to date. The auditor should also review any internal reports produced by the company's own staff and any board minutes on the contract.

The value of work completed and certified to date, less any payments on account, should be shown as part of the debtors' figure in the balance sheet. The company should have some means of identifying contracts which are likely to result in a loss being incurred. SSAP 9 requires that all foreseeable losses should be provided for immediately.

14.3 Investments

Very few companies will have a significant number of investments in stocks or shares. This means that it is often quicker to test all of the items in this account than to spend time reviewing the system. This section will restrict itself to the audit of investments of companies for whom trading in shares is a secondary activity. The audit of a financial institution would require much more attention to be paid to the reviews of inherent and control risks. The audit of this type of company is, however, outside the scope of this text.

14.3.1 *Detailed testing of investments*

It is unlikely that the company will keep the share certificates themselves. These should be deposited with a third party, such as a bank, for safekeeping. The custodian should be given explicit instructions as to the identity of the staff who are entitled to authorise the transfer or disposal of the investments. All instructions should be given in writing.

If the certificates are kept on the company's premises, then the company should ensure that they are properly protected, perhaps in a fireproof safe. Those who are responsible for recording transactions or for authorising acquisitions and disposals should not have access to the certificates.

The auditor should either physically inspect the share certificates at the year end or should request direct confirmation of their existence from the custodian. The authorisation for any transactions entered into during the year should be checked by referring to the appropriate board minutes and correspondence with the custodian.

The auditor should ensure that all of the benefits which should have accrued to the company during the year have been properly accounted for. There are a number of publications, such as Extel, which give details of dividends, issues of bonus shares and rights issues. The auditor should consult one of these and trace the receipt of all such distributions through the company's accounting system.

The company is entitled to value its investments at either their cost or market valuation. If they are stated at cost then market value will have to be disclosed if this is materially different. If they are stated at their market value then cost will also have to be stated. The market values of quoted companies are determined by trading on the Stock Exchange and are published in the Stock Exchange Daily Official List and in many newspapers.

It may be difficult to determine the market value of securities which are not listed on the stock exchange. A valuation must be determined in a subjective manner by reviewing the investment's prospects. The auditor must consider the validity of the company's assumptions and of the model which has been used to determine the value. The Companies Act 1985 states that any permanent diminution in value must be recognised in the financial statements.

The extent of the company's shareholding as a proportion of the investment's total equity must be investigated. If the company holds more than 10 per cent of the allotted share capital then the Companies Act 1985 requires that the name, country of incorporation and proportion of shares held must be disclosed in the financial statements. If the company's holding is sufficient to give it significant influence over the other company then it may have to be accounted for under the equity method in the company's consolidated financial statements. If the holding is sufficient to give it control, then the other company is deemed to be a subsidiary and should be reflected as such in the consolidated financial statements. Additional details concerning associates and subsidiaries must also be published in the notes to the financial statements.[6]

14.4 Bank

The figure for bank can be a significant component of a company's working capital. It may also be one which management may wish to distort. Readers of the financial statements may be afraid that the company will have liquidity problems if the balance is too low. An excessive bank balance can, however, imply inefficient management. It is relatively easy to manipulate the bank balance by advancing or delaying receipts or payments. The audit of bank is another figure for which the auditor can save time by concentrating on substantive testing.

14.4.1 *Detailed testing of bank*

The company's bank balance will normally be entrusted to the cashier. The cashier will be responsible for maintaining the cash book and will also write out any cheques which have to be prepared manually. The cashier should not be a cheque signatory.

At the end of every month, the bank will send a statement. This should be reconciled to the cash book by someone other than the cashier. The reconciliation is required because of the timing differences between the recording of transactions in the cash book and their appearance in the bank's records. Thus, some of the cheque payments and lodgements recorded by the company before the end of the month will not be on the bank statement. It is also possible that the bank will have deducted interest or charges and these will have to be entered in the cash book.

The auditor can ensure that this control has operated by inspecting the file of bank reconciliations. Reconciling items should be reasonably current and any long-outstanding differences should have been investigated.

The auditor will request direct confirmation of the balance from the bank itself. This is done by sending a standard confirmation request to every bank branch with which the company has had an account during the year. The wording of this request has been agreed between the APC and the clearing banks.[7] This asks for a list of every account held by the company at that bank along with the closing balance. The letter also asks for an extremely comprehensive list of disclosures including loans granted by the bank, security pledged to the bank and details of any contingent liabilities, such as guarantees given for the liabilities of third parties.

The auditor will then compare the figures on the bank's response to this request with the bank balance stated in the bank reconciliation as at the year end. The auditor will ensure that any outstanding lodgements recorded in the reconciliation are valid by inspecting the pay-in slips which should have been date-stamped by the bank before the year end. The outstanding cheques will be tested for understatement by selecting a number of payments recorded in bank statements after the year end and inspecting the cheques themselves to see whether they were dated before the year end. If they were, then they should appear as outstanding payments in the bank reconciliation. The figure according to the cash book should then appear in the balance sheet.

The auditor should look for signs of 'window-dressing'. The company could, for example, increase the bank balance to an artificial level by delaying the monthly payment of creditors until after the year end, thus raising the bank balance by the amount of a month's payments. Alternatively, debtors could be given an extremely attractive discount for settling their balances before the year end. It is also possible to alter the balance by taking out a loan for a few days which would be repaid just after the year end. All of these devices produce a bank balance which is misleading but which is, nevertheless, arithmetically correct at the year end. The auditor should ask for any such manipulation to be disclosed, at the very least by means of a note to the balance sheet.

14.5 Taxation

The company will have to disclose its tax charge in the profit and loss account and the liabilities in respect of tax in the balance sheet. It is common for the auditor to provide the company with tax advice as part of a separate engagement. This means that the auditor's tax department will have taken part in the estimate of the tax charge and will also have an agreement with the Inland Revenue that any correspondence concerning the company be directed to them. This forewarns the auditor of any major claims which the tax authorities are likely to make in respect of prior years or of any reservations which they have about the current year's computations.

The audit work on the general ledger will have provided the auditor with reasonable assurance that the various allowable and disallowable expenses have been properly accounted for. The auditor, or his colleagues from the tax department, should not have any great difficulty in making sure that the analysis of expenses for tax purposes has not been manipulated. If the tax computation for the year has been prepared by the company's accountant then the auditor should review the various assumptions made within it and discuss any which appear unreasonable.

If the company has paid or proposed any dividends during the year, then the auditor should ensure that Advance Corporation Tax (ACT) has been properly paid and accounted for. If this ACT is being carried forward as recoverable then the auditor should review the company's forecast profits and distributions in order to see whether a recovery is likely within the foreseeable future.

Deferred tax is a liability which arises because certain profits may not be taxable until some time, perhaps even several years, after they have been recognised in the financial statements. The company should calculate the value of such profits and make forecasts to see whether they are likely to result in payments within the foreseeable future.[8] The auditor should review these forecasts and calculations and consider whether they appear reasonable. The company should disclose the extent of any unrecognised potential liabilities in a note to the financial statements. The flexibility inherent in SSAP 15 has led for calls for its replacement with a rather more rigid set of rules which did not require any forecasts.

14.6 Long-term loans and equity

The value of any long-term debt will usually be tested by means of direct confirmation from the lenders, who should also be asked whether their loans are secured in any way. The confirmation requests will be sent to those who had loans outstanding at the beginning of the year, even if the company now claims to have settled them, and to any new lenders. New loans can be identified by reviewing the board minutes for details of negotiations or advances and by reviewing the cash book for any large receipts. Management should be asked to confirm that all long-term debt has been accounted for in the balance sheet.

The audit of share capital is unlikely to pose problems in the case of private companies. The audit of public companies could be more difficult because of the possibility of large numbers of transactions.

The company's authorised share capital can be agreed to the memorandum of association. The figure for the issued share capital should be compared with the total according to the register of members. In the case of large, quoted companies, these registers may be maintained by independent registrars. The authorisation for any dividends paid should be checked against the minutes of shareholders' and directors' meetings. The total amount paid can usually be checked by proof in total.

Any issues of shares occurring during the year should be examined to ensure that the issues had the necessary authorisation from the shareholders or had been provided for in the memorandum of association. The recording of each stage of the application, allotment and call process should be examined to ensure that the payments received from applicants and new shareholders have been properly accounted for and that the increase in the share capital has been properly dealt with. This would include the correct calculation and recording of any share premium.

Auditors have to consider the accounting treatment of equity and long-term liabilities very carefully. Both of these areas have been the subject of a great deal of manipulative accounting. Companies have used loopholes in the regulations to structure 'loans' in such a way that they did not have to be shown as such in the financial statements. They have also developed financial instruments which could be treated as share capital in the balance sheet, but which gave the holders of these the same rights (and the company the same obligations) as if they were debt. The ASB has attempted to curtail these activities by publishing FRSs 4 and 5. These require the 'economic reality' of any obligation to be shown rather than its legal form.[9]

The figures for reserves should require very little detailed audit testing. The profit statement should have been tested in detail. The auditor can, therefore, agree the opening balance to the previous year's audited accounts and the movements to the profit and loss account. This should produce the closing balance according to the company's balance sheet.

14.7 Summary

This chapter has dealt with the audit of those balance sheet figures which were not covered in Chapters 12 and 13, namely fixed assets, stock, investments, bank, taxation, long-term liabilities and equity.

This treatment has been relatively brief. A more detailed treatment can be obtained from the in-house manuals published by a number of accounting firms.[10]

REVIEW QUESTIONS

1. Should an auditor state the extent to which it has proved necessary to rely on the assistance of independent experts in the identification of specialised fixed assets or stocks during physical inspections?

2. What aspects of a report prepared by an independent surveyor should the auditor examine if the amount stated in it is to be included in the balance sheet?

3. The directors of a company have increased the value of the bank balance from an average level of £300 to the sum of £47,000 as at the year end. Within ten days of the start of the new financial year, the balance had slumped to £450. How could the auditor justify the need for a note to the financial statements which described the arrangements relating to bank at the time of the year end?

EXERCISES

1. YTR Ltd build houses and factories. During the year the company's own staff erected a new office building on a piece of land immediately beside their existing offices. This new building was required because of expansion which had taken place during the year. The costs incurred were as shown in Table 14.1. State how the cost of this new building should be audited.

2. Your client has a substantial balance deposited with the First National Bank of Mordovia. This balance is denominated in the local currency. Draft an audit program for the audit of this balance, suggesting how the approach taken differs from that which would be applied to the audit of a balance in a major UK clearing bank.

3. You are the auditor of JHG Ltd, a manufacturing company. This company maintains

Table 14.1 Costs incurred in building new offices

	£
Land – purchased from neighbour	90,000
Materials – bricks, cement, etc.	30,000
Labour – wages paid to employees while engaged upon the office project	70,000
Depreciation on construction machinery	10,000
Cost of resurfacing existing car park adjoining offices	5,000
	205,000

records of all stock issued and received, valued at standard cost. The computerised accounting system identifies the standard quantities and prices of each component contained in each item sold during the year and values these at their standard cost. The company plans to hold a stock count at its year end. There are fifteen depots spread across the country.

(a) Suggest how the auditor should go about deciding which depots to visit during the stock count.

(b) Identify the audit problems which would arise if the results of the physical stock-taking suggested that stocks were valued at £90,000 but the book stocks were worth £130,000. Assume that the £40,000 difference is material. Does it matter whether the company uses the book stock or the physical stock valuation?

4. The directors of LKJ Ltd prepared a forecast of expected profits and dividends and another of acquisitions and disposals of fixed assets in order to support their decision to treat ACT recoverable as an asset and to justify the inclusion of a very small liability in respect of deferred taxation.

The auditor examined these forecasts. They appeared reasonable in the light of previous trends and accorded with the impressions gained from discussions with various directors and managers about the immediate future for their areas of responsibility. The directors confirmed their confidence in the assumptions made when drafting these forecasts by reiterating them in the letter of representation.

Six months later, the company ran into severe and unexpected difficulties. They did not make any profit in the new financial year and were forced to dispose of some fixed assets, incurring tax on the related chargeable gains. The shareholders were extremely upset to discover that the figures for recoverable ACT and deferred tax in the previous set of financial statements had been based upon projections which subsequent events proved to have been optimistic.

Describe the extent to which LKJ's auditor could be accused of negligence. State the assumptions which you have made in arriving at your decision.

References and further reading

1. APB, SAS 420, *Audit of Accounting Estimates*, 1995.
2. For further information about the use of independent experts, see APB, SAS 520, *Using the Work of an Expert*, 1995.

3. Davies, M., Paterson, R. and Wilson, A., *UK GAAP*, Macmillan, 1994.

4. APC Auditing Guideline, *Attendance at Stocktaking*, 1983.

5. ASC Statement of Standard Accounting Practice 9, *Stocks and Work in Progress*, 1988.

6. The accounting treatment of associates and subsidiaries is dealt with by ASC, SSAP 1, *Accounting for Associated Companies*, 1982 and ASB, *Accounting for Subsidiary Undertakings*, 1992.

7. The text of this request can be found in the APC Auditing Guideline, *Bank Reports for Audit Purposes*, 1982.

8. The calculation of this liability is dealt with in Statement of Standard Accounting Practice 15, *Accounting for Deferred Tax*, 1985.

9. ASB, FRS 4, *Capital Instruments*, 1993 and FRS 5, *Reporting the Substance of Transaction*, 1994.

10. A number of firms have published their manuals. The most detailed treatment of the risk-based approach can be found in *Grant Thornton Audit Manual*, Longman, 1990.

PART IV

OTHER ROLES FOR AUDIT

The external audit of financial statements is by no means the only way in which the various theories and techniques discussed in the earlier parts of the book can arise. This section looks at some of the more constructive uses of audit both within companies as a service to management and externally in reviewing the company's impact on society.

Chapter 15 deals with internal audit. Most organisations of any size in the private sector and all public sector organisations have an internal audit function. This can provide management with some assurance that the controls and systems are operating as they should and can assist management in discharging their duties towards the company.

Chapter 16 looks at ways in which the concept of audit can be applied to maximising efficiency in either profit-making or not-for-profit organisations. This is a highly topical issue, particularly in public sector accounting.

Chapter 17 brings the book to a close with a discussion of some of the ways in which an organisation's impact on the environment can be monitored. Given the growing awareness that businesses have a much broader responsibility than the creation of wealth for their shareholders, this is a vitally important topic.

CHAPTER 15

Internal audit

This chapter will describe the function of the internal auditor within an organisation. Unlike the external auditor, whose principal duties are to the shareholders, the internal auditor acts in support of management. Internal audit is, to some extent, an extension of the system of internal controls. This may mean that the work done by the internal auditor will be of some relevance to the external auditor.

By the time you have completed this chapter, you should be able to:

- Explain the role of internal audit.
- Explain how the quality of internal audit work can be maintained.
- Compare the role of internal audit with that of external audit and explain how the external auditor can obtain evidence from the work done by internal audit.

15.1 The role of the internal auditor

Internal auditing has been defined as 'an independent appraisal function established within an organisation to examine and evaluate its activities as a service to the organisation. The objective of internal auditing is to assist members of the organisation in the effective discharge of their responsibilities'.[1] This definition is broad enough to encompass the many activities which are undertaken under the general heading of internal audit in both the private and the public sectors. There are, however, three distinguishing features of the internal audit function:

1   It involves the appraisal of activities.
2   It is independent of the activities which are under investigation.
3   It is intended to be a constructive service.

ACTIVITY

Some elements of the definition of internal audit seem to echo the definitions of internal control and also of external audit. Given that most organisations are required to have these anyway, why might they be willing to bear the additional cost of establishing an internal audit department?

The benefits of having an internal audit department will become more apparent in the course of this chapter. It is worthwhile, however, to introduce some of the issues at this stage.

Senior management have a statutory duty to protect the company's assets and to ensure that the financial statements give a true and fair view. They cannot delegate these duties to anyone else, including the external auditor. It might, therefore, be reassuring for them to know that the operation of the systems of internal control is being monitored by staff who are independent of routine operations. Controls may lapse without such a review and the system may tend to deteriorate. This may be picked up by the external auditors, although their reviews of the system tend to occur only annually and will only examine those aspects which are directly relevant to forming an opinion on the financial statements.

The internal audit department will also provide a pool of capable staff with a broad knowledge of the business. This could be an extremely valuable resource if, for example, the board wishes to commission a report or investigation.

The internal audit function has, historically, been associated with the review of accounting information within the organisation. This chapter will, therefore, concentrate on the accounting aspects of the discipline. Internal auditors are, however, becoming increasingly involved in the investigation of the efficiency of the organisations in which they are employed. This extension of the internal auditor's role, often referred to as 'management audit', will be discussed in Chapter 16.

15.1.1 *Internal audit as an extension of internal control*

Company directors have onerous statutory duties with regard to safeguarding the company's assets and ensuring that proper accounting records are being maintained. They must also base important resource allocation decisions upon internal management accounting information. The size and complexity of many enterprises make it impossible for their directors to monitor everyday operations in person. They must, therefore, rely heavily upon the controls built into the accounting and other systems in order to do this for them.

According to the standards published by the Institute of Internal Auditors (IIA), internal controls are intended to ensure the following:

- The reliability and integrity of information.
- Compliance with policies, plans, procedures, laws, and regulations.
- The safeguarding of assets.
- The economical and efficient use of resources.
- The accomplishment of established objectives and goals for operations or programmes.[2]

This definition is broadly similar to the one published by the APC for use in the context of external auditing.[3]

The emphasis placed on each of the goals included in the definition can vary from company to company. Some organisations will devote more attention to ensuring that management have reliable information and that fraud and theft are prevented. Others will be more concerned with the procedures which monitor the company's efficiency in the use of resources.

15.1.2 *Agency theory and internal audit*

The remoteness of senior management from routine operations creates similar agency problems to those which exist in the context of the shareholder–director relationship. Staff may have a motive to produce misleading records or reports in order to conceal fraud, secure promotion or higher salaries, or protect themselves from redundancy. The controls built into the accounting systems to prevent this abuse may fail to operate because of poor supervision. Control weaknesses could arise because of unauthorised changes to procedures.

The directors cannot monitor the operation of the system themselves. They can, however, appoint an internal audit department to carry out this function for them. Internal audit has been described as 'a managerial control which functions by measuring and evaluating the effectiveness of other controls'.[4] This implies that the internal audit department is not responsible for the design, operation, or supervision of the system. Instead, internal audit is expected to review the system to ensure that the controls within it are effective and that they are operating properly.

The importance attached to the review of accounting information would appear to depend largely on the organisation's management structure. A study in the United States measured the extent to which divisional managers were dependent upon their immediate superiors for promotion and other career prospects. It was discovered that greater importance was attached to the internal audit of accounting information in companies in which managers could be more easily influenced. It would appear that the directors are aware of the pressures which can affect the quality of information within the organisation and are prepared to use internal audit in order to ensure that they have credible information for management purposes.[5]

15.1.3 *Internal v. external audit*

The nature of an internal audit investigation may differ significantly from that of the external auditor's. The most important difference is that the internal auditor is not bound by statutory duties and is, therefore, able to concentrate upon those aspects of the system which are considered most important by senior management or which appear to have the greatest audit significance. It is also quite possible for internal audit's priorities to change and develop with the organisation's circumstances.

Internal audit activities could be scheduled using a variation of the risk-based approach to auditing. Audit risk would have to be defined in terms of the various goals of internal control with an appropriate weighting attached to each one. Greater attention could be paid to departments whose management have a greater motive to manipulate their internal reports or where senior management are simply suspicious of the information which is being produced. Alternatively, more attention could be paid to the departments where there appears to be the greatest scope for reducing costs or increasing effectiveness. The internal auditor can use many of the external auditor's techniques for assessing inherent risk and for conducting analytical review.

The internal auditor's review could be similar to that of the external auditor. Audit staff could evaluate the potential effectiveness of the controls within the system and conduct compliance tests. In some organisations there is a manual or set of standing instructions which describes the 'official' system. The auditor would then be more concerned with ensuring that these are being complied with.

The remainder of this chapter will concentrate upon the internal auditor's approach to the examination of the accounting systems. This will be structured round the IIA's standards. The chapter which follows will discuss the role of internal audit with regard to improving the efficiency of operations.

15.2 Professional standards for internal auditors

The Institute of Internal Auditors (IIA) represents the interests of internal audit specialists. Organisations are not required to restrict themselves to members of this body when selecting internal audit staff. IIA members are, however, required to pass examinations in various aspects of internal audit, management and computer audit.

One of the IIA's most obvious contributions is in the publication of a series of standards for internal auditing. These cover the vital areas as follows:

- Independence
- Professional proficiency
- Scope of work
- Performance of audit work
- Management of the internal auditing department.

These standards are not mandatory in the sense that internal auditors could be disciplined for failing to adhere to them. They are aimed at both managers and auditors. Management can refer to the standards in order to ascertain the role of internal audit and to measure its effectiveness. Internal auditors can use the standards as a guide to good practice. Thus, the standards have been written largely for educational purposes.

15.2.1 *Independence of internal audit*

Internal audit staff must be free to conduct whatever investigation is necessary to enable them to fulfil their objectives. They must also be able to report their findings honestly. There is little point in having an internal audit department if its staff can be influenced by those whom they are appraising. The IIA Standards identify two aspects of independence: organisational status and objectivity.

The status of internal audit is determined largely by the manner in which it is supervised. The internal audit manager should report to someone who has sufficient seniority to ensure that audit reports are studied and acted upon. The audit committee, if one exists, should be asked to supervise the activities of internal audit and to receive its reports on behalf of the board. This suggests that the internal auditor should not report to anyone who is directly involved in the supervision of the accounting system. There would be a conflict of interest if the results of audit investigations were being reviewed by a manager who had a vested interest in suppressing some or all of the findings.

The internal audit department's remit should be defined formally by the board. The internal auditor's powers to obtain access to information and documents should be defined in writing. Internal audit staff may have to demand material from members of the company who are, technically, senior to them. The department's work might be hampered if auditees refused to provide access to the necessary records or answer questions posed by audit staff.

The status of the internal audit department will also be enhanced if the board takes an active interest in the planning of internal audit activities and the review of the department's more significant findings.

Objectivity is an attitude of mind. It could be difficult for the internal auditor to maintain such an attitude. Internal audit staff are, after all, full-time employees of the organisation. It may become difficult to maintain an independent attitude when working closely with the same staff in the auditee departments for a prolonged period. This is in sharp contrast to external audit staff who are sometimes involved with several different companies in the course of a normal year.

Internal audit staff should not be sent into situations where they would face a conflict of interest. Staff should, therefore, be encouraged to inform their supervisors of any reasons why they should not be assigned to a particular investigation. Regular rotation of assignments reduces the risk of close friendships developing with staff in auditee departments. This also encourages a fresh approach. Staff who have spent too long on any given area may be reluctant to report any weaknesses or omissions which they have failed to discover during earlier audits.

It is undesirable for audit staff to have any operating responsibilities. This can create the possibility of staff being asked to investigate the effects of their own decisions. Staff who have been seconded to internal audit should not be asked to audit the activities of their old departments.

15.2.2 *Professional proficiency*

Internal auditors do not require to hold formal qualifications in order to practise. It is, however, vital that the staff assigned to an investigation have the necessary skills and experience to cope. These may go far beyond the traditional knowledge of accounting and bookkeeping skills which are usually associated with auditing. In many cases, internal audit departments will have to recruit staff with qualifications in a range of technical and managerial skills. Internal audit staff must also have the necessary social skills to enable them to communicate effectively with the subjects of their investigation and obtain their active cooperation.

Many accountants spend some time in internal audit after obtaining their professional qualifications. This is often seen as a means of obtaining experience of working in an industrial or commercial environment after the completion of a training contract in a professional office. Those who do not belong to a professional accounting body could be encouraged to take relevant training, perhaps sitting the IIA's examinations.

Internal audit staff should be required to approach their work with a similar degree of professionalism to that displayed by the external auditor. This should, however, be defined in the context of each individual engagement. Excessive diligence in the conduct of an investigation could prove disruptive and delay the completion of the audit.

The working papers produced by audit staff should be reviewed by their superiors within the department. This review will ensure that appropriate action has been taken with regard to any irregularities discovered during the investigation and can also be linked to a system of staff appraisal.

15.2.3 *Scope of internal audit work*

The IIA standards suggest that the internal auditor should evaluate the adequacy and effectiveness of the system of internal controls. The IIA's definition of internal control has been discussed earlier in this chapter. The scope of internal audit is, ultimately, a matter for senior management to decide. It may be that internal audit's role will be restricted to the compliance testing of accounting and administrative controls. Alternatively, the internal auditor could be expected to conduct thorough reviews of the efficiency of operations and may not be required to pay any attention to accounting matters.

15.2.4 *Performance of audit work*

The IIA standards suggest that 'audit work should include planning the audit, examining and evaluating information, communicating results, and following up'.[6] The approach taken to audit planning and to the evaluation of audit evidence is similar to that of the external auditor. Differences will, however, arise in respect of the detailed objectives of the audit and this could have implications for the nature of the information which should be examined. It is, for example, unlikely that internal audit staff will devote a great deal of time to substantive testing. This might, however, be necessary as part of an investigation into a suspected fraud or if a serious control weakness has been discovered and the audit staff wish to investigate its effect on the accuracy of the figures. Internal audit reports are significantly different from those prepared by the external auditor. An external audit report is a coded message whose wording hardly varies from one audit to another. An internal audit report is intended to describe the scope of the audit and the results obtained. It will, therefore, be much longer and will have to contain a much more comprehensive description of the work done.

The report represents the only tangible result of the auditor's activities. It is, therefore, the only means by which the board and the staff who are subject to the audit can evaluate the effectiveness of internal audit. The credibility of internal audit will be damaged if reports are unclear or misleading.

The auditor's findings must be presented clearly and accurately. Audit staff should, for example, be discouraged from reporting trivial items in order to expand the size of the audit report. Any minor control weaknesses or compliance deviations can be dealt with informally by discussing them with staff in the auditee department or by issuing a supplementary report to the main document.

Staff should keep detailed records of the work which they have done and their findings. They should be capable of substantiating any matters raised in the report if they are challenged. The effects of any problems should be quantified.

The content of the report should be discussed with the supervisors of the auditee department before it is submitted. The supervisor's comments should be noted and incorporated into the report. This reduces the tensions which might arise if the supervisor was not given the opportunity to respond to any implied criticism before it is reported to senior management.

The auditor might be required to make specific suggestions for the correction of any control weaknesses discovered. Each organisation should have its own policy on this matter. Auditor independence could be impaired in the future because audit staff have been involved in the design of the system. They might be reluctant to report problems which have arisen as a result of their modifications. This problem could, however, be overcome by regular rotation of assignments. If audit staff are encouraged to suggest improvements to the system, then they can make use of their training and experience. Indeed, the departmental managers might not be particularly well qualified to make the necessary changes.

The distribution of the report should be carefully controlled. The report could describe loopholes in the system which could be exploited by fraudulent staff. The subjects of the report could also be embarrassed if their apparent failings were likely to be broadcast throughout the organisation. Thus, reports should be regarded as confidential. One copy should be sent to the manager in charge of the department which has been audited. Another should be sent to that person's immediate superior in order to ensure that appropriate action is taken. A copy will have to be retained within the internal audit department for review purposes. Copies may also be requested by the audit committee and by the external auditor, perhaps in a summarised form.

The auditor should conduct a follow-up to the report in order to ensure that the suggestions contained in it have been heeded. The time scale for these improvements should be agreed with management during the discussion of the auditor's findings. Once this period has elapsed, the auditor should ensure that the problems have been remedied. This could require a special visit to the department or, if the problems have not been too serious, the auditor could request written confirmation that the matters raised in the report have been dealt with. A detailed description of the new procedures should be given to support such a claim.

15.2.5 *Management of the internal auditing department*

The final standard deals with the manner in which the internal audit function should be controlled and managed in order to achieve its maximum effectiveness. This requires a formal statement of the role of the internal audit department, its powers and responsibilities. This statement is, in any case, required in order to support the department's status within the organisation.

The activities of the internal audit department should be properly planned. A series of detailed goals should be established within the framework laid down by the statement of internal audit's responsibilities. These goals should be translated into work schedules, with the greatest priority attached to the areas of highest risk or where there is a greater possibility of savings. These schedules can, in turn, be used to prepare budgets for staffing and expenses.

Large internal audit departments might require official audit manuals, similar to those produced by firms of external auditors. If this is not considered cost-effective then the department's policies should be recorded in other ways, perhaps by means of occasional memoranda. This will ensure that audit staff adopt a consistent approach in their work.

There should be a formal programme of quality control procedures to ensure that the work of the department is up to the required standard. This would include the supervision of staff and the review of their working papers by senior members of the department. There should also be quality control reviews to ensure that work is being done to the required standard throughout the department.

15.3 Internal audit as a source of audit evidence

The external auditor might be able to place some reliance upon the work of the internal auditor, thereby reducing the external audit fee. The potential savings can be increased still further if the internal and external auditors agree to reduce the extent to which they duplicate each others' efforts. Finally, it is possible to make substantial savings by seconding internal audit staff to the external auditor.

ACTIVITY

What factors will the external auditors take into account in determining the extent to which they will rely on the work of an internal auditor department?

The normal factors which determine the reliability of audit evidence will still apply. The external auditor will look for some evidence that the work done by the internal audit department is of a high quality and is unlikely to be undermined by the actions of the staff being audited. This means that the internal audit department must display a combination of both technical proficiency and independence.

These issues will be developed throughout the remainder of this section.

15.3.1 *Reliance on internal audit*

Internal audit can be seen as an extension of internal control. The factors which the external auditor should take into account in placing reliance on the work of the internal auditor are described in an SAS.[7] This suggests that the external auditor should consider such criteria as:

- The relevance of internal audit work (compliance testing of controls will be much more relevant than, say, investigations into the potential for cost-cutting).
- The professional proficiency of the internal audit staff (training, qualifications, etc.).
- Supervision and review of internal audit working papers and files.
- The extent to which internal audit findings are supported by appropriate evidence and testing.

- The extent to which internal audit reports tend to bear out the external auditor's findings on areas of overlap.

If each of these factors is satisfactory, then the auditor may be able to place some reliance upon the internal audit function. The materiality of individual figures and the levels of inherent risk associated with them should be borne in mind when making this assessment.

There have been a number of studies on the relative importance attached to the various criteria by which the external auditor measures the relevance of internal audit. A study by Schneider[8] suggests that the quality of the internal audit department's work was the most important factor, followed by the competence of its staff as measured by their qualifications and experience and then by objectivity. This is supported to some extent by another study which suggested that auditors paid most attention to competence and the quality of work but attached very little significance to objectivity.[9] This rather low weighting for objectivity does, however, conflict with the findings of another survey[10] in which it was discovered that the independence of the internal audit function and the extent to which it had been considered reliable in previous years were the most important variables. All of these studies were, however, based upon case studies. There is a possibility that the importance of certain variables will be affected by the circumstances described in each case.

15.3.2 *Coordination of audit work*

It has been suggested that management should adopt a much more proactive approach to the reduction of audit fees by encouraging the internal audit department to liaise more closely with the external auditor with a view to reducing the extent to which audit work is being repeated.[11]

This approach would involve much more than simply comparing the interests of the two groups of auditors and looking for opportunities to reduce costs. The head of internal audit should consult with the external auditor and develop a coordinated auditing strategy. The external auditor should be required to quantify the extent to which the audit fee was being reduced because of the collaboration with internal audit.

Such an approach may be met with resistance from both the external and internal auditors. The external auditor is unlikely to display any enthusiasm for a proposal to reduce the audit fee. There is, however, nothing to prevent the company from appointing another firm on the understanding that it will work closely with the internal auditor. Thus, the external auditor is virtually obliged to comply with management's wishes. There is no reason why an external auditor cannot place some reliance on work done by the internal audit department.

The internal auditor may feel that the work done in support of the external auditor will interfere with the department's other responsibilities. This could be a valid argument if important aspects of internal audit were neglected in order to reduce the audit fee. The selection of goals for the internal audit function is, however, a matter for the board to decide.

15.3.3 *Secondment of internal audit staff*

It has been suggested that the internal audit department could second staff to the external auditor. These staff could act in support of the auditor, perhaps by collecting documents for examination or possibly even assisting in audit testing.[12]

The extent to which savings can be made from the various strategies is illustrated by a practical case in which an external auditor suggested that a full scope internal audit investigation of 425 hours in duration could reduce the time taken for the external audit by 60 hours, a ratio of 7.08:1. A more limited internal audit investigation taking 575 hours, carried out under the direct supervision of the external auditor, could replace 450 hours on the external audit, a ratio of 1.28:1. If internal audit staff were seconded to assist in the external audit then it would be possible to achieve a 1:1 substitution ratio for internal to external audit hours.[13]

The fact that there is a relatively poor trade-off between internal and external audit hours when the internal audit staff are working independently does not imply that internal audit is inefficient. The investigation which resulted in the substitution ratio of 7.08:1 would have produced other benefits in addition to the reduction in the audit fee.

15.4 Summary

Internal audit exists to serve management. It does so by ensuring that the various controls implemented by management in order to ensure that the company is efficient and that the accounting records are accurate are operating properly.

The role of internal audit should be defined by senior management. This is partly to ensure that the department is reasonably independent of the various managers and supervisors on whom the internal auditor must report as part of his duties.

The Institute of Internal Auditors has attempted to improve the quality of internal audit work by publishing a series of standards. The cover the main areas of independence, professional proficiency, scope of work, performance of audit work, and management of the internal auditing department.

The work of the internal audit department could have some relevance to that of the external auditor. It is not in the best interests of the company for the work of the two groups of auditors to overlap. The internal audit department could be instructed to provide the external auditor with as much assistance as possible in order to reduce the audit fee.

REVIEW QUESTIONS

1. In 1990, the APC published an Auditing Guideline entitled *Guidance for Internal Auditors*. This would appear to support most of the arguments developed in the IIA standards. Why would the APC wish to publish a document which is intended to improve the quality of internal audit work?

2. The APB has made its standards mandatory. Discuss the difficulties associated with publishing a mandatory set of standards for internal auditing.

3. Many organisations deliberately recruit newly qualified accountants from professional firms to join their internal audit departments. These appointments are viewed as a means of giving staff a broad overview of the systems. They are expected to move into managerial positions after two years or so. Discuss the advantages and disadvantages of this policy for the professionalism of the internal audit function.

4. Should the external auditor be encouraged to use staff seconded from internal audit to conduct detailed audit testing? What precautions should be taken?

EXERCISES

1. The Wyetown branch of XZ Ltd has forty administrative staff and more than 200 manufacturing staff. Internal audit staff are visiting each branch in order to evaluate the effectiveness of the debtors' ledger systems. The following notes have been prepared on the Wyetown system:

(a) There are three clerks in the sales ledger department. The ledger is split alphabetically. Smith handles the section from A to K, Jones deals with L to N, and Brown with O to Z. There are equal numbers of accounts in each section.

(b) Sales invoices are typed in the accounts department. Each member of the debtors' ledger staff then records the invoices in a sales day book, one for each section of the ledger. The clerks total the sales day books and inform the nominal ledger clerk of the grand total each month. The sales day books are then used to update the debtors' ledger.

(c) Most of the incoming mail contains either cheques from customers or, increasingly, queries about the monthly statements prepared by the debtors' ledger clerks. Smith, Jones and Brown take it in turns to collect the mail from the reception area each month. The person collecting the mail is responsible for opening it and passing any correspondence addressed to other departments to the relevant person.

(d) Cheques received through the post are recorded in the debtors' ledger. They are kept in a locked cash box until the end of the week when whichever of the debtors' ledger clerks is least busy takes them to the bank. The cash book and nominal ledger accounts are updated from the bank pay-in slips.

You are required to do the following:

(a) Identify the weaknesses in the above system and suggest how they should be rectified.

(b) Describe the actions to be taken if:
  (i) the branch manager agrees to implement the proposed changes, or
  (ii) he refuses to change the system on the grounds that the staff are long-serving, trusted employees.

2. The chief accountant at XZ's head office requests an audit investigation at the Wyetown branch. Shortly after the receipt of your report on the Wyetown system, it had been noticed that the turnover of debtors was slowing down rapidly. This was unexpected because the company had started to grant a discount for prompt payment which had speeded up the payments collected by other branches.

One of the clerks at Wyetown has started to enjoy a much more lavish lifestyle, having bought an expensive house and car. The clerk claims to have inherited some money, but the branch manager suspects that he is stealing incoming cheques and concealing the theft by 'teeming and lading'.

Suggest how the requested investigation should be conducted.

References and further reading

1. Institute of Internal Auditors, *Standards for the Professional Practice of Internal Auditing*. These standards are reproduced as appendices to the following texts: A.D. Chambers, G.M. Selim and G. Vinten, *Internal Auditing*, Pitman, 1987; G. Courtemanche, *The New Internal Auditing*, Wiley, 1986. These texts are also highly recommended as a source of further information about internal auditing.
2. Institute of Internal Auditors, *ibid*.
3. APB, *Glossary of Terms*, 1995.
4. IIA, *The Statement of Responsibilities of the Internal Auditor*, 1971.
5. San Miguel, J.G. and Govindarajan, V., 'The contingent relationship between the controller and internal audit functions in large organisations', *Accounting, Organisations and Society*, vol. 9, no. 2, 1984, pp. 179–88.
6. Institute of Internal Auditors, *Standards for the Professional Practice of Internal Auditing, op. cit.*
7. APB, SAS 500, *Considering the Work of Internal Audit*, 1995.
8. Schneider, A., 'Modelling external auditors' evaluations of internal auditing', *Journal of Accounting Research*, Autumn 1984, pp. 657–78. The same author describes this study in 'Consensus among auditors in evaluating the internal audit function', *Accounting and Business Research*, Autumn 1985, pp. 297–301.
9. Margheim, L.L., 'Further evidence on external auditor's reliance on internal auditors', *Journal of Accounting Research*, Spring 1986, pp. 194–205.
10. Brown, P.R., 'Independent auditor judgement in the evaluation of internal audit functions', *Journal of Accounting Research*, Autumn 1983, pp. 444–55.

11. Berry, L.E., 'Strategies for controlling audit costs', *Sloan Management Review*, Fall 1985, pp. 63–8.
12. Wallace, W.A., 'Internal auditors can cut outside CPA costs', *Harvard Business Review*, March-April 1984, pp. 16 and 20.
13. Wallace, W.A., 'Enhancing your relationship with internal auditors', *The CPA Journal*, December 1984, pp. 46–53.

CHAPTER 16

Management auditing

The traditional role of both external and internal auditors has been to add credibility to financial information. Their investigations are sponsored by shareholders, managers, or other interested parties who wish to be able to rely upon that information for decision-making purposes. Auditors are not usually expected to comment upon the performance or the viability of the organisation or department under consideration. This is usually left to the readers of the audited figures.

Management auditing provides a new dimension to the audit function. Instead of checking the accuracy of accounting statements, the management auditor looks at the efficiency of the organisation's operations and reports upon ways in which costs could be reduced or profitability improved. This examination can extend to the review of the organisation's strategies and can even consider its interaction with society and the environment. This branch of auditing was first introduced in the audit of local and central government and has since spread into the private sector.[1]

This chapter will concentrate upon the implications of management audit for the private sector, drawing from the literature on the experiences of the application of this concept in public sector organisations.[2]

By the time you have completed this chapter you should be able to:

- Explain what is meant by a management / value for money audit.
- Compare and contrast the objectives of economy and efficiency audits against effectiveness audits.
- Describe the problems associated with management audit reporting, including the controversy over whether reports should be made public.

16.1 What is management auditing?

Management auditing can be defined in many ways. The term also has several synonyms, such as 'operational audit' or 'systems audit'. Rather than become entangled in semantics, the following definition will be adopted in this chapter:

> Management audit is an objective, independent, informed and constructive appraisal of the effectiveness of managers/teams of managers in their achievement of company objectives and policies in order to identify existing and potential weaknesses and strengths in all functions and operations within an organisation and to recommend ways to rectify these weaknesses and potential weaknesses. It must be seen as a managerial function, and as such must assist management, and in doing so, strengths and not only weaknesses must be reported upon.[3]

This definition was devised from responses to a questionnaire survey which was distributed to senior managers, partners in accounting firms and academics. It was endorsed by over 70 per cent of the respondents. The following lines of enquiry were deemed to fall within the scope of a management audit by at least 80 per cent of the respondents:

1   Is the structure of the organisation sound; does it support the aims of the business and utilise the resources available to it effectively?
2   Are management systems of planning and control adequate, understood and continuously used?
3   Are control techniques, such as budgetary control, providing management with proper and timely information?
4   Are management systems of planning and control reviewed and updated regularly?
5   Are the objectives of the business being met?

ACTIVITY

Given that management audit does not appear to be an accounting activity as such, why might accounting firms be keen to offer this service in addition to (or even instead of) the traditional external audit?

Management audit tends to be less labour-intensive than external audit and so can be more profitable. External auditors may feel that they have an advantage in offering this type of service because of their knowledge of the business, particularly since the development of the risk-based approach. This type of audit will also enable the auditor to enhance the profitability of the company and so provide management with something which is perceived as useful. This could help the auditor to sell even more services.

One of the reasons for the widespread agreement on the wording of this definition and the selection of goals for management audit is the fact that much of the foregoing is highly ambiguous. There are a number of contentious matters which would have to be resolved in the implementation of a management audit.

The first difficulty is in the definition of 'management'. The management auditor could be appointed by the shareholders to report upon the performance of senior management.[4] This is in sharp contrast to the suggestion that the audit should be commissioned by senior management in order to evaluate the organisation's middle and junior management.

The selection of suitable topics for management audit investigations can also prove difficult. The greatest benefits could be obtained from an evaluation of the company's fundamental strategies and key operating policies. Senior management could, however, see this type of review as interference in their duties and reduce the auditor's role to the study of the manner in which the board's strategy has been implemented. The nature and content of the auditor's report is another difficult area. It is not, for example, clear whether the report should be published. These issues will be developed later in this chapter.

16.1.1 *Management v. financial auditing*

Management auditing differs significantly from its financial counterpart. The management auditor is concerned with forming an opinion on the strengths and weaknesses of the organisation and its management. The financial auditor adopts a neutral position on these matters and simply ensures that the readers of his report are provided with information from which to make this type of decision for themselves.

There is no official definition of a management audit. The management auditor's attention can be focused on specific areas within the organisation's performance. Senior management could devise a schedule for a management audit which would cover each of the major functional or geographical areas of the organisation in turn over a number of years. Such rotation of emphasis is unacceptable in the case of a statutory audit.

There are, however, some similarities between the two types of audit. It is, for example, vital that both the statutory and the management auditor are independent of the activities which they audit. The management auditor's independence could be protected by the employment of an outside consultant or by the use of an internal auditor whose objectivity was protected by the techniques described in Chapter 15.

Management auditors are required to collect and evaluate evidence in exactly the same manner as a financial auditor. Different types of evidence will be relevant to each type of audit. The attributes of reliable evidence are, however, the same in each case.

Each type of audit should result in a report. The financial auditor reports to the members of the company, having measured the truth and fairness of the financial statements against professional and statutory standards. The management auditor must report in accordance with the terms of the engagement. This may require the development of a benchmark against which to measure the effectiveness of the managers under investigation. The form and content of the management auditor's report will be determined in the context of the engagement.

16.1.2 *Who should conduct a management audit?*

It has been argued that the organisation's external auditor is best qualified to carry out a management audit. The external auditor is trained and experienced in the collection and evaluation of evidence. A management audit requires an independent attitude and a thorough knowledge of the business. The external auditor can offer both of these attributes.[5]

A counter-argument might be that the external auditor's experience tends to be restricted to the examination of accounting information. The management auditor may have to be qualified in systems analysis, marketing, or in whichever functional area is under review. This could mean that an independent management consultant would be a more suitable auditor.[6] The risk-based approach to auditing forces the auditor to develop a much greater awareness of the company's business environment. Its increasing application to both internal and external audits may invalidate the case against the auditor's role as a management auditor.

The internal auditor's training and skills are similar to those of the external auditor. Arguably, the internal auditor will have a more detailed knowledge of the company. The internal auditor does not, however, have direct access to a consultancy division for specialist advice and might have to second staff from other departments or seek the assistance of independent consultants.

16.2 The scope of a management audit

The phrase 'value for money auditing' has been used to describe the concept of a management audit, particularly in the public sector. The National Audit Act 1983 and the Local Government Finance Act 1982 require both internal and external auditors to consider value for money in the conduct of their examinations.

16.2.1 *The 3 E's*

Value for money is often expressed in terms of the '3 E's' of economy, efficiency and effectiveness. These three concepts are interrelated.

> *Economy*
> 'refers to the acquisition of the appropriate quality and quantity of financial, human and physical resources at the appropriate times and at the lowest cost'.

Efficiency

'refers to the use of financial, human and physical resources such that output is maximised for any given set of resource inputs, or input is minimised for any given quantity and quality of output provided'.

Effectiveness

'refers to the achievement of the objectives or other intended effects of programmes, operations or activities'.[7]

ACTIVITY

Management audits have often been criticised for concentrating too heavily on either economy and efficiency or effectiveness. In particular, there tends to be a heavier emphasis on economy and efficiency. Why might this be?

Management audits cannot examine both economy and effectiveness because of the inverse relationship between the two. It is almost always possible to improve effectiveness if one is willing to bear some additional cost or to make savings if one is willing to tolerate a lower level of service.

Auditors may prefer to concentrate on economy and efficiency because these are much easier to measure than effectiveness. This is particularly true in areas such as health or education where the outputs are extremely difficult to quantify.

A value for money audit can be either reactive or proactive in approach. The auditor can either examine the results actually obtained for a given level of investment or examine the plans and budgets to see whether management's targets are realistic.

16.2.2 *Economy and efficiency audits*

Most management audits concentrate upon economy and efficiency. These attributes are easier to measure than effectiveness. The organisation must establish a policy for the selection of activities to audit. One possibility is to establish a long-term plan which would involve the examination of every major functional area over a period of, say, five years. This plan could be modified in response to opportunities for savings. A department which appeared to be overspending in comparison to others or a cost which appeared to be out of control in relation to its budget might be investigated.

It is impossible to measure efficiency unless there is an appropriate set of standards. It is important that these standards are chosen carefully. The credibility of management audit will suffer if the performance of departments is measured against irrelevant standards. The evaluation of staff against invalid standards could have more damaging consequences. Managers may attempt to satisfy an impossible standard by making sub-optimal decisions. The buying department could, for example, react to unrealistic expectations about the price of materials by purchasing poorer qualities.

Standards could be determined by comparison with similar departments or units either within the organisation or in other organisations. The auditor would, however, have to ensure that the comparisons are fair. A comparison of manufacturing costs in two similar factories could be misleading if one factory has more modern equipment than the other. This could affect the cost of labour. Different amounts of depreciation will also be charged.

If efficiency is to be measured in terms of comparative statistics, the auditor will have to ensure that the standards which are being applied are sufficiently stringent. The fact that one department is more efficient than the others does not necessarily mean that there is no room for improvement.

The actual conduct of the efficiency audit is similar in many respects to a financial audit. The auditor must obtain evidence to support the assertion that a department is efficiently run or that further savings could be made or revenues generated. One of the most fruitful sources of such evidence is to be found from a review of the systems which have been implemented to maximise profitability.

As part of the audit of, say, stock control, the auditor could review the procedures which are intended to minimise the amount of money tied up. There are several mathematical models which can be used to ensure that stock is ordered at optimal intervals and that the risk of running out of stock is kept within acceptable levels. There should be a system for monitoring stock holdings. One of the most dramatic examples of a failure to manage stocks properly occurred when a new management team was appointed to take charge of the Woolworth group of companies. They introduced a new stock control system and discovered that the company had sufficient lime green zip fasteners to satisfy demand for 500 years. They also discovered that one-fifth of retail floor space was occupied by product lines which sold five or fewer items per store per year.[8]

The review of systems should include some consideration of the cost-effectiveness of the monitoring procedures. A highly sophisticated inventory control system which requires large numbers of staff to operate could cost more to operate than the savings which could be generated from the improved information.

An economy and efficiency audit could have a motivational effect on the staff who are to be reviewed. Managers will aim to match the standards against which they are to be evaluated. The standards do, however, have to be carefully chosen. Managers also have to be encouraged to put the overall effectiveness of their departments first, even if these aims are in conflict with the statistical basis upon which they are to be assessed. Thus, a manager should be prepared to authorise staff overtime if this is necessary in order to meet the requirements of an important customer. This should happen even if the overtime will result in an adverse labour variance.

16.2.3 *Effectiveness audits*

It is impossible to state that a department has provided value for money unless it has met its objectives. In a sense, there is little point in measuring efficiency unless it can also be demonstrated that the department is also fulfilling its intended role within the organisation. It can also be misleading to measure efficiency in terms of costs. Certain expenses can be reduced quite easily, but at the risk of causing the company considerable harm. Maintenance and advertising are good examples of these. The costs of lost production or sales associated with limiting the amounts spent in these areas could outweigh the savings generated.

The first step in conducting an effectiveness audit is to determine the precise objectives of the activity under review. In the public sector these might be expressed in terms of the service being provided, such as health care. In the private sector, these are likely to be expressed in terms of maximising shareholder wealth or in terms of a surrogate measure such as profitability or share price.

It is not part of the auditor's role to determine the duties of the department under investigation. These should be defined by senior management as part of the engagement. The audit will be rendered almost impossible if the auditor and auditee cannot agree upon the department's objectives.

The objectives of the department should be consistent with those of the organisation as a whole, although there should be a specific set of objectives for each department. Thus, the purchasing department could be responsible for obtaining materials of an acceptable quality at the lowest possible price. They should also ensure that the production department has sufficient stocks for operating purposes. To the extent that these objectives conflict, perhaps because the more reliable suppliers might also tend to be more expensive, senior management should rank them in order of priority.

The auditor's examination of effectiveness can concentrate upon one or more of goal analysis, audit of operations, and audit of systems.[9] Managers must translate their general objectives into specific, meaningful goals. The auditor might start by examining these and ensuring that they are consistent with the general objectives. The manager in charge of vehicle maintenance might have a general responsibility for the safe and reliable operation of the company's fleet of cars and vans. This might be translated into a series of individual goals such as ensuring that all vehicles are serviced at regular intervals in accordance with their manufacturers' recommendations. Service intervals and the quality of the department's workmanship should be such that breakdowns because of mechanical failure are infrequent. The residual value of vehicles should be maximised. The calculation of the optimal service interval may be based upon mathematical formulae which have been developed for this purpose.

The audit of operations involves the measurement of actual effectiveness and its comparison with objectives. This may require some form of investigation.

Market research techniques could, for example, be used to measure the effectiveness of an advertising campaign in increasing the company's brand image.

It may be almost impossible to measure effectiveness in a scientific manner. If, for example, the auditor is investigating health and safety practices, it is difficult to quantify the severity of accidents. If the extent to which accidents could have been avoidable is also to be taken into consideration, then this will complicate matters still further.

It has been suggested that the auditor ought to accept that the review of effectiveness is likely to require subjective assessment.[10] This could, to some extent, be overcome by making use of expert advisers. The auditor could, for example, request a peer review of a factory's safety record to be conducted by the safety officer at another factory in the company.

The examination of systems might also enable the auditor to identify areas for improvement. The auditor could investigate the nature of management's own systems for monitoring effectiveness. If the performance measures are valid then the auditor might be able to base the audit upon statistics which are readily available. If management are monitoring a valid measure of their performance then this could, in itself, improve effectiveness.

16.3 Management audit reporting

The management auditor will report in a similar manner to any other internal auditor. The scope of the audit should be described in detail. The report should, for example, state whether the investigation was of economy and efficiency or effectiveness. The auditor should identify the basis upon which efficiency or effectiveness was measured. This will enable the reader to evaluate the relevance of the findings.

The auditor's findings will then be stated and quantified wherever possible. These should be accompanied by specific recommendations and the responses of the departmental management. If the audit has been restricted in any way, perhaps because information has been withheld or could not be obtained, then this should also be reported.

16.4 Statutory management audits

Management audits were introduced in the public sector to compensate for the lack of a profit motive to spur managers. This problem might not seem relevant to the private sector where badly run companies are in danger of being taken over. The shareholders can also remove the directors from office if the company's performance does not match expectations. There is, however, a case for conducting a management audit anyway. The fact that a company's results are reasonable does not mean that there is no room for improvement. Furthermore, management could be maximising short-term profits at the expense of the company's future.

Langenderfer and Robertson have derived a model for an external management audit from the postulates of financial auditing proposed by Mautz and Sharaf.[11] This assumes that a management audit should be a service to the shareholders and not management. This is based largely upon the apparent information needs of the users of financial statements, who are often more interested in non-financial measures of the performance of management.

The management auditor should be expected to evaluate management performance rather than measure it. This distinction is important because of the higher degree of objectivity and precision implied by measurement. The need for subjectivity is largely a result of the lack of standards against which to measure management performance. The fact that performance cannot be quantified objectively is not seen as a problem. It could actually be advantageous in that reports will have to be much more carefully written and the scope of the audit described in much greater detail than for financial audits.

While Langenderfer and Robertson make a valuable contribution to the development of management audit, they do not cover such vital issues as the need for a statutory report or the extent to which such a report should be published. A survey of the opinions of practising accountants, corporate managers, investment analysts and institutional investors did not discover unequivocal support for the idea of a compulsory management audit.[12] This could, however, have been so partly because the authors suggested that such an audit should be conducted by the company's external auditors. Some respondents could have relatively little confidence in the abilities of financial auditors to form a valid opinion on the standards of management. The authors concluded that the need for a management audit was evident regardless of the attitudes of those surveyed. The idea might become more attractive if the concept of a management audit could be more clearly defined. Boys explored some of the issues relating to management auditing in a survey of accounting firms and industrial and commercial companies.[13] This suggested that there was some support for the concept of management audit.

The need to publish the auditor's findings appeared to create a number of problems. Management would not wish the auditor to publish a report which consisted of a list of weaknesses. This would lead to criticism from the shareholders and could impair the working relationship between the auditor and management. It would be more appropriate for the auditor to express an opinion on the overall quality of managerial performance. Such a report is difficult to justify because of the lack of generally accepted management standards.

Three possibilities were proposed to overcome the problem of arriving at an opinion on management. The financial statements could simply state that a management audit has been conducted without going into further detail. A detailed report of all of the audit work done could be published. The APC could extend the Auditing Standards to require some management audit testing. The scope paragraph of the existing financial audit report would then imply that a management audit had been carried out by virtue of the reference to the application of Auditing Standards.

Boys suggests that the accountancy profession should become involved in the development of techniques and methodologies for management audits. This could lead to the accountant becoming more heavily involved in this activity. Auditors should also attempt to provide as much constructive advice as possible during their normal audit of the financial statements.

16.5 Summary

A management audit is essentially an appraisal of managerial performance. The management auditor can attempt to assist management by evaluating individual sections within the organisation. Alternatively, the audit could be intended to satisfy the shareholders that the company was being run properly. Such audits tend to involve a great deal of subjective judgement if only because there are no generally agreed standards against which to measure managerial performance.

Management audits can concentrate either upon economy and efficiency or upon effectiveness. These concepts are not mutually exclusive, although the former concentrates more upon the inputs into an activity and the latter on its output. The auditor can, and should, investigate the methods by which management measure their own performance in these areas. If they have adopted inadequate standards then this should be brought to their attention.

There have been suggestions that management auditing should become mandatory in the private sector. This is already the case in the public sector. A number of issues would have to be resolved if this were to be the case, including the selection of an appropriate auditor and the manner in which the auditor should report.

REVIEW QUESTIONS

1. If inefficient companies are liable to be taken over, do shareholders really require management audits?

2. To what extent could a management auditor base the evaluation of economy and efficiency or effectiveness upon statistics obtained from the published financial statements of similar companies?

3. Should the cost-effectiveness of a value for money audit department be measured in terms of the cost savings which it generates?

4. Discuss the relative merits of the different methods described in 16.4 for the publication of the results of a management audit report.

——————— EXERCISES ———————

1. The managing director of Trendy plc always watches a business affairs programme on television. The latest edition contained an item about management auditing. This prompted discussion at the next board meeting and it was agreed that the external auditor should be commissioned to conduct a review of the economy and effectiveness of the company's marketing function.

The auditor requested a statement of the marketing function's goals. The only response was 'Selling, we suppose'.

(a) Suggest the difficulties which the auditor will face in dealing with the manager in charge of the marketing department, and in preparing a report to the directors because of the lack of a clear set of departmental objectives.

(b) Suggest how efficiency and effectiveness could be measured if the department's goals had been defined as 'The maximisation of revenues by the promotion of the company's products using the most cost-effective sales techniques'.

2. Compare and contrast the difficulties of measuring the efficiency and effectiveness of the personnel management function with that of public relations.

References and further reading

1. An overview of auditing in the public sector can be obtained from Buttery, R. and Simpson, R., *Audit in the Public Sector*, ICSA Publishing, 1993.
2. There is a detailed review of the work on management auditing in the public sector in Glynn, J.J., *Value for Money Auditing in the Public Sector*, Prentice Hall, 1985.
3. Santocki, J., 'Meaning and scope of management audit', *Accounting and Business Research*, Winter 1976, pp. 64–70.
4. Sherer, M. and Kent, D., *Auditing and Accountability*, Paul Chapman Publishing, 1983, p. 113.
5. Ponder, E.H., 'Operational auditing by CPA firms', *The CPA Journal*, October 1984, pp. 38–50.
6. This attitude is reflected in the policy of one accounting firm whose audit staff conduct only regulatory audits. Management audits for the same clients are conducted by members of the firm's management consultancy staff. Some of these would have been trained in auditing, others would have been recruited from other backgrounds. See Tomkins, C., 'Local Authority audit under the Audit commission and what it means to one private sector professional firm', *Financial Accountability and Management*, Spring 1986, pp. 35–51.
7. All three definitions have been taken from the CICA Value for Money Auditing Standards which are reproduced in Price Waterhouse, *Value for Money Auditing Manual*, Gee and Co., 1983.
8. These facts came to light during an attempted takeover of Woolworth (now known as Kingfisher) by Dixons. See, for example, Peston, R., 'Woolworth shows its new colours', *Investors Chronicle*, 16 May 1986, p. 97.
9. Quoted in Glynn, J.J., *Value for Money Auditing in the Public Sector*, Prentice Hall, 1985, p. 62.

10. Grimwood, M. and Tomkins, C., 'Value for money auditing: towards incorporating a naturalistic approach', *Financial Accountability and Management*, Winter 1986, pp. 251–72.

11. Langenderfer, H.Q. and Robertson, J.C., 'A theoretical structure for independent audits of management', *The Accounting Review*, October 1969, pp. 777–87.

12. Smith, C.H., Lanier, R.A. and Taylor, M.E., 'The need for and scope of the audit of management: a survey of attitudes', *The Accounting Review*, April 1972, pp. 270–83.

13. The results of this survey are summarised in two articles by Boys, P., 'Value-for-money test spreading in private sector', *Accountancy*, July 1984, pp. 118–20 and 'Growth of VFM: what role for the profession?', *Accountancy*, January 1985, pp. 132–3.

CHAPTER 17

Environmental audit

Diane Walters

Environmental auditing has become more prominent in recent years. This aspect of auditing has grown in tandem with the increased demands of members of the public and of legislators for companies to improve their corporate environmental performance. More pressure is being put on organisations to produce environmental reports in addition to the normal financial reports, and the environmental audit is seen as part of the environmental reporting process.

Environmental auditing is a term which covers a large variety of different activities. These activities range from the assessment of a company's compliance with current or future legal standards on air pollution, to company energy efficiency audits. Environmental auditing is a new task which no single profession is currently able to undertake alone. This is an area where the 'financial' auditors find themselves working alongside auditors with different specialist skills, such as scientists and lawyers.

By the time you have completed this chapter, you should be able to:

- Explain what is meant by environmental audit.
- Describe the various types of environmental audit.
- Describe the basic approach to an environmental audit.
- Explain how environmental audit is affected by standards and legislation.

17.1 What is environmental auditing?

In the last few years more and more companies are reaching the conclusion that they cannot disregard environmental matters or exploit natural resources without regard for the consequences.[1] Many businesses are now considering their impact on the environment, and are trying to ensure that their activities conform to standards set by regulatory bodies, as well as those standards expected by the general public. An assessment of the processes, practices and techniques used within the business can help determine where problems may arise, and also show where greater efficiencies can be made through improved environmental performance. This assessment is known as an environmental audit.[2]

The term means exactly what it says – the audit of a business to assess its impact on the environment. The European Commission's definition describes environmental audit as:

> a management tool comprising a systematic, documented, periodic, and objective evaluation of how well organisations, management and equipment are performing with the aim of contributing to safeguard the environment by facilitating management control of environmental practices, and assessing compliance with company policies, which would include meeting regulatory requirements and standards.[3]

Another definition from the Confederation of British Industry explains in a more simple way how wide-ranging environmental audit can be. It defines the activity as:

> the systematic examination of the interactions between any business operation and its surroundings. This includes all emissions to air, land and water; legal constraints; the effects on the neighbouring community, landscape and ecology; and the public's perception of the operating company in the local area.[4]

Although these definitions may seem to be describing an activity which is very different from financial auditing, the two are in fact very closely related.

17.1.1 *The aims of the environmental audit*

The environmental audit is designed to identify the environmental problems associated with the production of goods or services, to develop benchmarks of good practice, and to act as the basis of an evolving corporate strategy. But within these general aims, organisations may have quite diverse ideas about why they need to concern themselves with environmental audits.

Some companies may wish to ensure compliance with the growing body of environmental legislation. Other companies might be determined to improve their market competitiveness, or to sharpen the market focus of their products, by developing a visibly 'green' public image. For some companies, the environmental audit may be thrust upon them, in the form of demands from insurers or investors.

Environmental audits may be undertaken simply in order to facilitate compliance with the law. But they have a wider remit, in that the audit should be viewed as a means to ensure that the company's policies, practices and processes are operating effectively and efficiently, and in accordance with the long-term goals and objectives of the company.

17.1.2 *Who benefits?*

When a company decides to embark on an environmental audit programme, it is likely to experience several benefits as a result. These benefits may include:

1   Better corporate risk control. The company will reduce its costs associated with poor environmental performance, and be less exposed to litigation and penalties or fines.
2   Public image enhancement in the market place and improved public relations. The company may even increase its profitability because of its new 'green' image.
3   Competitive advantage by not merely complying with legislation, but by anticipating it.
4   Improved operating efficiencies such as recycling, reduced packaging and lower energy usage.

It is not only the company which benefits, of course. Companies which have given the environment high priority have found that employees have benefited from increased morale, and third parties such as customers and investors gain comfort that the organisation is taking its environmental obligations seriously.

Of course, not all of the effects of introducing environmental auditing to a company will have a positive effect on the company (although its introduction will ultimately have a positive effect on the environment itself). The major possible disadvantage for a company is that the public's perception of the company and its products become more negative. Almost all companies which actively and voluntarily involve themselves with environmental audits are likely to be at the positive end of the corporate environmental health spectrum. However, in the United Kingdom at present, most companies are contributing in a negative way to the health of the environment. One of the problems encountered by companies which are prepared to make public information about their environmental performance is the negative public reaction. It may be difficult to explain to the public that every other company in the same industry is much more environmentally damaging, but simply avoids environmental audit.

17.1.3 *Environmental audit characteristics*

The practice of environmental auditing shares many characteristics with the practice of auditing a set of financial statements. It involves the collection of information, the evaluation of the information collected, formulating conclusions, and making recommendations in the form of a report.

The exact form of any particular environmental audit will depend on its specific purpose, but will generally involve similar procedures to those found in a traditional audit. For example, the audit objective may be to ensure that internal control systems designed to monitor compliance with pollution legislation are in place and operating effectively. The environmental auditor will review the internal control system to ensure its effectiveness, and will carry out compliance testing to ensure that the internal controls are operating consistently throughout the year.

17.1.4 *Organisation of the environmental auditing profession*

Environmental auditing requires professional skills such as assessing and analysing systems, assessing risk, making decisions based on the results of audit tests, and preparing reports. These are all skills found in traditional auditing. Because environmental auditing has so many similarities with traditional auditing, it makes sense to use the traditional auditing profession's experience and methods as the base for environmental auditing.[5]

However, environmental auditing will often require professional competence within technical areas such as environmental legislation, technology and science. It therefore makes sense that environmental auditors adopt a team approach, with various professionals bringing their own particular expertise to the audit. A recent report published by the Danish accountancy profession[6] recommended that because of this need for a multi-disciplinary approach, it should be firms, and not individual persons, who are authorised as environmental auditors.

In the United Kingdom, individuals may register with the Environmental Auditors Registration Association. At present registration is voluntary, but all members must agree to follow a code of practice.[7] The National Accreditation Council for Certification Bodies also has a role in regulating environmental auditors who are engaged in work specifically aimed at assessing compliance with certain EC and UK environmental standards.

17.2 Classifications of environmental auditing

Environmental audits can vary significantly in their scope and level of detail. When developing an environmental management system, a company may wish to undertake a comprehensive review of performance across the full range of its activities. At other times, managers will want to focus on particular aspects of their business. The following list of types of environmental audits is by no means exhaustive, since every company will have its own unique set of environmental circumstances.

17.2.1 *Comprehensive environmental performance review*

This involves a review of all aspects of the company, looking at how the business impacts on the environment. It may require significant resources, and a wide range of skills and expertise. It may be the first step for a company to address environmental issues, since it will provide a baseline from which to judge future improvement. The following areas would be included in this type of audit:[8]

Materials and energy
- Are the resources renewable?
- Are the resources extracted in a sustainable way?
- Are there any secondary effects (e.g. deforestation)?
- What is the source and usage of energy?
- What transport is used?
- Do suppliers have a sound approach to the environment?

Processes
- Is waste kept to a minimum?
- Is pollution controlled?
- How well is waste managed?
- What is building and plant maintenance policy?
- How are products transported out?
- What is the environmental impact during product use?

Products and outputs
- How much energy does the product consume?
- Could packaging be reduced/improved?
- Can the product be recycled?
- What are the effects of product disposal?
- Is there any potential for resource recovery?

This type of audit may be carried out internally, or by an outside team of environmental audit specialists. Either way, they require the close cooperation of all relevant members of staff, and the commitment of management to ensure that recommended changes and solutions are acted upon.

17.2.2 Compliance audits

This type of audit assesses whether or not a company is meeting the requirements of current and proposed legislation and regulations. In practice, compliance audits may focus on a specific operation (such as chemical waste discharged) or on all operations carried out at a particular site. They may also focus on assessing compliance with company policies and standards. Finally, they may be used to assess compliance with industry guideline standards.

As the volume and variety of environmental legislation are increasing at a very fast pace, particularly from the European Commission, it is likely that this aspect of environmental audit will become more and more prominent.

17.2.3 Environmental Impact Assessment (EIA)

These are carried out before major projects are undertaken. EIA tries to identify and predict the effects of a new development on the environment. If it is likely that these effects will be adverse, possible alternatives can be sought (for example, locating a new factory in a different location, or using more expensive but less harmful chemicals as part of a production process). Where there are no better alternatives, it may be that the project is abandoned altogether.

Since 1988, EC legislation[9] has required that all major projects which are subject to some sort of planning permission, and which are likely to have a significant effect on the environment, should be subject to EIA.

17.2.4 *Acquisition audits*

When a company is considering taking over another company, it will carry out a great deal of investigation into every financial aspect of its target. Increasingly, companies being considered for acquisition are being subjected to an environmental audit. This is designed to protect the purchaser from ending up with considerable environmental liabilities which it did not realise it was acquiring. And so an investigation will be carried out into any potential liability for remediation or clean-up costs, and any potential legal actions, penalties or fines. The level of concern, and hence the level of audit detail, will vary depending on the type of company being taken over. A chemical manufacturing company will obviously be riskier than a nursing home. The acquisition audit is also a good time to review the environmental policies of the potential acquisition, in order to assess how well these policies accord with those of the parent company.

17.2.5 *Supplier and customer audits*

Supplier audits are carried out to ensure that products and services bought in by a company meet the standards applied within that company. This type of audit is most commonly found in the retailing sector, with several large supermarket chains adopting the technique. Without an analysis of where products come from, it is difficult to make claims about being 'green' or 'environmentally friendly'. The effect has been to force suppliers into adopting more sound environmental practices, and so the use of this type of audit is responsible for spreading green awareness.

Customer audits are usually carried out only where a company sells a product which is potentially environmentally dangerous, such as industrial chemicals. These audits are carried out to ensure that the customer is properly treating and storing the product. The intention is to avoid a situation where an environmental problem gives rise to poor publicity and possible legal liability, which may in turn affect the supplier.

17.3 Conducting a corporate environmental audit

External auditors increasingly find themselves considering environmental matters when carrying out a normal statutory audit. If the financial statements are to show a true and fair view, the auditor must ensure that any contingent environmental liabilities have been included in the accounts. The auditor of statutory financial statements will need to consider the following questions:[10]

1 Are there any contingent liabilities, such as remediation costs of contamination?
2 Has stock become obsolete, through possible change in legislation or standards?
3 Have the lives of fixed assets become shortened due to changing legislation making existing processes illegal?
4 Does depreciation reflect any changes in the lives of fixed assets?
5 How viable are the company's product lines in the future, given changing legislation and public tastes?
6 Is there any evidence of illegal acts related to the environment, such as dumping waste products illegally?

Until these questions are answered satisfactorily, the auditor will be unable to give an opinion on the financial statements. Many of these questions are difficult for an auditor who is professionally qualified as an accountant, but not as a scientist, to answer. A few of the large accountancy firms have started to train their staff in the environmental implications of the statutory audit. Other audit firms rely on their own management consultancy departments, while smaller firms may have to rely on the advice of third party experts.

17.3.1 *Basic steps in an environmental audit*

There are three essential phases in carrying out an environmental audit. These are planning, gathering information, and concluding the audit. The planning of this type of audit is just as important an activity as planning a financial audit. For example, it is essential that the correct people are selected to carry out the audit. The actual work carried out will most probably include compliance as well as substantive testing, and the auditor will be required to produce a report on the work carried out. The types of activities involved at each of these three essential stages are:

Planning stage
- Identify the audit objectives (for example, is the purpose to check compliance with management environmental control procedures, or to identify inefficiencies in those procedures?).
- Define the scope of the audit (the whole company or only one specific site?).
- Determine who is the audience for the environmental audit (for example, management, regulatory authorities, or the public).
- Obtain all relevant background information.
- Determine the audit approach.
- Ascertain, evaluate and document the relevant environmental systems and controls operating.
- Prepare a detailed audit programme.
- Select the audit team on the basis of skills and experience.

Audit testing
- Select the items to be tested.
- Carry out detailed compliance and/or substantive testing.

Concluding
- Post-audit research and verification of the findings from the site visit.
- Analysis of audit findings, identifying any deficiencies, discrepancies and good performance practices.
- Preparation of an audit report, outlining the objective and scope of the audit, the methods employed, a summary of the results, and an indication of action areas.

17.4 Standards and legislation

In the United Kingdom there are two environmental standards which many companies are striving to meet. The first is a European Commission initiative, the Eco-Management and Audit Scheme (EMAS), and the other is British Standard 7750, Environmental Management Systems. Both standards define a voluntary system for environmental management. There are considerable market benefits to companies which comply with the systems, and outside parties such as suppliers, consumers and lenders may exert pressure on companies to participate in the schemes.

17.4.1 Eco-Management and Audit Scheme (EMAS)[11]

This scheme, adopted by the EC in 1993, requires member states to introduce a voluntary scheme whereby industrial companies which register for the scheme are committed to the following:

1. Define and adopt an environmental policy.
2. Set achievement targets.
3. Evaluate their performance in meeting those targets.
4. Make the information available to the public.

The information must be validated by an independent, accredited environmental auditor. This auditor, or 'verifier', is responsible for checking the environmental management system and validating the completeness and reliability of the information presented. Successful organisations may use an official 'statement of participation' and graphic which indicate their involvement with the scheme.

17.4.2 British Standard 7750

Like EMAS, this standard is voluntary, and it has been in effect since 1992. It was revised in 1994 to make it as compatible as possible with EMAS. The British Standard shares many of the features of the EC scheme, with one exception –

there is no requirement for a public environmental statement. An independent environmental auditor must be involved, in this case to assess the company's environmental management plan.

The extent to which companies apply for and are accredited under both BS7750 and EMAS is an indicator of the willingness of businesses to self-regulate, rather than relying on legislation to force them to conform. Companies which comply with the standards are not necessarily as environmentally sound as possible, but show a willingness and ability to manage their environmental performance.

17.5 Summary

Companies are set to produce more and more information on their environmental performance, partly as a response to public demand, and partly because of statutory intervention. Most of this information is at present not subject to audit, but this is changing. Within the next few years it is likely that all companies will be required to produce a detailed environmental report as part of the annual corporate report. Moreover, it is likely that this environmental report will require to be audited.

There is an important role for financial auditors in providing environmental audits, but the profession needs to be willing to work as part of multi-disciplined teams. The auditing profession also requires to develop environmental auditing guidelines, and to change the various accountancy bodies' education syllabuses to reflect this new type of audit.

REVIEW QUESTIONS

1. It has been argued that environmental auditing is merely a passing fad, and that soon auditors will be turning their attention to some other fashionable topic. Will environmental audit exist in twenty years' time?

2. Some companies have carried out an environmental audit, but have not produced or implemented any action plan as a result. Is there a danger that the environmental audit is being used as a marketing tool?

3. Is the accounting profession the best source of environmental auditors?

4. In Belgium, certain companies have a statutory requirement to produce specific environmental reports, disclosing details of production processes and emission levels. Should this become a statutory requirement in the United Kingdom?

5. In 1994, of the *Financial Times* top 100 companies, thirty-four published environmental reports, and six obtained independent verification of their contents. Is this good or bad news?

———————————————— **EXERCISES** ————————————————

1. You are the chief internal auditor of Waystit Ltd, a manufacturing company. The board of directors is concerned that the company is not managing its energy utilisation efficiently. The directors have asked you to undertake a company-wide energy audit, in order to identify how and where·fuel and power are consumed in the organisation, and to identify how performance could be improved. Draft an outline energy audit programme for Waystit Ltd.

2. You are an independent environmental auditor. A medium-sized local company, Alex Ltd, has approached you for advice. Alex Ltd is currently considering whether or not to instigate a full environmental audit of all aspects of its performance. This is partly as a result of public pressure, and partly because of a growing awareness on the part of the directors that they need to recognise the link between profitability and sound environmental practice. The directors intend to publish the results of the environmental audit as part of the annual corporate report.

Before embarking on this major exercise, the directors have asked you to produce a report explaining to them the advantages and possible disadvantages for the company of:

(a)   Carrying out an environmental audit, and
(b)   Making the results public.

3. Devise an audit programme for a comprehensive environmental performance review of a small hotel.

———

References and further reading

1. For a general discussion of business and the environment see Davis, J., *Greening Business: Managing for sustainable development* (Blackwell, 1991) and Hutchinson, C., *Business and the Environmental Challenge* (Conservation Trust, 1991). For an overview of the role of the accountant in this area, see Gray, R.H., Bebbington, J. and Walters, D., *Accounting for the Environment* (1993).

2. For further reading on the topic, see Elkington, J. *The Environmental Audit* (WWF, 1990).

3. European Commission, *Proposal for a Council Regulation establishing a Community Scheme for the Evaluation and Improvement of Environmental Performance in Certain Activities and the Provision of Relevant Information to the Public* (Eco-Audit) (1991).

4. The Confederation of British Industry, *Narrowing the Gap: Environmental auditing guidelines for business* (1990).

5. These ideas and recommendations for action are discussed in detail in a report produced by the Canadian Institute of Chartered Accountants, *Environmental Auditing and the Role of the Accounting Profession* (1992).

6. Institute of State Authorised Public Accountants, *Proposal for Organization of the Environmental Auditing Area* (1992).

7. The code of practice is contained within the Environmental Auditors Registration Association, *Revised Guidelines* (1995), which also gives details of application procedures and registration requirements.

8. These are based on the KPMG *Environment Briefing Note*, Number 5 (1990).

9. This was as a result of the EC *Directive on Environmental Assessment* (85/337).
10. Other areas related to environmental issues which should receive the attention of the auditor are identified and discussed in a report produced by the Institute of Chartered Accountants of England and Wales, *Business, Accountancy and the Environment: A policy and research agenda* (1992).
11. Further information on EMAS can be found in Hillary, R. *The Eco-Management and Audit Scheme: A practical guide* (Letchworth Technical Communication, 1993).

Proposed structure of Statements of Auditing Standards

Series 001/099   Introductory matters
010   The scope and authority of APB pronouncements

Series 100/199   Responsibility
100   Objective and general principles governing an audit of financial
                   statements
110   Fraud and error
120   Consideration of law and regulations
130   Going concern
140   Engagement letters
150   Subsequent events
160   Other information in documents containing audited financial
                   statements

Series 200/299   Planning, controlling and recording
200   Planning
210   Knowledge of the business
220   Audit materiality
230   Documentation
240   Quality control for audit work

Series 300/399   Accounting systems and internal control
300   Audit risk assessment
310   Auditing in an information systems environment

Series 400/499   Evidence
400   Audit evidence
410   Analytical procedures
420   Audit of accounting estimates
430   Audit sampling
440   Management representations
450   Opening balances and comparatives
460   Related parties
470   Overall review of financial statements

Series 500/599   **Using the work of others**
500   Considering the work of internal audit
510   The relationship between principal auditors and other auditors
520   Using the work of an expert

Series 600/699   **Reporting**
600   Auditors' report on financial statements
610   Reports to directors or management
620   The auditors' right and duty to report to regulators in the financial sector

Series 700/799   **Engagements other than audits of financial statements**

Series 800/899   **Particular industries and sectors**

–   Glossary of terms

Index